Healthy City Planning
From Neighbourhood to National Health Equity

Healthy city planning means seeking ways to eliminate the deep and persistent inequities that plague cities. Yet, as Jason Corburn argues in this book, neither city planning nor public health is currently organized to ensure that today's cities will be equitable and healthy.

Having made the case for what he calls 'adaptive urban health justice' in the opening chapter, Corburn briefly reviews the key events, actors, ideologies, institutions and policies that shaped and reshaped urban public health and planning from the nineteenth century to the present day. He uses two frames to organize this historical review: the view of the city as a field site and as a laboratory.

In the second part of the book Corburn uses in-depth case studies of health and planning activities in Rio de Janeiro, Nairobi, and Richmond, California to explore the institutions, policies and practices that constitute healthy city planning. These case studies personify some of the characteristics of his ideal of adaptive urban health justice. Each begins with an historical review of the place, its policies and social movements around urban development and public health, and each is an example of the urban poor participating in, shaping, and being impacted by healthy city planning.

Jason Corburn is an Associate Professor at the University of California, Berkeley and is jointly appointed in the Department of City & Regional Planning and the School of Public Health.

Planning, History and Environment Series

Editor:

Ann Rudkin, Alexandrine Press, Marcham, UK

Editorial Board:

Professor Arturo Almandoz, Universidad Simón Bolivar, Caracas, Venezuela and
 Pontificia Universidad Católica de Chile, Santiago, Chile

Professor Nezar AlSayyad, University of California, Berkeley, USA

Professor Scott A. Bollens, University of California, Irvine, USA

Professor Robert Bruegmann, University of Illinois at Chicago, USA

Professor Meredith Clausen, University of Washington, Seattle, USA

Professor Yasser Elsheshtawy, UAE University, Al Ain, UAE

Professor Robert Freestone, University of New South Wales, Sydney, Australia

Professor John R. Gold, Oxford Brookes University, Oxford, UK

Professor Sir Peter Hall, University College London, UK

Professor Michael Hebbert, University College London, UK

Selection of published titles

Planning Europe's Capital Cities: Aspects of nineteenth century development by Thomas Hall (**paperback 2010**)

Selling Places: The marketing and promotion of towns and cities, 1850–2000 by Stephen V. Ward

The Australian Metropolis: A planning history edited by Stephen Hamnett and Robert Freestone

Utopian England: Community experiments 1900–1945 by Dennis Hardy

Urban Planning in a Changing World: The twentieth century experience edited by Robert Freestone

Twentieth-Century Suburbs: A morphological approach by J.W.R. Whitehand and C.M.H. Carr

Council Housing and Culture: The history of a social experiment by Alison Ravetz

Planning Latin America's Capital Cities, 1850–1950 edited by Arturo Almandoz (**paperback 2010**)

Exporting American Architecture, 1870–2000 by Jeffrey W. Cody

Planning by Consent: The origins and nature of British development control by Philip Booth

The Making and Selling of Post-Mao Beijing by Anne-Marie Broudehoux

Planning Middle Eastern Cities: An urban kaleidoscope in a globalizing world edited by Yasser Elsheshtawy (**paperback 2010**)

Globalizing Taipei: The political economy of spatial development edited by Reginald Yin-Wang Kwok

New Urbanism and American Planning: The conflict of cultures by Emily Talen

Remaking Chinese Urban Form: Modernity, scarcity and space. 1949–2005 by Duanfang Lu (**paperback 2011**)

Planning Twentieth Century Capital Cities edited by David L.A. Gordon (**paperback 2010**)

Planning the Megacity: Jakarta in the twentieth century by Christopher Silver (**paperback 2011**)

Designing Australia's Cities: Culture, commerce and the city beautiful, 1900–1930 by Robert Freestone

Ordinary Places, Extraordinary Events: Citizenship, democracy and urban space in Latin America edited by Clara Irazábal

The Evolving Arab City: Tradition, modernity and urban development edited by Yasser Elsheshtawy (**paperback 2011**)

Stockholm: The making of a metropolis by Thomas Hall

Dubai: Behind an urban spectacle by Yasser Elsheshtawy (**paperback 2013**)

Capital Cities in the Aftermath of Empires: Planning in central and southeastern Europe edited by Emily Gunzburger Makaš and Tanja Damljanović Conley

Lessons in Post-War Reconstruction: Case studies from Lebanon in the aftermath of the 2006 war edited by Howayda Al-Harithy

Orienting Istanbul: Cultural capital of Europe? edited by Deniz Göktürk, Levent Soysal and İpek Türeli

Olympic Cities: City agendas, planning and the world's games 1896–2016, 2nd edition edited by John R Gold and Margaret M Gold

The Making of Hong Kong: From vertical to volumetric by Barrie Shelton, Justyna Karakiewicz and Thomas Kvan (**paperback 2013**)

Urban Coding and Planning edited by Stephen Marshall

Planning Asian Cities: Risks and resilience edited by Stephen Hamnett and Dean Forbes (**paperback 2013**)

Staging the New Berlin: Place marketing and the politics of reinvention post-1989 by Claire Colomb

City and Soul in Divided Societies by Scott A. Bollens

Learning from the Japan City: Looking East in urban design, 2nd edition by Barrie Shelton

The Urban Wisdom of Jane Jacobs edited by Sonia Hirt with Diane Zahm

Of Planting and Planning: The making of British colonial cities, 2nd edition by Robert Home

Healthy City Planning: Global health equity from neighbourhood to nation by Jason Corburn

Healthy City Planning:
From Neighbourhood to National Health Equity

Jason Corburn

Routledge
Taylor & Francis Group

LONDON AND NEW YORK

First published 2013
by Routledge
2 Park Square, Milton Park, Abingdon, Oxon OX14 4RN

Simultaneously published in the US and Canada
by Routledge
711 Third Avenue, New York, NY 10017

Routledge is an imprint of the Taylor & Francis Group, an Informa business

This book was commissioned and edited by Alexandrine Press, Marcham, Oxfordshire

British Library Cataloguing in Publication Data
A catalogue record of this book is available from the British Library

Library of Congress Cataloging in Publication Data
   Corburn, Jason.
   Healthy city planning : from neighbourhood to national health equity / Jason Corburn.
      pages cm. — (Planning, history and environment series)
   Includes bibliographical references and index.
   ISBN 978–0–415–61301–9 (hardback) — ISBN 978–0–415–61302–6 (pb) —
   ISBN 978–0–203–77224–9 (ebook)
      1. Urban health. 2. Cities and towns—Health aspects. 3. Urban ecology (Sociology)—
   Health aspects. 4. Public health—Environmental aspects. I. Title.
   RA566.7.C672 2013
   362.109173'2—dc23

                         2012049458

ISBN: 978–0–415–61301–9 (hbk)
ISBN: 978–0–415–61302–6 (pbk)
ISBN: 978–0–203–77224–9 (ebk)

Typeset in Aldine and Swiss by PNR Design, Didcot

MIX
Paper from
responsible sources
FSC
www.fsc.org FSC® C013056

Printed and bound in Great Britain by
TJ International Ltd, Padstow, Cornwall

Contents

Preface

If city planners were doctors, they would need to respond to claims of medical malpractice from today's urban poor residents. For the past century or more, urban planners, city managers and national policy-makers – in the global North and South, rich and poor countries alike – have systematically neglected the conditions in neighbourhoods of the urban poor that contribute to disease, injury and premature death. While this book argues that city living is generally health-promoting, since it often provides greater opportunities for accessing safe housing, food, health care, education, employment, and expression of political, gender and cultural rights, where you live in a city and how that city is governed can determine who gets sick early, suffers unnecessarily and dies early. The failure to plan for growing urban populations and to promote the physical, social, economic, institutional and political conditions that can make all city residents healthy is the negligence that city planners must now reverse. This book offers a new way forward for all those interested in shaping a more equitable, sustainable and healthy urban planet.

The modern disciplines of urban planning and public health emerged together to fight epidemics of infectious diseases ravaging cities in Europe and North America. Planners aimed to clean up cities from filth, pipe in clean water and dispose of waste, all with the hope of eliminating disease and stopping premature death. These sanitary interventions deserve some credit for reducing disease, but so too do scientific insights from bacteriology and, perhaps most importantly, progressive public policies that increased wages, rights and safety for urban workers and that promoted and protected children, minority groups, women, immigrants and indigenous populations. When city planners, public health workers and public policy-makers acted together in the nineteenth and sometimes in the twentieth century, they often viewed the city as a *field site*, or an intricate, nuanced place needing in-depth study, often with urban poor residents, to understand how best to improve health and prevent, not just treat, illness. The importance of urban field work is often told through the stories of public health heroes, such as Alice Hamilton's 'shoe leather' epidemiology in Chicago and John Snow's work on preventing cholera in London. Healthy city planning in this era combined multiple forms of expertise to improve the economic, living, workplace, social and political conditions of the urban poor.

As laboratory science began to replace field-site investigations in public health, and clinicians replaced field workers and planners, urban health moved further into the body, not the neighbourhood. The *laboratory view* of the city approached urban health challenges like fixing a machine, where professional mechanics often took apart and treated the individual parts of a city separately, much like some clinicians would isolate the parts of an ailing human body. The laboratory and machine-like view of the city tended to separate the parts from the complex whole and excluded the expertise of the urban residents suffering the most from participating in problem solving. 'Community planning malpractice' today reflects this approach, since the multiple and cumulative forces that influence health in the most vulnerable city neighbourhoods are routinely ignored by most clinicians, public health professionals, urban planners and city governments more generally. Instead, we focus on one disease, one 'unhealthy behaviour' and one physical urban design change at a time, hoping that fixing these separate parts of the urban machine will somehow come together to heal sick neighbourhoods and the people living in them.

Yet, practice is changing as we enter the twenty-first century. Insights from decades of research and activism around the world, from Latin American social medicine, Asian 'barefoot' health workers, new urban social and environmental justice movements, and experiments from the Healthy Cities Movement worldwide, are all contributing to new urban health equity focused city planning. Policies and practices linking neighbourhoods to national policy are recognizing that we cannot continue to treat people only to send them back into the living and working conditions that made them sick in the first place.

I wrote this book both to expose the historical forces and events that separated city planning and public health from some of their 'field site' and social justice origins and to explore how history can inform a new way forward for twenty-first century healthy and equitable city planning. As I suggest in the book, the way forward will not come from innovations in the global North, from corporations or privatizing the city, but rather from new collaborative and participatory practices and national policies focused on urban equity that are implemented by social movements and local governments and held accountable through monitoring, evaluation and on-going learning. While new science and technology can help, they will never be the solution. One example of the limits of technology, which I review in detail in the chapter on Nairobi, is the dynamic in this city's informal settlements where over 80 per cent of slum dwellers own or have daily access to a mobile phone that allows them to browse the internet, communicate using social media and conduct online banking transactions. Yet, while these folks tweet, fewer than 10 per cent have access to a private, safe and hygienic toilet in their homes. This book offers ideas for changing the chronic political inequities that keep the urban poor unhealthy.

As I show in this book, insights and innovations for twenty-first century healthy and equitable city planning are coming from cities, neighbourhoods and social movements in the global South and poor communities in the North. From Rio de Janeiro to Nairobi, to the San Francisco Bay Area, I highlight innovative healthy city planning efforts that are changing and improving the conditions that make all of us healthy – from basic human needs for food, water and shelter, to political and cultural recognition, to reducing pathogenic exposures of toxins and violence, to holding corporate polluters accountable, to increasing economic, social and medical care services. Most importantly, the innovations are generated by and for the most marginalized urban residents, such as those living in segregated communities. As the evidence offered here suggests, twenty-first century healthy city planning is fundamentally about social, racial and economic justice and improving the health of the least well off. This results in better health and quality of life for everyone.

City planners, public health professionals, engineers, doctors and others that read this book may find some of the approaches and suggestions unsettling. Yet, that is one of my aims, since conventional approaches in these and other professions have largely failed to focus on addressing the chronic inequalities in cities that are driving persistent health inequalities. I suggest such 'radical notions' that the effectiveness of medical and curative interventions and the work of epidemiologists depends on a greater appreciation of how the histories of urban neighbourhoods and the biographies, or life experiences, of people get 'into our bodies' to influence well-being. I also suggest that city planners should stop segmenting the profession into different sectors, such as land use, transportation, design, housing, etc., and incorporate insights from over a century of urban sociology, epidemiology, and other disciplines where integrated approaches focused on how people move through and experience their world, and the coping and resilience strategies they develop, offer the best clues for effective policy interventions and institutional approaches to reducing urban inequities. I call on public health researchers and other scientists to stop pretending to be value-neutral and apolitical in their work, and recognize the need to engage more explicitly with how national and municipal public policies and government institutions more generally are shaping urban vulnerability. I also call on all those involved in public health to be more attentive to the insights from planners, medical anthropologists and others who understand that a complex set of inter-related urban neighbourhood characteristics influence health – not just built environment features – and that strategies for greater urban health equity must embrace this complexity and not try to isolate individual variables that influence urban health.

Perhaps most frustrating for some reading this book will be my definition of healthy city planning. I suggest that healthy city planning is not one thing or a single end-point. Healthy city planning is an on-going process of policy experimentation, intervention, monitoring, learning, and adaptation, with the aim of constantly improving the conditions that promote health for all populations, but with a particular focus on improvements that change the inequities currently experienced by segregated, poor, racial and ethnic minority populations and their more wealthy neighbours.

In these and other ways, this book enters into an on-going conversation about city living, policy-making, sustainability and survival on an increasingly urban planet. It aims to inject new ideas and voices – particularly those too often ignored and made invisible – into decision-making from the neighbourhood to the nation that promote greater equity and human health. My hope is that it will help us avoid further 'city planning malpractice' by ensuring equity anchors healthy city planning in this century of the city.

Acknowledgements

This book is the result of multi-year collaborations and partnerships and sharing of experiences and practices. I could not have written it without the insights, expertise, inspiration and involvement of my friends and colleagues around the world. Of these folks are already engaged deeply in the practices of healthy city planning and I have learnt so much from and with them. In Brazil, Daniel Becker, Katia Edmundo, Ives Rocha from CEDAPS; Cristiano Boccolini from UERJ; Francisco Inacio 'Chico' Bastos, Christovam Barcellos from FIOCRUZ; Fernando A Proietti, Observatório Saúde Urbana de Belo Horizonte; Fernando Cavallieri, City of Rio de Janeiro. Most importantly, my collaborator at UERJ Eduardo Faerstein.

In Nairobi, I have many people to thank, too many to name, but some collaborators that made the content of this book possible include: Jane Weru, Irene Karanja, David Mathenge, Joseph Kimani, Jane Wairutu Jason Weweru, Lamech Machuki, Charles Baraka, George Kirui, Francis Gitau, Edwin Simiyu, from Muungano. Professor Peter Ngau at the University of Nairobi. My dear friend Jack Makau at Slum/Shack Dwellers International (SDI). Some of my participation in the Nairobi work was supported by a grant from the Rockefeller Foundation and supported by Robert Buckley, Suman Sureshbabu, and Susan Kagondu. Mark Hildebrand, formerly of UN-Habitat and the Cities Alliance, has been extremely helpful and supportive of the informal settlements upgrading work.

In Richmond, California and the Bay Area: Shasa Curl, Gabino Arredondo, Lina Velasco, LaShonda White, Devone Boggan, and Bill Lindsey at the City of Richmond; Wanda Sessions and Wendell Brunner at Contra Costa Health Services; Nile Malloy, Greg Karras and Bill Gallegos at CBE; Roger Kim, APEN; Juliet Ellis and Sheryl Lane formerly of Urban Habitat; Henry Clark, West County Toxics; Deputy Mayor, Jeff Ritterman. My involvement in Richmond has been supported by grants from the California Endowment and supported by Diane Aranda and Tony Iton.

My father for the cover, and of course, AS, SR and JJ are, and continue to be, my inspiration.

Introduction

The Pursuit of Health Equity on a Planet of Cities

On an urban planet, healthy city planning is about global health. Few topics are more important to health than city and community planning and development. Yet, neither planning nor public health is currently organized to ensure that our planet of cities will be equitable and healthy. A new strategy for planning and managing cities and metropolitan regions is necessary for planetary sustainability and survival. This book offers a framework for planning healthy and equitable cities where neighbourhood-scale innovations are linked to national policy initiatives. Healthy city planning here is about eliminating the deep and persistent inequities that plague cities and the new knowledge, practices and participants that must become central features of urban policy-making and urban institutions in order to promote greater urban health justice.

Today, where you live and how that place is managed can determine when and if you get sick, receive medical treatment and whether you die prematurely. Cities throughout history have been beneficial for the wellbeing of most urban dwellers (Dye, 2008). Cities offer great advantages for what the United Nations calls the social determinants of health, those resources that often determine if you will get sick, access care and live a healthy life. Urban areas generally offer more people opportunities to benefit from economic and educational opportunities, medical services, political and gender rights, housing and basic infrastructure, and cultural and religious expression. This holds true in both rich and poor cities of the global North and South. Yet not everyone in cities can take advantage of these socially produced resources. Some experience health inequities: differences in access to health promoting resources that are unnecessary, avoidable and unfair. As the UN-Habitat and World Health Organization stated in their 2009 report, *Hidden Cities: Unmasking and Overcoming Health Inequities in Urban Settings*:

Health inequities are the result of the circumstances in which people grow, live, work and age, and the health systems they can access, which in turn are shaped by broader political, social and economic forces. They are not distributed randomly, but rather show a consistent pattern across the population, often by socioeconomic status or geographical location. No city – large or small, rich or poor, east or west, north or south – has been shown to be immune to the problem of health inequity.

The Spatial and Relational Complexity of Urban Health Inequities

Consider Paris, the San Francisco Bay Area in California and Nairobi, Kenya. In 2011, Emmanuel Vigneron, Professor of Geography at Université Montpellier 3, published a map which showed mortality rates by neighbourhood along the Paris Metro. The more affluent the Parisian neighbourhood the lower the risk of dying (figure I.1). In the San Francisco Bay Area, an African-American child born in West Oakland will die, on average, 15 years earlier than a white child living just a few kilometres away in the Oakland Hills (ACPHD, 2009) (figure I.2). In the Bay Area, life expectancy for everyone increased between 1960 and 2006, yet the difference in life expectancy between whites and African-Americans has persisted and is increasing. This is what public health researchers call the social gradient and this reflects a health inequity; an avoidable difference that is unfair and unjust. We could repeat these maps (and they have been made) for Washington DC, London, Rio de Janeiro, Cape Town, Mumbai, etc.

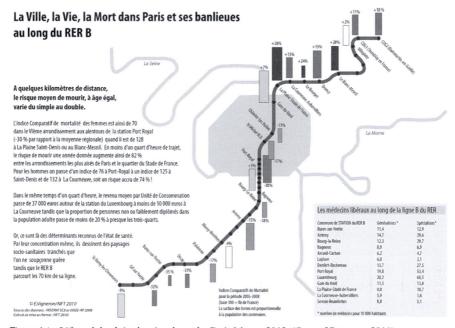

Figure I.1. Life and death in the city along the Paris Metro, 2012. (*Source*: Vigneron, 2011)

In Nairobi, infant mortality is higher in the slum population than the city more generally and higher than for those living in rural areas (APHRC, 2002) (figure I.3). In Nairobi's Mathare slum (figure I.4), discussed in more detail in Chapter 5, the reasons behind health and illness are much more complex that just differences between slum and non-slum dwellers. For example, in Mathare private toilets are rare and those

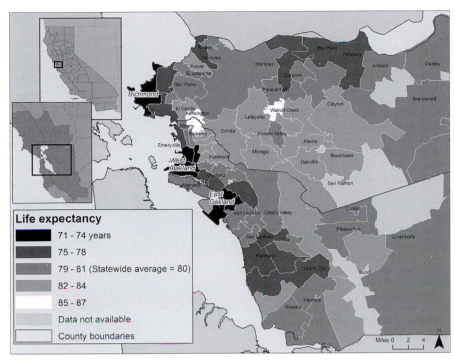

Figure I.2. Life expectancy in Contra Costa and Alameda counties by ZIP code. (*Source*: ACPHD, 2008)

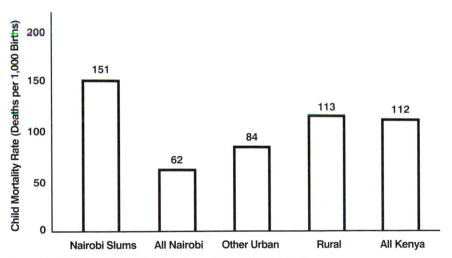

Figure I.3. Child mortality in Nairobi's slums. (*Source*: APHRC, 2002)

that do exist are not connected to any waste treatment, so using them can concentrate pathogens and increase risk for children playing outside as waste flows openly into the streets. The toilet might also be under lock and key, controlled by a local gang that extorts a high price for each use. The cost may adversely impact the disposable income of a family. The toilet may also be unsafe especially for children and women. If the

Figure I.4. Mathare informal settlement, Nairobi, Kenya. (*Source*: Photo by author 2009)

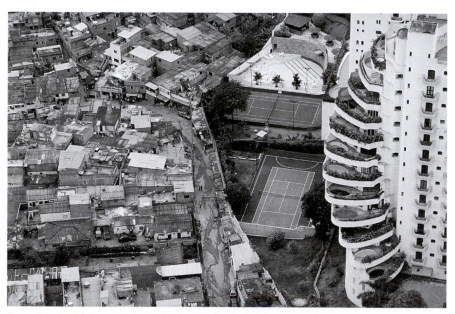

Figure I.5. Spatial disparities in São Paulo. (*Source*: Tuca Vieira, used with permission)

toilet lacks security and lighting at night, as almost all do in Mathare, they become sites for rape and sexual violence against women. Rape and sexual violence is known to spread HIV/AIDS and other sexually transmitted diseases. A rape victim or an HIV positive woman is often stigmatized in the slum, leading to additional abuse and difficulty finding employment. Such women may be forced into sex work to buy food, which regularly consumes over two-thirds of slum dwellers' monthly income.

Understanding these cascading and related impacts of a toilet in an urban community such as the informal settlements of Nairobi is crucial for healthy city planning. Yet, the last century of public health, urban planning and urban policy has approached health in the city much as one would fix a machine or the human body; find each broken part, separate it from the rest and use parts experts for the repair and reinstallation. In planning, housing policy is segmented from land use, land use from the environment, environment from economic development, and so on. This is reflected in the practices and institutions of both planning and public health. Most urban health departments are organized around specific diseases or behavioural changes, not neighbourhoods, social justice, democracy or other suspected determinants of wellbeing. Eventually, I argue, we will have to turn to an analysis of science, particularly laboratory models of evidence generation, to understand better why and how this fragmentation took hold in both planning and public health, and the ways we might recast science for healthy city planning. Healthy city planning is, borrowing from the landmark Healthy Cities report by Trevor Hancock and Len Duhl in 1986, about:

continually creating and improving those physical and social environments and expanding those community resources which enable people to mutually support each other in performing all the functions of life and in developing their maximum potential.

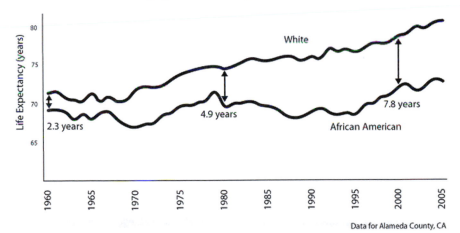

Data for Alameda County, CA

Figure I.6. Life expectancy by race in Alameda County, San Francisco Bay Area. (*Source*: ACPHD, 2008)

From Health in Cities to Healthy City Planning

What else helps to explain the persistence of the health inequities in Paris, San Francisco Bay Area and Nairobi to which I referred above? Most urban health interventions are focused on bringing social services, primary care, economic opportunities and physical improvements to urban residents or their neighbourhoods. Interventions tend to focus either on people or places, but rarely both at the same time. Interventions are generally

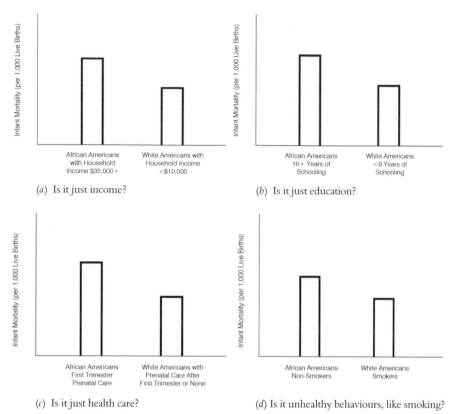

(a) Is it just income?   (b) Is it just education?

(c) Is it just health care?   (d) Is it unhealthy behaviours, like smoking?

Figure I.7. What explains racial health inequities in America? (*Source*: Mathews and MacDorman, 2012)

conceptualized and led by experts, and focused on one disease, one risk factor, one hazardous exposure, one population group, or one suspected 'cause' of poor health, such as poverty. More care, more places offering care, more prevention and more services are also intervention targets. This is the *health in cities* approach.

The health in cities approach has failed to generate a response to why spatial and racial inequities persist even when interventions aim to address the fundamental social determinants of health? As shown in figure I.7, inequitable health outcomes, such as infant mortality, persist between whites and African Americans, even when the latter have middle class or higher incomes, are educated, receive pre-natal care and do not smoke. The health in cities approach might continue to treat these social factors but still not change inequities.

Healthy city planning argues for a fundamentally different approach from the health in cities approach. While the latter has achieved important improvements in population health, the fragmented research and interventions of health in cities is not up to the task of promoting twenty-first century urban health equity. Healthy city planning is about rejecting the fragmentation of issues, risks and expertise. As I will explain in more detail throughout this book, healthy city planning is an orientation to research, policy and practice that is explicitly:

1.   *Anti-reductionist* – avoids a focus on single behaviours, diseases, or risk factors, and reifying some social groups or neighbourhoods as if they were homogenous, such as Latinos in the US or informal settlements in the global south.

2.   *Anti-determinist* – rejects that only biology, genetics, behaviours or physical living and working conditions determine health and disease.

3.   *Anti-positivist* – questions the neutral, disembodied and placelessness of science and technology; embraces historically situated epistemology.

4.   *Anti-elitism* – acknowledges that urban expertise is always co-produced by 'experts' with a diversity of life experiences; focuses explicitly on reversing privileges obtained through social structural inequalities according to wealth, ethnicity, gender, sexual orientation and other forms of discrimination.

New Science for Healthy and Equitable Cities

In February 2008, the journal *Science* released a special issue on cities. The journal noted that cities were important sites because they were responsible for many inputs (economy, people, consumption more generally) and outputs (pollution, ideas, health care) that are core aspects of research and policy in the sciences. While *Science* made no sweeping conclusions, the journal suggested that scientists would need to consider using complex systems analysis for planning future cities (Batty, 2008).

In October 2010, the journal *Nature* also published a special issue on cities. The journal asked why scientists do not pay more attention to the issues of and in cities and called for scientists across many disciplines to collaborate with leaders in other sectors of society. In 2011, the International Council of Scientific Unions released a report *Health and Wellbeing in the Changing Urban Environment: A Systems Analysis Approach*, which outlined a multi-year effort by global scientists to develop a new approach to studying the relationships between the urban environment and human health based on complex systems analysis. The report noted that complex systems analysis can 'enable us to see the patterns of disease as well as factors promoting health and wellbeing that underlie these patterns, the so-called 'causes of the causes' (ICSU, 2011).

In 2012, a Lancet Commission issued a report entitled, *Shaping Cities for Health: Complexity and the Planning of Urban Environments in the 21st Century* (Rydin et al., 2012) and argued for taking a complex systems approach to healthy cities. The Lancet Commission issued five recommendations to implement this twenty-first-century complex systems approach:

1.   City governments should work with a wide range of stakeholders to build a political alliance for urban health.

2.   Attention to health inequalities within urban areas should be a key focus when

planning the urban environment, necessitating community representation in arenas of policy making and planning.

3.   Action needs to be taken at the urban scale to create and maintain the urban advantage in health outcomes through changes to the urban environment, providing a new focus for urban planning policies.

4.   Policy-makers at national and urban scales would benefit from undertaking a complexity analysis to understand the many overlapping relations affecting urban health outcomes.

5.   Progress towards effective action on urban health will be best achieved through local experimentation in a range of projects, supported by assessment of their practices and decision-making processes by practitioners.

What these major reports all have in common is the attention to a new science of and for the city rooted in complex systems thinking rather than linear machine-like fixing (Wilkinson, 2012). Yet, all the reports, except *The Lancet*, failed to mention explicitly the existence of, and importance to reverse, urban health inequities and the role for community-based organizations as leaders in this new science for the city. Finally, none of the reports gives a clear indication of what historical events and policies shaped unhealthy cities and how these insights might inform their recommendations for a new science of healthy city planning.

Despite their limitations, these special reports represent a major shift in the scientific and public health community that this book builds upon. Namely, these reports acknowledge that scientific 'business as usual' is insufficient for understanding and addressing the major challenges our planet faces in the twenty-first century, from climate change to urban health. Further, for city planners and other social scientists attention to social justice must be central aspects of this new orientation to science.

On Methods

The first part of the book explores the histories of city planning and public health from the nineteenth century to the present day. I use a combination of original documentation and secondary literature to piece together my account of key events, actors and institutions. The review is not intended to be exhaustive, but rather focused on highlighting the expressions and interpretations of the field site and laboratory views of the city that frame each of the historical reviews.

The second part of the book uses in-depth case studies of health and planning activities in Rio de Janeiro, Brazil, Nariobi, Kenya, and Richmond, California, to explore the institutions, policies and practices that constitute healthy city planning. The field research began in 2008 and continued through 2012. I used interviews, original data collection, and participant observations to develop and analyze the cases.

In each, the analytic frame explored how health was defined, who participated in this framing, what institutional structures were established to promote equity and health, which municipal and national policies influenced organizational work, and what the actors learned along the way? In all three cases, I am working on some aspect of the planning projects described in the study. While this closeness to each site surely biases my interpretation of events, the insider perspective has allowed me to understand process and project significance with local residents, policy-makers and researchers. I also participated in survey data collection and analyses in both Nairobi and Richmond, giving me access to unique original data.

Why These Cases?

Rio de Janeiro is an important case and place because Brazil is a global leader in health policy, investing in informal urban settlements or *favelas*, and more recently successfully reducing poverty. I begin with a case from the global south in part to demystify the notion that health equity oriented urban planning can only emerge in cities of the North with significant fiscal resources, technical expertise and long-established democratic governance. Brazil and Rio flip all these assumptions on their head. Rio de Janeiro is also an important place because much of the policy innovation in Brazil, from one of the most successful strategies to prevent and manage AIDS to universal health care delivered at the community scale, to integrated urban planning, has its origins in Rio and particularly its community-based social movements.

The Nairobi case focuses on planning work driven by slum dwellers in the Mathare informal settlement. Mathare is one of the largest slums in Nairobi and East Africa and the case suggests that understanding and planning for the different needs and cultures across the same slum are crucial aspects of healthy city planning. Much of the literature on improving informal settlements suggests that, especially in the worst-off places like Mathare, land rights, improved water and sanitation and other services are needed, but few explore the processes necessary to decide if these are the priority interventions for each place, how improvement schemes can be accountable to local residents and how planning can build local power for broader social change. The planning for health and equity in Mathare offers insights for the global struggle to improve the wellbeing of those living in informal settlements everywhere.

Richmond is a city with an important civil rights and social activist history and a place struggling to get out from under the grips of one of the world's largest multi-national corporations and polluters, Chevron. Richmond emerged as, and has largely remained for much of its history, a 'company town', but my case highlights how environmental justice activists have shifted the balance of power and helped to make the city a national leader in healthy planning. While much recent urban planning and health work in the US, and to some extent Europe, focuses on narrow notions of physical planning, this case is important for understanding how an integrated equity framework that includes an explicit focus on racial justice can organize healthy city planning.

Outline of the Book: Learning from the South

Extending earlier work, this book makes a case for a new science of the city by offering a detailed framework of what, in Chapter 1, I call *Adaptive Urban Health Justice*. Adaptive urban health justice builds from complex system ideas, but recognizes that these concepts tend to be too abstract and divorced from urban residents' lived reality. Thus, I combine a complex systems approach with frameworks from eco-social epidemiology, science and technology studies and adaptive ecosystem management to define the core constructs and practical challenges of adaptive urban health justice.

Chapters 2, *The City in the Field*, and 3, *The City as Laboratory*, briefly review key events, actors, ideologies, institutions and policies that shaped and reshaped the modern era of urban public health and planning. I use two frames to organize these chapters, the view of the city as a field site and as a laboratory.

The field view of the city suggests that urban health practitioners and institutions were driven by a commitment to empirical observations 'in the streets' to understand and intervene to improve urban health. In the field site view of cities, professionals and lay people act as surveyors, cartographers, and interviewers, to detail the uniquely particular features of places that help explain the distributions of disease and death across time, space and culture. As Chapter 2 suggests, field site researchers defined the new discipline of sanitary science, influenced national health legislation and the structure of municipal bureaucracies.

As sanitary science gave way to germ theory and bacteriology as the driving theory of what explained disease, the view of the city shifted to the laboratory. In the laboratory view of the city, as I detail in Chapter 3, research and policy-making aimed to emulate the values and credibility of laboratory science. In the lab, the researcher seeks distance from the researched, mechanization and standardization of instruments is valued, and the inquiry is insulated from and restricted to those who know how not to contaminate the experiment. As I will show in more detail, the lab view not only shifted the type and focus of urban health research, it shaped urban health interventions and institutions. The laboratory view of the city proposed universal urban improvement schemes that could be applied anywhere, no matter the population, geography, social or cultural characteristics of that place. Yet, as I will show in both chapters, but emphasize in Chapter 3, neither the field nor lab views was absolute, and in practice what often emerged were hybrids of both. Perhaps the most important hybrid field-lab urban health strategy was the community health centre, where clinical medicine was combined with attention to health equity issues of economic and social justice and democratic participation. The community health centre was and remains an important practice for healthy city planning.

Chapters 2 and 3 are critical histories. Many modern city planning and public health histories are stories of North American and European male heroes, from Edwin Chadwick and John Snow to Ebenezer Howard, Daniel Burnham, and Frederick Law Olmsted. In these accounts, modern epidemiology and city planning are largely stories of triumph over adversity and saving society from impending doom. An underlying narrative of unfettered progress also permeates these histories. While Chapters 2 and 3 discuss the male 'heroes' of the two fields, I also try to uncover work by women and minority-led social movements. While far from comprehensive, my review will raise critical questions that set the stage for understanding the strengths and weakness of more contemporary experiments in healthy and socially just city planning and urban policy-making.

Chapters 4, 5 and 6 offer case studies of practices that personify some of the characteristics of my ideal of adaptive urban health justice outlined in Chapter 1. Each case begins with an historical review of the place, its policies and social movements around urban development and public health. In each case I focus on the events that seemed to most directly impact the urban poor, since all my contemporary case studies explore how the urban poor are participating in, shaping and being impacted by healthy city planning.

In Chapter 4, *Favela Health: Planning and Policy in Rio de Janeiro*, I explore the overlapping policies and practices that are aiming to improve the lives and living conditions for *favela* residents. Brazil has implemented a set of social policies that are enabling neighbourhood health planning to improve living conditions in *favelas*, such as Favela-Bairro, by setting up health clinics and introducing community health workers, while also providing national leadership for poverty alleviation, such as through its conditional cash transfer programme called *Bolsa Família*. This chapter emphasizes that these contemporary policies emerged from a particular urban health policy history, which opens the chapter. Most important, I analyze how *favela* communities are shaping, implementing and benefiting from policy change in Brazil through the work of the Center for Health Promotion (CEDAPS), a civil society group that supports community-based health planning and facilitates Rio's Healthy Cities Network. I show that the combination of municipal and national health and social policies, a set of rights emerging from the Brazilian Constitution, and active networks of civil society groups connected across the city's many *favelas*, is contributing to healthy and equitable planning in Rio de Janeiro.

Chapter 5, *Collaborative Planning in Nairobi's Informal Settlements*, explores the potential for healthy city planning when the state is absent or unresponsive to the needs of the urban poor. I follow the healthy planning work of a network of slum dwellers called *Muungano wa Wanavaijiji*, as they organize residents, gather data and plan for community improvements and policy change. This chapter highlights the importance of slum dweller networks, within a city, across the country and internationally, for enabling healthy city planning and explore how Slum Dwellers International (SDI) supports the neighbourhood-scale planning in Nairobi's slums. I also offer a detailed historical review of city planning and public health in Nairobi and suggest that a legacy of colonial era policies and more recent national initiatives have created both challenges and opportunities for healthy slum planning. I will show that while the living conditions in Nairobi's informal settlements are different from those in Rio's *favelas*, lessons for healthy and equitable city planning emerging from both places have some similar qualities, such as the importance of community-based institution building, multi-issue policies at the municipal and national scale and short-term projects that build incrementally toward structural changes.

Chapter 6, *Planning for Urban Environmental Health Justice*, explores how activists in Richmond, California, and local government are turning decades of dumping, divestment and despair into 'a stone of hope' to borrow from Martin Luther King, Jr. Richmond sits across the Bay from San Francisco, but has historically been an industrial dumping ground for the region. Home to many poor people of colour, it has one of the lowest life expectancies and highest rates of disease (see figure I.2 for one example) in the entire region. The new hope for Richmond comes from a set of inter-related planning activities, including drafting and implementing California's first health-equity focused General Plan, reducing pollution from a Chevron oil refinery that dominates Richmond's landscape, and institutionalizing the Richmond Health Equity Partnership – a coalition of government agencies, the school district, and community-based organizations working collaboratively to promote health equity. The chapter includes a historical review of development and racial politics in Richmond in order to situate the current healthy city efforts. Importantly in this case, land use, and corporate, and environmental regulatory decisions gave rise to some of the first environmental justice (EJ) organizations in the US, the West County Toxics Coalition and Communities for a Better Environment (CBE). A coalition of EJ groups, the Richmond Equitable Development Initiative, emerged from early environmental health struggles against Chevron's refinery pollution burdening the African-American, Latino and Asian-American population in Richmond and extended their work to include housing, job creation and land-use planning.

Community organizations conducted research, challenged elected officials and Chevron, and drafted policies prompting the city to work with them to develop an integrated health equity strategy that is being incorporated into the day-to-day management of Richmond. The case explores the events and organizations behind these changes, the important role of the environmental justice movement in framing the issues and the evidence-based data to justify action, and how health equity is being institutionalized across all the functions of city management. While an on-going process, I suggest that the Richmond Health Equity Partnership is the result of active and on-going community organizing focused on environmental health and equity-focused coalition building among activist groups. This chapter argues that the work in Richmond highlights that sustainable health city planning in rich countries with very poor cities cannot be primarily about changing urban design, the built environment or reforming governmental planning institutions; there has to be an equity strategy.

The book concludes with Chapter 7, *Towards a Planet of Healthy Cities*, by highlighting some of the lessons from the case studies and reflecting on my ideal model of Adaptive Urban Health Justice. The cases all offer insights for and the barriers to linking neighbourhood innovation and accountability with national urban equity policies and resources. I suggest that new metaphors integrating a new science for the city, democratic policy-making and multi-issue, relational planning are needed to move away from the machine-fixing approach that now dominates both public health and city planning. I also conclude with some significant challenges healthy city planning will face on a planet that is increasingly urbanized and increasingly stratified by a minority of those who have the resources and capabilities to be healthy and a majority that struggle every day to survive. Eliminating inequities and promoting health equity must be the guiding framework if we are to move towards a twenty-first century planet of healthy cities.

Chapter 1

Adaptive Urban Health Justice

Of Machines and Butterflies

In planning, policy-making and public health, scientific metaphors shape much of how we interpret and intervene in the world. Policy science and management often tacitly view challenges like urban health much like a machine; if something seems to be broken the best approach is to take it apart, understand how all the parts work, fix each one, and put it back together. Public health often aims to emulate Western medicine where curing the body can also be like machine repair and focused on individual parts not the complex whole. In policy science as machine, the internal workings take priority since less is known about how to control the entire system and the ambient environment that might be influencing the machine's functioning. Not everyone can repair or even understand the workings of the policy-making machine, so the theory goes, and only specially trained experts are trusted to participate.

Planning for health equity in cities, as I will argue in this chapter, confronts many of the core assumptions of the machine metaphor. Cities have many unpredictable parts, are variegated and the sum of their parts rarely equate easily with the functioning of the whole. People in cities find ways to interpret and assign meaning to places in surprising and unexpected ways, even when certain aspects of the city are 'hard-wired' for a particular function, such as roads and parks. Cities are constantly built and rebuilt socially, physically and interpretively. The interpretations and possibilities of cities are influenced by forces from within their neighbourhoods and municipal boundaries, but also by policies and institutions outside at the national and international scales. With all this complexity, the rational machine-like approach to policy change and management has proved inadequate.

This chapter argues that cities are complex systems characterized more by uncertainty, indeterminacy and ignorance than certainty, functions and rationality (Batty, 2008; Tsoukas, 2005). A complex system must develop processes of adapting to change, since it is near impossible to model and predict the future of complex systems. This concept is the driving idea behind adaptive urban health justice.

In complex systems small, localized events can have an unexpectedly large influence on the entire system. In chaos theory, this is known as the butterfly effect, first coined by Edward Lorenz. Lorenz postulated that in the complex and uncertain meteorology system, a butterfly flapping its wings in the Amazon today can affect the formation of a hurricane thousands of kilometres away in the near future. The butterfly can have this impact if the initial conditions when the wings are flapped are sensitive to the small movement.

So, in complex cities, we might image our butterflies as neighbourhood actions working in unpredictable ways to radically alter not just the city, but an entire metropolitan region. Healthy city planning is about creating the enabling conditions for the butterflies to take flight and preparing to learn from and adapt to the unpredictable impacts that may result. Yet, healthy city planning is not agnostic about the existing conditions that currently do or do not exist in cities that might enable butterflies; identifiable policies, institutions, social movements, cultural practices, ideologies and so on have helped shape inequities that plague cities today, and deliberate changes to these same forces are necessary to enable healthy and equitable city planning.

To make this abstract discussion more concrete, this chapter turns to existing frameworks to offer more details of the processes and practices that must underwrite adaptive urban health justice. The existing frameworks include eco-social epidemiology (Krieger, 2011), sustainability science as framed by science and technology studies (Kates *et al.*, 2001; Gibbons *et al.*, 1994) and adaptive ecosystem management (Norton, 2005; NRC, 1999).

Eco-Social Epidemiology

The first concept that helps link the complexity of cities and urban systems with public action for health equity is eco-social epidemiology. First articulated by Nancy Krieger in 1994, eco-social epidemiology explicitly asks 'who and what drives current and changing patterns of social inequalities in health?' (Krieger, 2011, p. 213). Thus, the starting point for urban adaptive health justice is inquiry into and a commitment to address social injustices. Eco-social epidemiology is an important framework for urban policy-making because it seeks to understand what explains the *distribution* of morbidity and mortality over time and place. This is different from asking what might cause a specific disease, a point I will return to later in this chapter.[1] As Krieger (2011) has described, eco-social epidemiology has four core constructs that together direct inquiry and action.

Embodiment

The first concept of eco-social epidemiology is embodiment, which suggests that 'we literally embody, biologically, our lived experience', particularly the material and social worlds in which we live 'thereby creating population patterns of health and disease' (*Ibid.*, p. 215). Thus, the foundation of understanding and acting to reverse health inequities is knowing the histories of people, groups, places and the social, political and economic decisions that over time have shaped these histories. Embodiment is not a static concept but rather a dynamic on-going event, much like our complex urban system. For instance, eco-social embodiment emphasizes the constant interactions between genes and ever changing social environments – the expression of genes rather than just the presence of a particular genetic sequence. As Krieger emphasizes, embodiment is a *verb* for 'our bodily engagement (soma and psyche combined) individually and collectively, with the biophysical world and each other' (*Ibid.*, p. 222). People and the world they help shape are always active participants not passive subjects, in the processes of embodiment.

Embodiment can link epidemiology to city planning in currently under-hypothesized ways. City planning activities regularly shape the physical, cultural and social worlds of urban dwellers, but the field has not engaged with the bodily implications of its practices as much as fields like sociology and anthropology (Bourdieu, 1990; Emirbayer, 1997; Burawoy, 1998). Krieger explains the far-reaching intentions of eco-social embodiment and potential for linking currently disparate disciplines, describing it as:

A useful bridge to novel twenty-first century research in the cognitive and neurosciences, which are providing new evidence on the centrality of bodily sensory-motor experiences and interactions (with both organisms and the broader biophysical context) to the development and expressions of both cognition and behavior. Thus, embodiment conceptually stands as a deliberate corrective to dominant disembodied and decontextualized accounts of 'genes', behaviors and mechanisms of disease causation, offering in their place an integrated approach to analyzing the multilevel processes, from societal and ecological to subcellular, that co-produce population distributions of health, disease and well-being. (Krieger, 2011, p. 222)

Thus, for adaptive urban health justice, understanding history and context must be the starting points for exploring the relational interactions between society and biology.

Multiple Pathways of Embodiment

The second construct of eco-social epidemiology builds on the first and emphasizes that there are always multiple pathways of embodiment. Too often in public health and medicine we look for the 'one big cause' that can explain illness or promote wellbeing, such as sugar, dietary fats, smoking or physical activity (Taubes, 2008; Freedman, 2010). Public health also tends to model just one exposure at one point in time, often discounting multiple exposure pathways that change over one's lifetime. Eco-social epidemiology posits that multiple exposures happen at a range of scales, from the individual to the city/region to the global, and can include such pathogens as social and economic deprivation, environmental pollutants and toxins, discrimination and other trauma, targeted marketing of harmful commodities, inadequate health care and the degradation of life-supporting ecosystems (Krieger, 2011, p. 214). Here again city planners must understand how urban policies, institutions and practices shape and influence these factors, such as policies promoting racial residential segregation, taxation and government spending, infrastructure, transport and environmental policies and inclusive or exclusive decision-making processes.

Weathering Hypothesis

One hypothesis that can help city planners understand the bodily impact of multiple social, economic and other stressful exposures is called 'weathering' (Geronimus, 1992). The weathering hypothesis states that stressors on the body from social, economic, political and environmental deprivation and pathogens, from *in utero* throughout the life course, constantly wear down or weather the immune and neurologic systems leading to a range of diseases and possibly premature death (*Ibid.*). The hypothesis draws on a century of research into the effects of racism on health, from W.E.B. Du Bois and Kelly Miller in the late nineteenth and early twentieth centuries through studies by Frantz Fanon in the 1960s to twenty-first century articulations of structural racism (Du Bois, 1906; Fanon, 1968; Kelly, 1897; Williams, 1999). The idea of 'weathering on the body' is like the weathering sea salt air might do to the paint on the exterior of a building – a constant wearing away that reduces the paint's ability to protect the surfaces underneath and ultimately the inhabitants of the building. However, human weathering is not on the surface but to the human body's neuroendocrine system which reacts to socially produced, unnatural, stressors such as chronic unemployment, poverty, housing instability, lack of medical care, and the fear of crime (McEwen, 2000) (figure 1.1).

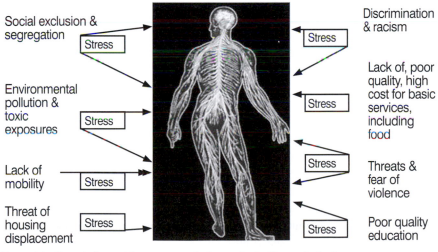

Figure 1.1. Cumulative social stressors on the human body. (*Source*: Author)

Under 'normal' stressful situations, the human body has a range of physical and chemical responses but primarily epinephrine (adrenaline) and cortisol are released to bring the endocrine and immune systems back to homeostasis. This adaptation is the body's ability to maintain stability under change and has been called allostasis (*Ibid.*) (figure 1.2). The weathering hypothesis states that under constant stressors the 'allostic load' continues to increase and the chemical release of 'fight or flight' hormones does

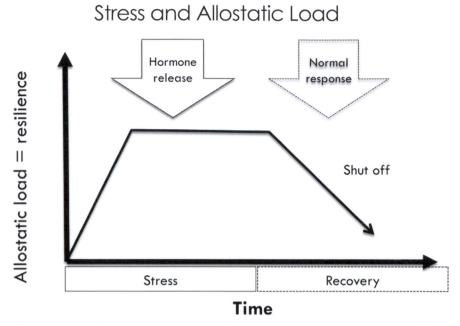

Figure 1.2. Normal biologic response to stress. (*Source*: Author, adopted from Geronimus, 1992)

not properly regulate or shut-off. The hypothesis states that increased allostatic load wears away at the immune system as it overworks to manage the hormonal releases and attempt to return to homeostasis. In addition, the weathering hypothesis suggests that the over-secretion of cortisol and adrenaline can trigger other biologic responses like poor glucose regulation and constant feelings of hunger that can contribute to chronic diseases such as overweight and obesity, diabetes, hypertension, cardiovascular disease, stroke, asthma and other immune-related illnesses (figure 1.3). While the weathering hypothesis was developed initially to explain poor birth outcomes for African-American women, there is reason to believe that the hypothesis can help guide city planners and others interested in understanding and addressing socio-economic inequities in health. Consistent with eco-social epidemiology, the weathering hypothesis demands that adaptive urban health justice identifies and articulates the institutional practices, routines and policies that are likely contributing to, mitigating or working to eliminate social stressors on a city's most vulnerable populations and places before rushing to offer ameliorative interventions.

Relational Framing: Exposure, Susceptibility and Resilience

The third core construct in eco-social epidemiology is that there is constant 'interplay between exposure, susceptibility and resistance, at multiple levels (individual, neighbourhood, regional or political jurisdiction, national, inter- or supra-national) and

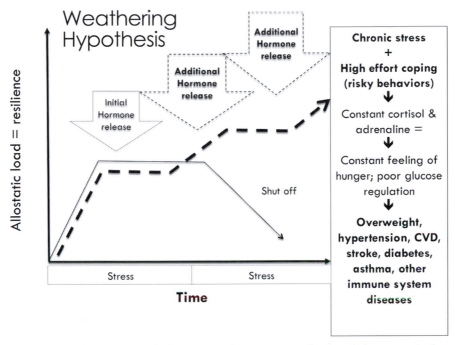

Figure 1.3. Weathering: constant biologic wearing from stressors & related morbidity. (*Source*: Author adopted from Geronimus, 1992)

in multiple domains (e.g. home, work, school, other public settings)' (Krieger 2011, pp. 222–223). What this means is that healthy city planners cannot be content with only studying morbidity and mortality but must also take seriously the institutional and individual forces that promote resilience and decrease susceptibility to illness for people in particular urban places. Too often public health researchers assume that if they reveal forces that seem to contribute to vulnerability and susceptibility to disease, eliminating these forces will result in greater resilience and even reduce health inequities between groups. Yet, just as public policy and behavioural economists have highlighted that reducing 'negative' behaviours is very different from inducing 'positive' ones, so too must urban public health focus on appreciative inquiry. No place, no matter how harsh the conditions, is all bad; people find ingenious ways to survive and thrive in unexpected ways and public health and city planning have for too long ignored these people-centred innovations.

The interplay of resilience and susceptibility in urban health equity was highlighted by Klinenberg's study of the 1995 heat wave in Chicago (Klinenberg, 2002). In a sophisticated analysis combining historical review of policies and places, quantitative data of populations and neighbourhoods, spatial mapping and ethnography, Klinenberg revealed that economic deprivation can be partially mediated by place-specific supportive social networks. These social supports probably helped prevent heat-related deaths of poor elderly residents in some Chicago neighbourhoods. The *Heat Wave* study explored why the African-American community of North Lawndale had higher heat-related deaths than the neighbouring Latino community of South Lawndale, called Little Village? The study found that a combination of public policies including racial residential segregation, policing and incarceration and 'redlining', that discouraged bank lending and investments, combined to shape physical and social despair in North Lawndale. Elderly African-Americans in North Lawndale were subsequently stranded among abandoned lots and fearful to leave their homes due to street violence during the heat wave. These same policies did not have the same effect in the largely Latino Little Village neighbourhood. Despite high individual and family poverty in Little Village, the community had a robust informal local economy, and cultural and religious activities that contributed to more street life and social interactions. Elderly residents in Little Village were less fearful than those in North Lawndale and got out of their homes to cool-off during the heat wave. The social interactions also encouraged social workers and church members to check up on vulnerable residents during the heat crisis. For Klinenberg, place-specific protective social networks were shaped by public policies, and the policies were shaped by structural racism against African-Americans that was not present against Latinos. In this case, only focusing on individual vulnerabilities would have missed the interplay between social structures, public policies and neighbourhood-level factors that can shape individual vulnerability and resilience (*Ibid.*).

Box 1.1. Relational approach to health equity: tackling HIV/AIDS in Brazil. (*Sources*: BMH, 2001; Engel 2006; Galvao, 2005; Nunn *et al.*, 2009; Oliveira-Cruz *et al.*, 2004; Parker, 2009).

In the 1980s, Brazil faced an AIDS epidemic, with one of the highest infection rates in the world. Activists organized to pressure the government to act. Public health leaders travelled to San Francisco, to learn what that city was doing to confront its rising AIDS crisis among the gay population. Returning to Brazil, activists and health professionals designed a multi-pronged strategy that was implemented over multiple years.

First, an educational campaign was launched that addressed the stigma of the disease, focused on free testing and preventing the spread of infections through programmes such as free condom and clean needle distribution. This was a radical approach in a country dominated by the Catholic Church. Activists worked to engage religious leaders in these campaigns.

Second, national laws were passed to outlaw discrimination against HIV positive individuals in employment, housing and other areas of society. A law was also passed guaranteeing the right of all Brazilians to have access to free anti-retroviral drug (ARV) treatment. Legislation required active social movements to ensure their implementation.

continued on page 21

continued from page 20

Third, Brazil rejected international trade rules on drug patents and began producing their own ARVs. In order to get enough ARVs to give them out free, Brazil invoked a clause in international trade law that allowed governments to break patents on drugs if there was a public health emergency. Brazil issued what are called compulsory licences, which allowed a domestic pharmaceutical industry to emerge and begin producing ARVs.

Fourth, Brazil's new national health care system was anchored with neighbourhood health clinics and community health workers, and hundreds of clinics were established and thousands of lay outreach workers trained and hired. A health system focused on prevention, not care, was institutionalized and delivered at the community-scale, reaching millions of poor Brazilians previously shut out of the health system.

Finally, coalitions of civil society groups organized geographically, such as in São Paulo and Rio de Janeiro, develop regional and national AIDS advocacy networks that are increasingly powerful in holding government accountable and altering electoral politics.

Brazil's AIDS programme was and remains the most successful in the world. No other country, rich or poor, has taken such an integrated and comprehensive approach to arrest the spread of AIDS.

Relational Characteristics of Urban Places

The *Heat Wave* study also highlights the variegated and relational aspects of urban communities and neighbourhoods that are too often glossed-over in public health and urban planning. As I have described elsewhere (Corburn, 2009, p. 14) 'place' is a concept that urban adaptive health justice should not treat simply and must be viewed relationally. A relational approach to place means emphasizing the interactions among the physical and social characteristics of places (not treating these as covariates in a formula) and the meanings that people in different places assign to these characteristics and their places more generally. A place might labelled 'safe' or 'dangerous' and planners must work to understand how these meanings are constructed and reconstructed over time, how some get stabilized and institutionalized to become 'taken for granted' and how some get reconstituted and influence the allocation of resources to the place (Escobar, 2001; Simone, 2004).

Place in healthy city planning is not just the background where economic, social, behavioural, and other transactions occur. Urban places express state and corporate power and are sites of resistance. This should come as no surprise since political change, from the Prague Spring of 1968 to the Arab Spring of 2011, often originates and builds oppositional power in metropolitan areas. The *La Via Campesina*[2] international movement that includes millions of peasants, farmers, landless and indigenous people is an important exception here, but even this movement organizes most of its main events in cities.

Places have agency, since people and institutions build things. This is another way places exert power. Places also take on monetary value such as through ownership and control of land, further distributing power. Places are sites of politics since social movements often organize in places but governments also organize electoral and representational politics by creating place-based political districts. Gerrymandering in numerous countries and attempts to depoliticize the boundary drawing process, such as the Boundary Commission in the UK, are just two examples of how place-based geographies of power are exercised. State-defined places take on further power distribution roles through taxation of land and catchment areas for such services as schools, hospitals, fire and emergency, and sanitary districts. Place politics is increasingly about boundary making – who and what is invited in – as competition among metropolitan areas replaces nation-states for business, cultural and other investments (Scott, 1998).

Community is another relational concept that is often treated synonymously with place. Communities in planning and urban health practice are often defined *a priori* as geographic locations, or around a particular milieu in which people gather, such as a church or recreation centre. Communities can also be defined by a shared set of interests, language or perspectives that may cut across geographic boundaries. Like place, community is not just a 'noun' to be found in the world, but rather is actively made and remade, enabled and stymied, valued or discounted by institutions and people.

In these ways, place and community in healthy city planning are about embracing *inter-sectionality and rejecting essentialism* – or the notions that no one person, group or place has a single, easily stated, unitary identity and that no absolute 'truth' from any single perspective exists (Corburn, 2005, p. 59). Thus, inter-sectionality and anti-essentialism demands that healthy city planning theory and practice acknowledge that not all places with the same health inequities will require the same ameliorative interventions because the suffering of an Afro-Brazilian community in a *favela* in the North Zone of Rio de Janeiro may be different than that of a lesbian Kikuyu single mother in a Nairobi informal settlement and still different than an African immigrant young male in the suburbs of Paris.

Accountability and Agency: Identifying Responsible Institutions

The *Heat Wave* case study by Klinenberg also helps highlight eco-social epidemiology's fourth construct that emphasizes 'accountability and agency for both the actual health inequities and for ways in which they are monitored, analyzed and addressed' (Krieger, 2011, p. 225). Agency can apply to researchers framing issues, defining problems and emphasizing some evidence over others, community organizations and civil society groups more generally that mobilize to reframe science policy issues (i.e. Epstein, 1996), corporations that use the inherent uncertainties of science to pollute and kill

(Markowitz and Rosner, 2002), and governments and inter-governmental institutions that legislate, regulate, enforce and re-interpret the rules that govern society. Urban adaptive health justice must identify the agents and institutions that are responsible for helping to create the social inequalities that contribute to health inequities in cities. This must include historical and contemporary institutional and policy analyses.

This eco-social construct also emphasizes *monitoring*. Surveillance is already a recognized function of public health and planners regularly collect reams of data on land use, socio-demographics and so on. However, turning data into monitoring indicators requires value judgments over what is important to measure, at what frequency and to what end? Monitoring can also imply assigning responsibility for a particular trend, and this too is rarely done in current planning and public health practice.

For example, burden of disease estimates have tended to focus on the whole world or specific geographic regions (Murray and Lopez, 1997; Wurthwein *et al.*, 2001). These data can mask intra-city differences and global data may not be relevant for informing national or municipal policy making. Public health has developed metrics for single pathogenic exposures or risk factors, but these measures often ignore both community assets that promote health equity and cumulative impacts on health from exposure to a range of urban environmental, economic and social stressors that characterize twenty-first century urban health inequities in the global north and south (Steenland and Armstrong, 2006; Harpham, 2009). Recognizing these population health challenges, the Commission on Social Determinants of Health (2008) called for 'health equity to become a marker of good government performance' (CSDH, 2008, p. 11) and for the UN to 'adopt health equity as a core global development goal and use a social determinants of health indicators framework to monitor progress' (*Ibid.*, p. 19).

More recently, the 2011 World Social Determinants of Health Conference and the Pan-American Health Organization's Urban Health Strategy called for the development of new urban health equity indicators that track the drivers of health inequities across place and time, particularly within a city neighbourhood (PAHO, 2011). Yet, the danger of indicator efforts is that they portray a too simplified picture of a complex reality and policy solutions may suffer the same defects. For example, indicators of single chemical exposures cannot produce policy-relevant knowledge about the environmental health consequences of multiple exposures. In a similar way, cross-sectional measures of single built and social environmental features of urban neighbourhoods tend to ignore the cascading and relational effects of inequalities in urban areas. Eco-social epidemiology demands that we critically examine the efficacy of traditional indicators that measure morbidity and mortality, since they tend either to place responsibility for improving health on the medical and public health communities alone or on vaguely identified institutions such as the economy, education or built environment. The result is an overemphasis on medical and public health solutions while failing to articulate the specific agents, institutions and policies that might need to change to promote greater urban health equity.

Science and Technology Studies for the City

The second core concept for urban adaptive health justice borrows from science and technology studies (STS) and aims to open-up science to wider democratic accountability and greater social problem solving. As mentioned in the Introduction, journals such as *Nature*, *Science* and *The Lancet* have all recently called for a new science of, and for, the city, particularly to address human health and sustainability issues. As I argue in more detail in Chapters 2 and 3, current scientific paradigms are partly to blame for some of the challenges facing healthy city planning today and new science-society paradigms are necessary for new practice. STS offers one such useful framework.

Scholars of STS, among others, have emphasized that the pursuit of science is now less in centralized research institutions and much more dispersed, context-dependent, and problem-oriented. That community members are monitoring the toxins they are exposed to in their homes and streets in partnership with community-based organizations and academics is just one example of this new model of science (Payne-Sturgess *et al.*, 2004; Corburn, 2005). Gibbons *et al.* (1994) have called this 'Mode 2' science and has the following characteristics:

◆ Knowledge that is increasingly produced in contexts of application (i.e. all science is to some extent 'applied' science).

◆ Science is increasingly transdisciplinary – that is, it draws upon and integrates empirical and theoretical elements from a variety of fields.

◆ Knowledge is generated in a wider variety of sites than ever before, not just in universities and industry, but also in other sorts of research centres, consultancies, and think-tanks.

◆ Participants in science have grown more aware of the social implications of their work (i.e. more 'reflexive'), just as publics have become more conscious of the ways in which science and technology affect their interests and values (Jasanoff, 2004, p. 234).

Ensuring the public accountability of Mode 2 science is challenging since typical methods of internal legitimacy, such as peer review, rarely if ever consider the social value of the work as a criterion (Jasanoff, 2005). Further, who the peers are and how they might be selected and what standards they might use for publicly accountable reviews is equally challenging.

Dissatisfied with the one-size-fits-all approach to peer review, Funtowicz and Ravetz (1992) proposed to divide the world of policy-relevant science into three nested domains with their own quality controls. First, they described normal science (borrowing from Thomas Kuhn's well known articulation) as ordinary or what we might call basic scientific research. A second modality for Funtowicz and Ravetz was consultancy science which is the application of science to well-defined problems. In both basic and consultancy science, traditional peer review might be effective in ensuring credibility. Finally, there was post-normal science, which they described as situations with highly uncertain and contested knowledge claims but where decisions need to made in a timely way, such as those over health and safety regulations. For Funtowicz and Ravetz, post-normal science demands what they call an 'extended peer review community' involving not only scientists but also the stakeholders affected by the issue. The aim of extended peer review is to ensure the public accountability and quality control of science policy decisions.

The implication is that science that continues to derive legitimacy solely from a socially detached position is too frail to meet the pressures placed upon it by contemporary problems, such as climate change, sustainability and healthy cities. Science must begin to focus more on gaining robustness from being embedded in, not increasingly detached from, society. However, as Jasanoff (2004) notes, this raises a serious challenge for how to institutionalize polycentric, interactive, and multipartite processes of knowledge-making within institutions that have worked for decades at keeping expert knowledge away from the vagaries of populism and politics. The question confronting the governance of science is how to bring knowledgeable publics into the front-end of scientific and technological production – a place from which they have historically been strictly excluded. This challenge raises the need for the third conceptual frame for healthy city planning, adaptive ecosystem management.

Adaptive Ecosystem Management

Adaptive ecosystem management and its related concept of sustainability science act as the third concepts in the healthy city planning framework. Sustainability science is one application or discipline that emerged in part as a response to the Mode 2 claims in STS (Kates *et al.*, 2001; Clark and Dickson, 2003; Kauffmann, 2009). It aims to reframe science around interactions between science and society, a focus on problems rather than disciplinary methods and coproducing knowledge for action.[3] Adaptive ecosystem management is a sub-field within sustainability science (Norton, 2005).

Adaptive ecosystem management was first articulated by Holling (1978) and was designed with insights from complex adaptive systems research and ecological management. Adaptive management acknowledges the failures of linear processes where narrow disciplinary scientists have aimed to develop complex models, predict long-term outcomes and suggest one-time policy standards. Instead, adaptive management begins with an acknowledgement of the inherent complexity and uncertainty within systems, that this complexity demands an iterative, ongoing learning process among a range of expert stakeholders, and policy interventions must be adjusted to reflect newly acquired knowledge (Lee, 1993; NRC, 2004). Another difference between adaptive management and conventional science policy is that adaptive management does not postpone actions until definitive causality is known about a system, but rather emphasizes the importance of action in the face of uncertain

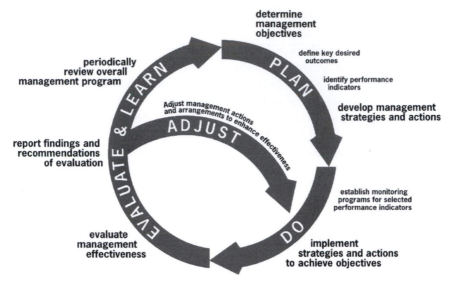

Figure 1.4. Adaptive management process. (*Source*: © Copyright CSIRO Australia, 2012. http://www. cmar.csiro.au/research/mse/)

science and couples these decisions tightly to rigorous monitoring (Norton, 2005). The National Research Council in the US has characterized adaptive management as an iterative process with the following characteristics (NRC, 1999, pp. 23–27) (figure 1.4):

1.   Management objectives that are regularly revisited and revised;

2.   A baseline model of change described for the system(s) being managed;

3.   A range of management choices;

4.   Monitoring and evaluation of choices;

5.   Mechanisms for incorporating learning into future decisions; and

6.   A collaborative structure for stakeholder participation and learning.

   The process of adaptive management is one where a broad group of stakeholders, from scientists to policy-makers to users of a resource, work together to generate evidence, make decisions, monitor the progress of those decisions, and make ongoing adjustments to decisions as new information emerges from monitoring. Gohlke and Portier (2007) call for greater capacity within public health institutions to adapt to new and emerging challenges, such as drug resistant infections and climate change, and that the field and discipline is currently ill-suited for adaptive science-based research and practice. Huang *et al.* (2011) also stress the importance of enhancing resources and training for the redesign of public health institutions to enhance the field's adaptive capacity.

Table 1.1. Traditional versus adaptive science policy.

Traditional Science Policy	Adaptive Science Policy
• Cross sectional data by few experts	• Broad stakeholder involvement – professionals & community
• Build predictive models	• Set management goals & act 1st
• Aim for short-term system equilibrium	• On-going, longitudinal data collection; Group monitoring, learning & evaluation
• Top-down policies of control & enforce	• Adjust policies & avoid problem displacement

Adaptive Urban Health Justice = Healthy City Planning

Building on the three concepts of eco-social epidemiology, science and technology studies, and adaptive ecosystem management, I turn to offer more specific details for the practice of Adaptive Urban Health Justice. Adaptive Urban Health Justice has five core components:

1. Democratic participation;

2. Integrated decision-making;

3. Multi-dimensional monitoring;

4. Social learning;

5. Adjustment and innovation.

1. Democratic Participation

The first construct of adaptive urban health justice is the design of democratic participatory processes where a range of expert stakeholders, professionals and lay people, can engage in the management process. As Healey (1998; 2003) and Innes and Booher (2010) among others have emphasized, collaborative policy processes are an important model in complex policy planning situations such as those confronting healthy city planning. Democratic participation is capable of addressing complex problem solving when associations of groups engage in 'communicative action' and connect local deliberative processes to others across a region, nation or even globally (Appaduri, 2002; Fung, 2006; Fraser, 2009). In these processes individual and organizationally affiliated agents are connected in a public process. They can often be networked across an entire city so that local or neighbourhood collaborative dialogues are linked to those across an entire city.

As I will show in Chapter 4, this is the model of the Rio de Janeiro Healthy Cities Network facilitated by the Center for Health Promotion (CEDAPS) in Brazil. Of course, participatory budgeting, which emerged in Porto Alegre, Brazil, is another example of networked democratic participation, where citizens directly deliberate over what they want but also elect representatives to engage with decision-makers in an ongoing way (Lerner, 2010). In Belo Horizonte, Brazil, participatory budgeting is already a central practice for promoting greater public participation in urban health and equity decision-making (see Box 1.2).

Box 1.2. Participatory budgeting and health in Belo Horizonte, Brazil. (*Sources*: Caiaffa *et al.*, 2005; Vlahov *et al.*, 2011)

Belo Horizonte is the fourth most populous city in Brazil, with approximately 2.3 million residents, vast income inequalities and a favela population only behind Rio and São Paulo. Belo Horizonte's Profavela Program includes participatory master planning, ongoing monitoring of community outcomes, and participatory budgeting. Participatory budgeting is a process that allows citizens to influence directly municipal budgetary priorities and expenditures.

In Belo Horizonte, participatory budgeting began in 1998 and includes an intersectoral, municipal government committee that creates and updates the master plan for the city (Plano Plurianual de Ação Governamental, PPAG). Representatives from five sectors (urban policy, urban planning, office for disadvantaged populations [social exclusion], environment, and sanitation) meet to discuss and develop the overall city blueprint. Citizens elect district committee representatives who meet directly with elected and government officials to decide issue and spending priorities. As part of the process of finalizing a project spending list, delegates make site visits to each proposed project site (the 'Priority Caravan'). After months of deliberation, selected projects undergo a general vote. Delegates from more vulnerable sub-regions – based on the number of slum dwellers – get a higher weighted vote per person.

Municipal funds are allocated using a formula that ensures half of the total budget is divided equally between the nine municipal regions. The other half of the budget is based on each area's rank according to an Urban Life Quality Index that measures community vulnerability based on water/sanitation service, social assistance, sports and cultural programmes, and infant mortality, premature births, and health access measures. The scores of each unit are combined to arrive at a total score for a region.

In 2006, 90 per cent of the population lived within 1,000 metres of a participatory budgeting project, half of the projects have been citywide infrastructure improvements, one-third were favela specific physical upgrading, 10 per cent constructed Family Health Centres, and the remaining built schools, sports fields, and cultural centres. In 14 years, approximately $300 million (only about 3 per cent of the annual municipal budget) has been spent on over 800 participatory budget capital projects while additional funds are secured for operation and maintenance.

2. Integrated Decision-Making

In adaptive urban health justice, decision-making comes much earlier in the process that traditional or rational policy-making. Under rational public policy-making, the 'ready-aim-fire' metaphor is common, while in adaptive management 'ready-fire-aim' is more common (Majone, 1989). What this means is that decisions are made acknowledging uncertainty, ambiguity and fallibility. Decisions are viewed as experiments, not end products.

As Norton (2005) emphasizes, adaptive decision-making integrates the range of perspectives and knowledges in the participatory process. Integrated action avoids the singe issue, disease or sector decisions that currently dominate planning and public health. Creativity and commitment to integrating perspectives will be necessary but knowledge alone is insufficient. Integrated decision-making aims to elicit what the public wants, to make apparent the possibility of unforeseen consequences and to make explicit the normative that often lurks within the technical.

Since 2004, Medellin, Colombia, has embarked on a programme called *Proyectos Urbanos Integrales* (PUI) that is an example of integrated urban equity planning. The project integrated the world's first modern urban aerial cable-car public transport system with comprehensive neighbourhood upgrading comprising new social housing, schools, parks, museums and other social services including direct support for micro-enterprises. Through a combination of active organizations of the urban poor and Mayoral leadership, the PUI identified priority projects and developed a staged implementation plan. According to Alejandro Echeverri, one of the principal architects of Medellin's transformation, planners worked closely with NGOs to prioritize projects. Some municipal planners were only assigned to working with community residents to imagine and plan 'integral projects'. Public spaces and projects that would benefit children were prioritized as were projects that would allow people from different classes and segregated parts of the city to interact. Local residents were hired for all the project construction labour. A participatory budgeting process ensures that local communities have a mechanism to participate in the allocation of resources to maintain and expand the initial investments. By integrating the cable car investment with other projects, the PUI has increased open space in the city, increased the number of local businesses operating around stations from 700 to over 1,000, built eighteen new parks and four new pedestrian bridges (Davila and Daste, 2012; Betancur, 2007; Fukuyama and Colby, 2011; Hylton, 2007).

3. Multi-Dimensional Monitoring

The third aspect of adaptive urban health justice involves multi-dimensional monitoring of decisions to track how well they are addressing health equity. Multi-dimensional monitoring requires the selection of indicators using a range of data sources and linking these to the pathways of embodiment as described in eco-social epidemiology. What we choose to monitor, and how, reflects the values that the adaptive process has towards:

◆   Legitimate sources of knowledge (the sources we consider trustworthy);

◆   Which research questions people pursue or ignore (e.g. do we study the poor or do we study which policies produce poverty?);

◆   The attribution of responsibility for health or illness;

◆   Appropriate targets for policy;

◆   How and where to use resources; and

◆   Whether health inequities are perceived as injustices or random outcomes.

For example, after receiving mediocre results on the Programme of International Student Assessment (PISA), a set of indicators tracked by the Organization for Economic Co-operation and Development (OECD), Germany initiated substantial educational reforms that continue to be tracked today. The Multi-Dimensional Poverty Index (MPI) developed in 2010 by the Oxford Poverty & Human Development Initiative is another example of multi-dimensional indicators (Alkire and Foster, 2011). In this process, a set of measures is compiled to relate poverty to education, health and living conditions (figure 1.5). Gulyani and Basset (2008) have also offered a multi-dimensional set of indicators, in their case specific to slum upgrading. For Gulyani and Basset two relational 'diamonds' display how, taken together, their multi-dimensional indicators track improvements to lives and living conditions (figure 1.6).

Yet, adaptive urban health justice indicators should do more than capture health outcomes, but also the determinants of health that often drive outcomes, including institutional practices and policy decisions made outside the health care and medical

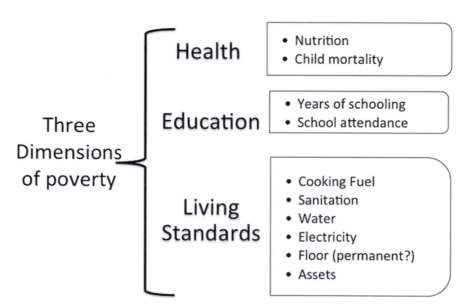

Figure 1.5. Multi-dimensional poverty index. (*Source*: http://www.ophi.org.uk/policy/multidimension al-poverty-index/)

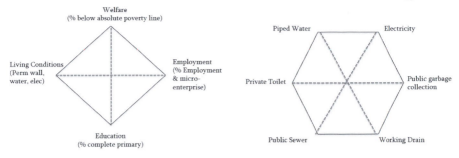

Figure 1.6. Relational diamonds of slum indicators: lives & living conditions. (*Source*: Gulyani and Basset, 2008)

sectors. Effective urban health equity indicators can monitor potential associations between determinants and health impacts by using data that are verifiable and easily accessible, and should be shared in a clear and compelling way by a range of interested stakeholders (table 1.2)

Yet, the multi-dimensional poverty index and the indicators offered by Gulyani and Basset do not capture the forces behind these outcomes or attempt to assign responsibility for the outcomes. The UN-Habitat Urban Indicators project aims to do this by including measures of governance, defined as the degree of decentralization in public decision-making, voter participation, the number of participants in civil society organizations, and the public transparency and accountability of local government institutions (UN-Habitat, 2011). Similarly, the World Health Organization's Urban Health Equity Assessment and Response Tool (HEART) also measures indicators that influence health equity such as government spending on health and education,

Table 1.2. Characteristics of adaptive urban health justice indicators.

Characteristic	Description
Simplicity	Easy to understand by a range of people and not requiring too much expert knowledge; tap into local knowledge and community expertise.
Relevance	They illustrate something about the system that residents and/or decision-makers need to know, and are collected frequently enough to influence action. They may also inspire people to see circumstances in new ways, including by disaggregating information by population groups, places, and/or presenting trends over time.
Reliability	Measures both assets and liabilities; public trust behind the information/methods of data collection; easily verifiable through available data.
Accessibility	The information is already available or regularly gathered and made publically available.
Responsibility	Identifies specific institutions, policies or processes that historically and currently contribute to inequities and those that work to promote greater equity.
Relational and Adaptable	Together, a set of indicators tells a compelling story about health equity; focus on relationships among measures, not just individual metrics.
Reporting	Develops reporting strategy from the beginning, identifies intended audiences, utilizes multiple forms of media/technology, and timed to inform various research and political decision-making processes.

voter participation, percentage of population completing primary education, and the proportion of the population covered by health and other insurance (WHO, 2010*a*).

Box 1.3. Participatory monitoring for a healthy municipality: Nossa São Paulo. (*Source*: http://www.nossasaopaulo.org.br/portal/)

Nossa São Paulo in Brazil is a civil society movement focused on the creation of democratic dialogue between citizens and municipal politicians and officials about quality of life indicators. The movement has over 600 participating organizations that are pooling their knowledge and resources to monitor various aspects of life in the city. The movement is modelled after Bogota Como Vamos, which started in Bogota, Colombia.

In its first 2 years from 2007–2009, Nossa SP established a publically accessible database of quality indicators for all of the city's sub-municipalities, including two annual opinion polls on the public's perception of life in the city. According to Mauricio Broinizi, director of Nossa SP, they made an explicit decision to have community members define indicators and not choose those defined by international organizations, or other cities in the global North or South. The best district average acts as the 'baseline' goal for the worst district. For example, Pinheiros's administrative unit has the best infant mortality indicator (5.98 per 1,000 live births) and Capela do Socorro has the worst (16.90 per 1,000) with Parelheiros not far behind (16.07 per 1,000). For households not connected to the sewer system, Sé was the best (0.75 per cent not covered) while Parelheiros was the worst (56.8 per cent). The numbers are meaningful to those that live there and those responsible for city services, but may not make sense to compare across other cities in Brazil or internationally.

These data helped Nossa SP influence the city's mayoral election, organize a campaign to lower sulphur in the diesel fuel and other campaigns that garnered widespread media attention. The district-level indicators include questions about equity from a household survey that included the city's favela residents. The group is also monitoring the city government's performance in a number of areas focused on resident-defined priorities, such as improving public space, increasing public and bicycle transportation, and citizen participation in district management. Another accomplishment of their indicators work was to influence the Mayor to present a Plan of Goals for the city and each district that the city and Nossa SP would monitor every 6 months.

The work of Nossa SP has been replicated in a dozen Brazilian cities and now forms the *Rede Social Brasileira por Cidades Justas e Sustentáveis*, which is linked to the Latin American 'Red de ciudades' movement. Community generated indicators with ongoing monitoring has led to a democratic social movement that is defining equity and wellbeing and using this process to hold local government accountable for promoting the conditions for greater equity and wellbeing in cities.

4. Social Learning

Monitoring can be a form of learning and the fourth characteristic of adaptive urban health justice is social learning. In the social world, learning is often constrained by the frame within which institutions must act. Just as historians disagree over what may have caused the rise or fall of particular political regimes, policy-makers may find it impossible to attribute their failures to specific causes. The origins of a problem may appear one way to those in power, and in quite another way to the marginal or the excluded. Adaptive learning requires assessment of the strengths and weaknesses of alternative evidence and explanations. As Argyris and Schon point out:

[T]he trouble people have in learning new theories may stem not so much from the inherent difficulty of the new theories as from the existing theories people have that already determine practices. We call their operational theories of action theories-in-use to distinguish them from the espoused theories that are used to describe and justify behavior. We wondered whether the difficulty in learning new theories of action is related to a disposition to protect the old theory-in-use. (Argyris and Schon, 1974, p. viii)

John Dewey believed that learning through experience was the 'progressive' alternative to traditional education. For Dewey, learning entailed a continuity of experiences or, as he put it, 'an experiential continuum'. Each experience should be influenced by prior experiences. He claimed that every experience 'modifies the one who undergoes it and this modification affects the quality of subsequent experience' (Dewey, 1938, p. 36). Collateral learning was another concept for Dewey and involved the process of acquiring new knowledge in one setting that could be carried forward to make sense of and assign new meanings to a subsequent setting. Dewey noted:

What avail is it to win prescribed amounts of information about geography and history, to win ability to read and write, if in the process the individual loses his own soul: loses his appreciation of things worth while, of the values to which these things are relative; if he loses desire to apply what he has learned and, above all, loses the ability to extract meaning from his future experiences as they occur? (*Ibid.*, p. 49)

Argyris and Schon (1996) expand on Dewey and argue for looped social learning where repeated experiences shared in group dialogues help detect a mismatch between intentions and consequences. For Argyris and Schon, 'single loop' learning involves changing behaviour only to address the challenging situation at hand but does not change the underlying routines that lead to the mismatch. In order for more meaningful learning to occur, they offer a 'double loop' learning process where the governing variables – the values and assumptions behind our understandings – are reconsidered and questioned. Meaningful learning occurs in the 'double loop' process because we do not merely solve problems but challenge the governing variables behind our 'theories-in-use' (figure 1.7).

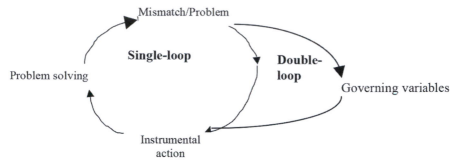

Figure 1.7. Double loop learning model. (*Source*: Argyis and Schon, 1996)

5. Adjustment and Innovation

A central feature of adaptive systems is the ability to learn and change as new information emerges from monitoring and is shared through democratic processes. Yet, adjustment needs a guide for change. Adjusting decisions will need to attention to the different temporal dimensions of health equity issues. Some decisions may need more time to take hold before adjustment while others will demand more frequent review. A core innovation of adaptive urban health justice is determining which decisions need frequent review and adjustment and what 'weight' of evidence triggers a review/adjustment and why? This is not a unique challenge to my framework, as public health and environmental policies have confronted this challenge for decades. The 'extended peer review' concept will be crucial here since these will inevitably be value judgments. Importantly, adapting must not be limited to the decisions themselves but also adjustment in the process, participants and goals of the adaptive management regime. Here I recognize that innovation frequently comes from both users and refusers, or those that engage with the subject (from the inside) and those that remain critics on the outside.

Building from Practice

This chapter has described the dimensions of adaptive urban health justice. The framework borrows from eco-social epidemiology, science studies and adaptive ecosystem management. The five dimensions outlined here mirror many of those of adaptive complex systems, but I have placed greater emphasis on having an explicit theory of health equity and neighbourhood changes stimulating wider system change – the butterfly effect. The brief examples offered here suggest that my proposed framework is not only possible but that many aspects are already being put into practice. While my framework is inherently iterative and dynamic, aiming for improvement as it moves forward, it is also keenly focused on learning. In the next two chapters I emphasize the importance of learning from the histories of city planning and public health to better inform our actions to promote greater health equity in city planning.

Notes

1. Eco-social epidemiology questions the biomedical explanation for the population distribution of health inequities that looks to genetics, and an individual's biology and behaviours as the primary explanations while barely acknowledging the influence of social and economic context.
2. See *viacampesina.org/en/*.
3. The journal *Sustainability Science* defines itself as providing 'a trans-disciplinary platform for contributing to building sustainability science as a new academic discipline focusing on topics not addressed by conventional disciplines. As a problem-driven discipline, sustainability science is concerned with addressing practical challenges caused by climate change, habitat and biodiversity loss, and poverty among others. At the same time it tries to investigate root causes of problems by uncovering new knowledge or combining current knowledge from more than one discipline in a holistic way to enhance understanding of sustainability'. (http://www.springer.com/environment/environmental+management/journal/11625)

Chapter 2

The City in the Field

Investigating Nineteenth-Century Urban Health Inequities in the Field

In early nineteenth-century Paris, a physician named Louis-René Villermé left his medical practice and began a research career. One of his landmark studies in Paris helps highlight the idea of 'the City as a Field Site' used in this chapter. Villermé was concerned with the controversies in his field at the time over whether disease was caused by contagion – the passage of illness from a sick to a healthy person through some yet unidentified process – or miasma. Miasma theory traced disease to the environment, broadly defined as filth, dirty air and noxious odours – commonly from rotting waste and dead bodies. Villermé was interested in investigating whether the environments of neighbourhoods including weather, altitude, proximity to the polluted Seine River, street width, housing density, trees and park space helped explain the distribution of mortality among populations in Paris (Porter, 1999, p. 68).

Villermé was sceptical of both the contagionists, who looked to biological explanations for the distribution of disease, and miasmists, and hypothesized that social forces, chiefly economic poverty, was a more important driver of ill health and death across city neighbourhoods. To investigate his hypothesis, he combined disparate data sets that had rarely been linked at the time to study urban health (Krieger, 2011, p. 78). First, Villermé gathered population data by Paris *arrondissement*, or neighbourhood district, collected in the 1817 census along with tax records from 1817 to 1820. Not limiting his investigation to quantitative information alone, he compiled detailed neighbourhood land survey information that characterized the qualities of the built environment along with handwritten field notes from the city's chief statistician (Coleman, 1982).

Villermé stratified his data into three categories, mortality, population density and income (Villermé, 1830). The mortality category used reports of 'at home deaths' from the census. Population density was calculated using land surveys and the number of inhabitants per square metre of area, taking into consideration space used for gardens, courtyards and streets. Finally, Villermé used a novel approach for estimating neighbourhood wealth by calculating the average rent per *arrondissement* and the ratio of taxes paid (or unpaid) to total rents paid per neighbourhood (Susser and Stein, 2009, p. 46).

Villermé constructed a table of his variables by *arrondissement*. He found that all the environmental factors had little relationship to mortality, including in-home and area densities and proximity to pollution. The strongest predictor of mortality was neighbourhood wealth, as measured by taxes paid and rents. For example, Villermé ulated that of all the neighbourhoods, the IXe *arrondissement* had the highest in-home mortality rate of 1 per 43 inhabitants (or about 221 deaths per 10,000 persons) but one of the lowest average rents at 172 francs per month, and 30 per cent of residents did not pay tax, meaning they were too poor to pay. He also found that the IIe *arrondissement* was the wealthiest with an average rent of over 600 francs per month, only 7 per cent of untaxed rents and a mortality rate of 1 per 63 inhabitants (or about 155 per 10,000 inhabitants). Villermé concluded that economic privilege or misery trumped neighbourhood factors in explaining mortality rates across urban Paris.

Villermé's findings were radical for the time because he questioned the prevailing theories of disease, namely miasma and contagion, and suggested that economic inequality was a more important factor in explaining why people in certain neighbourhoods died more frequently than others. His methods were also revolutionary, since he gathered a range of detailed data on the places and the populations living there, including quantitative and descriptive information. He also related detailed information of place to governance, namely taxation. In these ways Villermé combined aspects of both the field site view of the city and the laboratory view.

In the field site view of the city, professionals and city dwellers often act as surveyors, ethnographers, and analysts while developing a keen personal sensitivity to the uniquely revealing features of their particular place. The laboratory view of cities, which I describe in more detail in Chapter 3, orients urban research and policy-making to mirror the values of laboratory science, such as the detachment of researcher from researched, strict control of inputs and outputs that can be universally applied anywhere. Fieldwork often involves immersion in a site for a long period of time and developing embodied ways of feeling, seeing, and understanding. Yet 'the field' can carry with it a romanticized view of an unadulterated reality and that 'fieldwork' reveals things about a place that cannot be understood or replicated anywhere else.

This chapter traces some key actors and events in the early modern histories of city planning and public health, highlighting that the field site view was a major driving force in research and practice. Many nineteenth-century urban epidemiologists used the field framing to guide their investigations of disease and death and to investigate sanitary conditions more generally. The field site view helped reify miasma theory and often shifted attention away from hypotheses such as Villermé's finding that economic inequality was to blame. The field site view also had significant implications for urban governance, as the infrastructure projects it recommended needed to be publically financed and managed by expert bureaucracies, which were not yet institutionalized. New infrastructure management bureaucracies aimed to use health evidence to justify state interventions in the market economy and to regulate private industry activities, but evidence was increasingly difficult to gather. As a result, the field site view of the city began to move closer to modelling the laboratory view, even before laboratory science took hold and offered germ theory as a competing explanation to miasma.

Ultimately, the field site view weakened by the close of the nineteenth and early twentieth century, but not before significant institutions of urban planning and health were firmly established and legislation passed that sought to control the built environment in the name of public health. The field site view waned due to germ theory and bacteriology, and hygiene movements shifted their focus further and further inside the human body and less and less towards the environments – social, economic, built, etc – where people were exposed.

The 1840s: Competing Economic and Sanitary Explanations for Urban Disease

Villermé's findings did not convince the Paris Health Council to intervene in the growing economy. The Health Council continued to investigate noxious industries, garbage dumping, open sewage and adulterated food, but rarely challenged the growing economic liberalism in the city (Coleman, 1982). Yet, revolutionary ideas in Paris during and around 1848, particularly Socialist ideas, would call on medicine to be more active in urban governance in order to influence health.

Rudolph Virchow was a nineteenth-century German pathologist who studied disease and concluded, like Villermé, that government policies that perpetuated economic inequalities were to blame for differences in population distributions of disease and death. Virchow was employed by the Prussian government in 1848 to investigate a typhus epidemic in Upper Silesia, an area in North Prussia near the border with Poland. After extensive observations within the local hospital, interviewing physicians and patients, and field work in the community of Upper Silesia, Virchow wrote a report that included detailed case studies of the experiences of at least ten patients of different ages, sex, occupations and neighbourhoods (Ackerknecht, 1953). He concluded that there was no evidence of contagion as the cause of the epidemic. Virchow suggested that the history of place-based poverty, political oppression and disenfranchisement of Upper Silesians resulted in unhealthy living conditions and malnutrition, and that these economic and political factors were the cause of the epidemic. The local population had been subject to exploitation by the Prussians and lacking opportunities for political expression, Upper Silesians received nothing from their government. Full and unlimited democracy was the way to prevent typhus. Virchow recognized the radical nature of his findings, noting: (quoted from Porter, 1999, p. 107):

These are the radical methods I am suggesting as a remedy against the reoccurrence of famine and of great typhus epidemics in Upper Silesia… May therefore the next interval be used to preserve from the repetition of such scenes of horror by liberal institutions for the benefit of the people, which to the shame of the government has so far been inhabited only by poor and neglected people.

For Virchow, public health workers ought to be ambassadors or attorneys for the poor, advocating their rights as well as providing direct care. For him, changing social conditions would prolong and improve life more rapidly and successfully than improving medicine. He called on medicine to ensure that the state provided the material conditions that could prevent morbidity and premature mortality.

Filth and Urban Health

As the pace of industrialization increased in Britain, France, Germany and the United States in mid-nineteenth century, urban populations exploded as people sought work and a better life in cities. Rapid increases in population also meant that the physical infrastructure of cities, particularly housing and sanitation, could not keep pace. Buildings were quickly overcrowded as rooms were divided to house more workers and their families. Animal, human and industrial wastes accumulated dramatically in cities without systems for their removal. Common methods of waste disposal in cities, such as cesspools, regularly overflowed and contaminated water supplies and wells (Melosi, 2000; Tarr, 1996). Human and animal waste heaps were infested with flies and vermin, had unbearable odours and, when combined with the thousands of animals brought into the city for slaughter to feed the growing population, were logically seen as the culprit for infectious disease (Duffy, 1990). To make matters worse, as disease victims died in urban squalor, their bodies would often rot *in situ* for days as their families laboured or begged for the pennies to bury them (Wohl, 1984).

Chadwick and the Urban Sanitary Movement

For Edwin Chadwick, a lawyer working with Jeremy Bentham, eliminating disease required separating the labouring populations from the dependent poor. Chadwick was appointed to the Royal Commission of Enquiry on the Poor Laws in 1832, and his resulting report advocated reductions in government allowances to the poor, reforms implemented in the Poor Law Amendment Act of 1834. Chadwick would become Secretary of the Poor Law Commission and focused on studying the physical, rather than the social or economic, conditions where the poor lived. Chadwick hired medical officers assigned to the Poor Law to investigate London neighbourhoods with the highest typhus mortality. The doctors' reports described the squalor and crowded living conditions in these areas and Chadwick expanded his study to document sanitary conditions throughout Britain. Using hundreds of detailed case reports from these medical field workers, Chadwick would publish *The Report on the Sanitary Conditions of the Labouring Population in Great Britain* in 1842 (Chadwick, 1842).

Chadwick's report helped reveal the unsanitary living conditions afflicting the urban poor across Britain. He borrowed neighbourhood-scale maps that linked poor living conditions and death rates, such as the one produced by physician Robert Baker of Leeds in 1832 after a cholera outbreak (figure 2.1). Baker's map, reproduced in Chadwick's report, documented differing death rates by the wealth of populations, measured by employment and housing type, in different city neighbourhoods, including working, tradesperson and first class houses, along with population death

Figure 2.1. Sanitary map of Leeds, 1890s. (*Source*: Chadwick, 1842)

rates. The map seemed to link the highest death rates to districts with the lowest class of housing. To accomplish this, the map used symbols to note the locations of industry adjacent to housing, such as cotton and silk mills, and blue and red dots to identify the locations of deaths from cholera and other contagious diseases (Rosen, 1993).

Chadwick concluded that the only way to reduce death rates was to improve sanitary conditions. Chadwick did not address the issue of poverty directly. It is worth quoting Chadwick's report at length, from his concluding Section IX (Chadwick, 1842):

That the various forms of epidemic, endemic, and other disease caused, or aggravated, or propagated chiefly amongst the labouring classes by atmospheric impurities produced by decomposing animal and vegetable substances, by damp and filth, and close and overcrowded dwellings prevail amongst the population in every part of the kingdom, whether dwelling in separate houses, in rural villages, in small towns, in the larger towns, as they have been found to prevail in the lowest districts of the metropolis. That such disease, wherever its attacks are frequent, is always found in connexion with the physical circumstances above specified, and that where those circumstances are removed by drainage, proper cleansing, better ventilation, and other means of diminishing atmospheric impurity, the frequency and intensity of such disease is abated; and where the removal of the noxious agencies appears to be complete, such disease almost entirely disappears. That high prosperity in respect to employment and wages, and various and abundant food, have afforded to the labouring classes no exemptions from attacks of epidemic disease, which have been as frequent and as fatal in periods of commercial and manufacturing prosperity as in any others. That the formation of all habits of cleanliness is obstructed by defective supplies of water. That the annual loss of life from filth and bad ventilation are greater than the loss from death or wounds in any wars in which the country has been engaged in modern times.

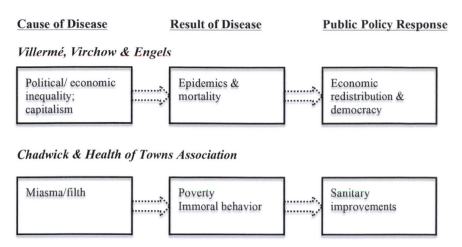

Figure 2.2. Different pathways to urban health in the nineteenth century: Villermé, Virchow & Engels.

Thus, even the upper classes, concluded Chadwick, were subject to disease if they lived in filth. These conclusions contrasted with those of Villermé and Virchow, but Chadwick's work would sway the field and government into action (figure 2.2).

Findings by the Committee on the Health of Towns agreed with those of Chadwick. A key report in 1840 linked the lack of planning in Manchester to unsanitary living conditions and disease, stating:

Manchester had no Building Act, and hence, with the exception of certain central streets, over which the Police Act gives the Commissioners power, each proprietor builds as he pleases... A cottage row may be badly drained, the streets may be full of pits, brimful of stagnant water, the receptacle of dead cats and dogs, yet no-one may find fault. Food is dear, labour scarce, and wages in many branches very low; disease and death are making unusual havoc. It is in such a depressed state of the manufacturing districts as at present exists that unpaved and badly sewered streets exhibit their malign influence on young and old. (Robertson, 1840)

The Health of Towns and Chadwick's report concurred that sanitary improvements such as 'drainage, the removal of all refuse of habitations, streets, and roads, and the improvement of the supplies of water' were necessary.

Changing the 'Immoral Traits' of Slum Dwellers

Two years after Chadwick's landmark report, Friedrich Engels published *The Conditions of the Working Class in England in 1844*, documenting that mortality rates around Manchester were stratified by three classes of streets and houses based on physical condition (Engels, 1968 [1844]). He also observed 'how the sufferings of childhood are indelibly stamped on the adults' (*Ibid.*, p. 115), resulting in a cumulative bodily impact from harsh working conditions, poor food, inadequate housing, and lack of medical care. Engels blamed locally polluting industries for creating unhealthy workplaces and neighbourhoods and argued that the antagonistic class relations of capitalism must be resolved in order to improve the public's health.

Chadwick believed sanitary improvements could accomplish what the Poor Law could not, namely 'cleaning-up' the bad habits of the urban poor. He noted in section IX of his 1842 report:

the removal of noxious physical circumstances, and the promotion of civic, household and personal cleanliness, are necessary to the improvement of the moral condition of the population; for that sound morality and refinement in manners and health are not long found co-existent with filthy habits amongst any class of the community.

This aspect of Chadwick's report was also influential with the Health of Towns Association, founded in 1844. This planning group would be even more explicit about the moral, not just health or economic, justification for urban sanitary interventions (Porter, 1999). Changing the living conditions of the urban poor was increasingly viewed by planners as a means to alter the social 'pathologies' of urban life, including violence, intemperance, and idleness (Boyer, 1983, p. 17). The 1848 report from the Health of Towns Association defined their position of moral environmentalism:

Thousands of human beings are here cooped up, filthy in habits, debased in morals, oppressed with want, abandoned and reckless – because without hope of relief – the proper subjects of disease and death engendered by the foulness which taints the air they breathe, the food they eat, the water they drink, covers the ground they walk on, ever clinging to them in close companionship with their persons, their clothing, their bed, and their board.

The Health of Towns Association report influenced the first British Pubic Health Act in 1848 (Porter, 1999). This Act established a General Board of Health and instructed local authorities to form local boards of health with powers over town infrastructure, including water and sewage, the regulation of industry and nuisances, to provide land for burials, and remove houses unfit for human habitation.

The Public Health Acts

The Public Health Act did not lead to widespread infrastructure investments as Chadwick and other sanitarians had hoped. Towns and cities pushed back against the idea of paternalistic central government directives and the wealthy objected to paying to clean-up the filth they blamed on the poor (Porter 1999, p. 120). Eventually, in 1854, Chadwick was removed from the General Board of Health and replaced by a physician, John Simon. Simon was a doctor-turned-statesman and, as Porter (*Ibid.*, p. 124) has argued, Simon would forcefully argue for medical professionals to advocate public policies and administrative changes to make the poor less poor. Legislation followed through the second half of the nineteenth century, including a new Public Health Act in 1858 and another in 1875. The 1875 Act gave the national government the power to prosecute local councils for failing to institute sanitary reforms (Wohl, 1984).

Decentralizing the responsibility for sanitary reforms to city governments was a key aspect of the 1875 Public Health Act. The Act codified such local tasks as housing form and street design and created local sanitary districts with the power to acquire land for public purposes. The Public Health Acts viewed local planning as the route to implement health policy goals (Porter, 1999).

John Snow and the Neighbourhood Field Site

After another cholera outbreak in 1848 London, the physician John Snow became interested in its cause after witnessing its devastating impact on his patients. Cholera was an illness where an upset stomach contributed to excessive fluid loss. The heart and kidneys struggle to function without fluid and eventually, especially in the nineteenth century, vital organs shut down. Victims died within forty-eight hours. The cholera epidemic of 1848–1849, by some estimates, claimed 50,000 lives in England and Wales (Johnson, 2006). Snow went to work investigating cholera by visiting neighbourhoods where the disease was most severe.

Snow visited Thomas Street in Horsleydown (now part of the London Borough of Southwark) and documented living conditions, finding that twelve poor families lived in connected cottages and shared a single well in a common courtyard. He noted that a wastewater channel drained into a cesspool adjacent to the drinking water well. According to Snow's report, in a two week period a dozen people from this building died from cholera. Snow also observed that in an adjacent building, residents shared a well from a different courtyard called Truscott's Court. During that same two-week period, only one person had died of cholera in the adjacent building. Snow hypothesized that something besides miasma was responsible for the disease since both buildings shared the same air and residents had similar housing and work place conditions (Johnson, 2006, p. 72).

As Snow would document in detail in his 1855 publication, *On the Mode of Communication of Cholera*, he used city death statistics disaggregated by London district to further investigate his hypothesis that perhaps ingestion of contaminated water, not foul air, was the source of cholera. He analyzed deaths by the source of a neighbourhood's water supply, since most areas received water from companies that siphoned water from the Thames River. What Snow found was that death rates were lower in neighbourhoods living north and east of the river than those in the central and southern areas. He hypothesized that those living further downstream were drinking more polluted water, since the city's street and industrial sewers drained into the river (Vinten-Johansen *et al.*, 2003).

Snow published these findings, and his hypotheses were widely rejected. During another cholera outbreak in 1854 in London, this time on Broad Street (now Broadwick Street) in Soho, Snow was commissioned to investigate by John Simon Chief Medical Officer at the General Board of Health. He documented the timing and location of all cases by house, the location of wastewater cesspools, and the water source of the victims. Two competing water companies provided water to Broad Street and both used water from the Thames that had been contaminated by sewage.

However, by 1853 one company, Lambeth Waterworks Company, had moved its intake source further upstream while the other, Southwark and Vauxhall Water Company, still supplied contaminated water. Snow undertook a door-to-door investigation of cholera mortality and asked specific questions of residents about the qualities – odour, clarity and taste – of their water supply. To his surprise, he learnt from residents that they preferred pump water and that users of the Broad Street pump did not complain about the water. Snow himself had observed that the pump's water was clear (Snow, 1854). He also visited the Lion Brewery on Broad Street to interview workers there who went about their work sipping the local beer throughout the day since it was part of their wage. Their beer was brewed with water from a private water supplier called the New River Company, not the local well.

As is now well known, John Snow used spatial maps of cholera deaths by street address to hypothesize that cholera was due to contaminated water from the Broad Street pump. He borrowed the idea of mapmaking from others, namely Edmund Cooper an engineer for the Metropolitan Commission of Sewers, to draft his own maps of the Broad Street area. The maps showed the highest death rates in homes closest to the Broad Street pump (figure 2.3). A public hearing was held to discuss Snow's and other's findings. *The Times* would report that Mr. Cooper of the Metropolitan Commission of Sewers had 'examined minutely the whole state of the district to ascertain the real cause of fearful outbreak of cholera…' and, referencing the report and maps, concluded assertively that:

[T]he sewers were not the cause of the cholera; that they were not in any way connected with the disease; but that the real cause of the calamitous occurrences in the locality to which Mr. Cooper's report referred was the filthy and undrained state of the houses. (*The Times*, 27 September 1854, p.12)

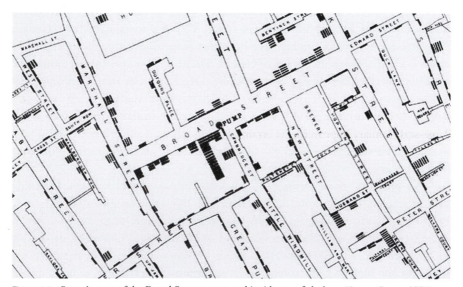

Figure 2.3. Snow's map of the Broad Street pump and incidence of cholera. (*Source*: Snow, 1854)

While Cooper focused his disease investigation on the general environment and putrid air emanating from 'undrained' houses, Snow focused on which individuals drank from which source of water. Snow's theory predated bacteriology and failed to resonate at the time with sanitarians or contagionists. Municipal and national policies were organized to clean-up urban environments, not monitor individual water sources. However, the combination of evidence gathered by Snow, from resident interviews, to water company activities, to the spatial mapping of disease, all contributed to the evidence behind his theory that contaminated water was the cause of cholera.

Private Interest and Urban Sanitary Action

As urbanization and industrialization grew rapidly in the mid-nineteenth century so did labour competition, and industrialists were keen to ensure their workers slept within walking distance of their workplace. Demand for homes near workplaces was high, and landlords commonly subdivided rooms, developed back gardens and courtyards, and even encroached into streets and alleyways, to increase their rentable space. One goal of the Health of Towns Association was to open up streets, pave, sewer, and redesign them to ensure they were open at both ends for the free through passage of air (Health of Towns Association, 1844, p. 5). A spatial theory of urban health took hold that built on Hippocrates's *Airs, Waters and Places* and believed that health was best promoted by connection, circulation and flow of street networks, air through homes, and pollution away from people (Sennett, 1995). Yet, expanding and regularizing streets, even in the name of public health, required public expenditure and curtailment of property rights. Town planners struggled to find the financial and political support to implement these design changes (Duffy, 1990).

The result was that sanitary and urban design approaches to health were piecemeal rather than comprehensive. In 1867, New York housing codes required one toilet inside a building and a sewer connection for every twenty people (Melosi, 2000). Fire escapes and interior rooms with fixed windows were later requirements. Parts of the building and the built environment were increasingly regulated. As Melosi (1980) has argued, it was not until sanitarians convinced business elites that they could disproportionately gain from sanitary reform – for example, fewer sick days and lower labour training costs and discounts on bulk water and sewer services – that more comprehensive and large-scale sanitary improvements occurred.

Koppitz (2005) has extended the idea that economic arguments, not public health justifications, brought on major urban sanitary changes. In a study of the Rhineland in Germany, he shows that financing and construction of sewerage systems took place only after planners convinced elite land owners that the new infrastructure would increase the value of marginal urban land, such as flood-prone and marshy areas, by draining it and keeping it permanently dry. The new dry ground would reap financial rewards for both municipal government and those that bought the new, improved land. Koppitz suggests that only after these revenues were extracted from the land was urban infrastructure in Germany constructed.

Urban Sanitary Governance in America

Building on the work of Chadwick and the miasma theory of disease causation in cities, John H. Griscom, New York City's Chief Sanitary Inspector, published *The Sanitary Conditions of the Laboring Population of New York* in 1845. Five years later in 1850, Lemuel Shattuck, Sanitary Commissioner in Massachusetts, published a similar study, the *Report of the Sanitary Commission of Massachusetts*. American sanitarians, like some of their European counterparts, advocated built environment improvements such as water and sewer infrastructure, refuse removal and street cleaning. A utilitarian approach to sanitary reform, much like Chadwick's, was part of the emerging American urban health and planning ethos (Duffy, 1990).

However, as in England, the costs associated with sanitary infrastructure and the lack of medical evidence at the time that the investments would indeed improve health for everyone, stymied construction. New public sanitary infrastructure required new urban and sometimes regional bureaucracies to provide long-term financing and ongoing management and maintenance. Efforts to engineer more healthy cities gave rise to multiple, and often fragmented, urban bureaucracies, including those concerned with waste collection, freshwater, sewerage, and housing (Peterson, 1979).

Piping in clean water for drinking and bathing did not by itself end environmental pollution or the spread of disease. Cities were now faced with disposing of vast quantities of dirty water. Physical and technical solutions dominated, as streets were paved to improve surface drainage and sewer pipes brought wastewater away from populated areas to marsh and coastal wetlands (Melosi, 2000). After studying infant mortality in England between 1870 and 1905, Millward and Bell (2001) suggest that the rising incomes of females of child-bearing age had the most significant influence on decline in infant mortality during this time, and environmental sanitation had a much less significant impact. Yet, the political and economic justification for infrastructure investments decoupled from poverty reduction continued through this era in Europe and North America (Schultz and McShane, 1978).

Engineers became the 'physicians of the street' and began to recognize that the incremental and piecemeal approach to infrastructure provision was vastly inefficient. They would lobby for centralized, permanent and professionally staffed bureaucracies to build, finance and manage regional infrastructure that would serve cities (*Ibid.*) (figure 2.4). There were few local ward politicians, private entrepreneurs or corporations in urban America with the economic capital, power (to control land

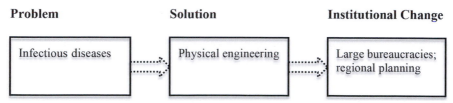

Figure 2.4. Urban sanitary reform in America.

uses) or interest in public health to risk the costs and uncertain returns in building and maintaining water, sewer, transportation or electricity networks to serve large urban populations (Peterson, 1979). Some engineers were convincing, such as Ellis S. Chesbrough, the Chief Engineer in Chicago, who was allocated $10,0000,000 by the city to build 54 miles (86 km) of sewers and raise streets as much as 12 feet (3.7 m) to allow for gravity-fed drainage (Cain, 1972).

New bureaucracies were established to acquire land for drinking water reservoirs and to take land for aqueducts and trunk sewer pipes. Regional authority was now needed, since water and wastewater systems rarely conformed to the geography of municipal borders. Boston's Metropolitan Sewer Commission, founded in 1889, was granted the authority to manage activities within the watershed servicing the city. These were vast and unprecedented powers that contradicted the New England tradition of home-rule governance. Sanitarians and their quest to build urban infrastructure was radically altering American politics (Duffy, 1990).

Surveying the City

In both the US and Europe engineers from the military were given authority and civil service job protections to make autonomous decisions seemingly in the interest of the public good (Schultz and McShane, 1978). As they gained this social status, engineers also began to redefine the healthy city as a whole ecosystem that was efficient only when all its parts functioned in unison. Some engineers saw themselves as the caretakers of these ecosystems, much like the physician took care of a family:

The city engineer is to the city very much what the family physician is to the family. He is constantly called upon to advise and direct in all matters pertaining to his profession... He does know the character, constitution, particular needs and idiosyncrasies of the city, as the family physician knows the constitutions of the family ... the city engineer is becoming the most important director of the material development of cities... To him, even more than to the successive mayors, falls the duty of serving as the intelligence and brains of the municipal government in all physical matters. (Olmsted, 1894)

As good caretakers engineers developed methods of cataloguing the built environment of cities through detailed field investigations.

Sanitary surveys were developed in the 1880s to describe the features of every street, structure, and individual lot within many cities. The hope was to document enough so as to uncover the locations where diseases 'breed' and where a change in environmental conditions could upset the spread of disease (Peterson, 1979, p. 90). The Memphis sanitary survey followed a similar study supported by New York City merchants who recognized that a reputation for an unhealthy environment hindered economic growth (Duffy, 1990, p. 134). Employing physicians, chemists, engineers, and others, the Memphis survey canvassed neighbourhoods house by house and block by block, eventually recommending a comprehensive, citywide approach to guiding city planning, including hiring a sanitary officer to oversee all work that included:

building a new water supply and sewer system; condemning and destroying buildings such as shanties and other buildings; damming bayous and developing a park along the shoreline; and repaving streets (Peterson, 1979, p. 90). While rejecting the piecemeal 'field site' view of earlier sanitarians, the work of these engineers was limited to the sanitary not the urban environment, and social factors were also routinely ignored (*Ibid.*, p. 91).

Social Reformers and the Urban Field Site

In part a response to the rising technocratic framing of urban health planning, popular social movements organized to demand greater labour and health protection and participation in urban reforms. In most industrializing cities during the mid- to late-nineteenth centuries, children were a major part of the manufacturing labour force. They worked in mills, glass factories, canneries and home industries instead of going to school or playing. Children suffered disfigurement, disease, and death from strenuous working conditions; stunted growth, curvature of the spine, tuberculosis and bronchitis were common among child labourers (Porter, 1999). As labour movements grew, they advocated legislation protecting against child labour and compulsory education for children. Social movements pushed back against industrialists, organized urban workers and demanded that the state intervene in the economy to protect the health and safety. Addressing public health and social change in the United States, Porter (1999, p. 156) notes:

Major strikes between 1877 and 1892 and the assassination of President Garfield in 1881 indicated the potential for civil disorder. In such an atmosphere, social reform took on a new urgency. New political movements … campaigned for income tax, an eight-hour [work]day, social insurance, labor exchanges for the unemployed, the abolition of child labor, workmen's compensation and public ownership of the railroads… Increasing numbers of social reform movements developed during the last quarter of the century aimed at ameliorating social crises and preventing revolution and anarchy. Health reform played a significant role in this context which exemplified the new social consciousness.

Social reformers, especially women, were particularly active in changing urban living conditions and participating in national policy debates.

The American park and playground movement emerged during the Progressive Era to advocate for safer play spaces for children, particularly those living in crowded ethnic enclaves in urban areas. Women advocates challenged the idea that urban parks should be places of leisure and contemplation only for the economic elite, an idea of an earlier generation of park planners and landscape architects in Europe and America such as Fredrick Law Olmsted (Gagen, 2000). The playground movement sought to build urban recreation spaces to keep children off the streets and provide structured playtime (figure 2.5). Many playgrounds were located next to schools so that gymnasiums, reading rooms, and baths could all be used for children's recreation, literacy, and hygiene. However, the playground movement often perpetuated gender

Figure 2.5. Children's playground, Poverty Gap. (*Source*: Jacob Riis, 1888. Used with permission from the collection of the Museum of the City of New York)

roles by targeting outdoor recreation for boys while girls were taught domestic roles (*Ibid.*). The movement was also known for teaching immigrant children 'cooperative play and obedience to authority' (Boyer, 1983). A private charity, the New York Association for Improving the Condition of the Poor (AICP), built one of the first public baths for the poor, driven largely by the belief that slum dwellers needed to be cleansed of moral failures and physical dirt (Williams, 1991, p. 24).

Under the leadership of wealthy white women, the urban playground movement was different from an increasingly visible American environmental movement that advocated and won national legislation for large parks and preserving land in wilderness areas.

Wilderness and the City

The American environmental movement emerged out of an anti-urban, romantic sentiment that was reflected in the art and literature of the day, such as Henry David Thoreau's *Walden*, published in 1854, and the transcendentalist painters of the Hudson River School. For these elite Americans, enlightenment could be found in unaltered nature and there was an intrinsic value in preserving wild lands (Cronon, 1992). Of course, the nature and wild lands that these early American environmentalists referred to was already the home of native peoples, but they were regularly forcibly evicted from their land to make way for new conservation areas. Yosemite Park in California was designated by the state as conservation land in 1862 and Yellowstone Park in Wyoming became the first national park in 1872. The national parks movement was a visible national social movement deeply engaged in American politics with access to legislators in Washington DC, including the President. The movement was under the leadership of wealthy white men, such as Scottish born naturalist, John Muir the first leader of the non-governmental organization, the Sierra Club.

John Muir would describe preserving wild lands as a spiritual endeavour, calling Yosemite 'his church'. In a now classic political struggle in early twentieth century American politics, Muir and the Sierra Club waged a campaign to prevent the damning of the Toulame River to form the Hetch-Hetchy reservoir in Yosemite. The reservoir would quench the growing thirst of the City of San Francisco and agricultural in its surrounding area. Muir would appeal directly to President Theodore Roosevelt, an avid outdoorsman, to intervene and stop the project. Despite his appeals, Muir and the Sierra Club lost and water flowed into San Francisco to continue the American expansion and urbanization of the West. However, the Sierra Club campaign galvanized American preservationists and spawned a social movement, which continues today, that viewed cities as separate from the worthwhile 'environments' needing political attention for protection (Gottlieb, 1993).

As William Cronon has noted, nature was viewed as wild, untouched and transcendent, while cities were viewed as dark, dirty and decaying. The racial politics were clear; white and good was nature and dark and dirty was urban. The mythic frontier naturalist was always male, rugged and strong, while urban living was portrayed as soft and feminine. Cronon (1995), in his essay, 'The Trouble with Wilderness; or, Getting Back to the Wrong Nature', notes that the nineteenth- and twentieth-century American narrative that tied wilderness to individualism had profound impacts on the cultural, political and financial status of American cities. He writes (*Ibid.*, p. 87):

Putting the city outside nature meant sending humanity into the same exile – isolating human life from the ecosystems that sustain it. The boundary between natural and unnatural shades almost imperceptibly into the boundary between human and non-human, with wilderness and the city seeming to be at opposite poles – the one pristine and unfallen, the other corrupt and unredeemed.

Convinced of our own omnipotence, we imagine nature retreating to small islands – 'preserves' – in the midst of a landscape which otherwise belongs to us. And therein lies our dilemma: however we may feel about the urban world which is the most visible symbol of our human power … we unconsciously affirm our belief that we ourselves are unnatural. Nature is the place where we are not.

For Cronon, this narrative also represented an attempt to escape from history and responsibility for past injustices in both urban and non-urban areas. The romantic ideology of wilderness contributed to a growing anti-urban American politics.

Yet, urban social reformers, such as those in the Settlement House Movement, advocated for and won changes aimed at improving urban health. Settlement houses were places where the poor could come to live and receive education, food, day care, bathing facilities, libraries, art, and social events. Hull House in Chicago, founded by Jane Addams in 1889, was one of the best known settlements and housed many of the era's progressive reformers such as Alice Hamilton and Florence Kelley (Hamilton, 1943). These women, influenced by the burgeoning Chicago School of Sociology that initiated the study of the neighbourhood effects on wellbeing, worked with residents to document unsanitary neighbourhood and workplace conditions and advocated for new social policies on behalf of residents (Deegan, 2002; Hull House Maps and Papers, 2007 [1895]).

The Atlanta Neighborhood Union was an African-American, women-led neighbourhood organization in Atlanta, Georgia, started in 1908 by Lugenia Burns Hope, and chartered in 1911. The Union focused on self-help and social services in the aid of African-American families. Like those in Hull House, the Union residents investigated living conditions in different areas of the city and advocated for programmes focused on education, home and personal hygiene. Importantly, the Union helped launch health clinics and established after-school programmes while also advocating for street, schoolhouse, and sanitary improvements for residents, and increased salaries for African-American teachers.

Hull House resident Florence Kelley lead a study of poverty in Chicago for the US Congress in 1893 called, *A Special Investigation of the Slums of Great Cities*. She worked with local residents to design a social and physical survey of neighbourhood conditions and residents mapped their findings. Residents of South End House in Boston published a report of their living conditions in 1898 called *The City Wilderness* (Woods, 1898). These studies personified the field site view of the city, as residents and professional researchers 'discovered' their place by being embedded in it. They generated local data that began to help connect poverty and poor health outcomes, not just general living conditions and the sanitary environment (figure 2.6).

Eugenics, Racism and the City

Social reformers struggled to confront the ideology that inherent racial inferiority was to blame for differences in disease and death rates between whites and African-Americans living in urban America. Many elite, including scientists and physicians, perpetuated ideas that the poor, immigrants, and especially African-Americans had genetic defects that led to their immoral behaviour and explained the origins of infectious diseases. This racist science (figure 2.7) was called eugenics and argued that race was a valid biological category and that the genes that determined race were linked to those that determined health (Kevles, 1985). A Eugenic society of biologists gained prominence in cities as leaders looked to blame the poor and non-whites for their problems rather than seeing these as social responsibilities requiring public resources (Galton, 1904).

The groundbreaking work of W.E.B. DuBois, among others, challenged the dominant medical and scientific view at the time that inherent racial inferiority was to blame for health disparities between whites and blacks. Inequities in life expectancy

Figure 2.6. Anna I. Grosser, US Children's Bureau, Department of Labor, with chart showing infant mortality rates according to fathers' earnings, 1923. (*Source*: Library of Congress)

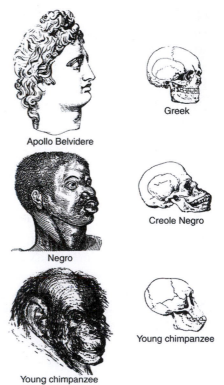

Figure 2.7. Eugenic study comparing intelligence to skull shape. (*Source*: Nott *et al*., 1854, p. 458)

between African-Americans and whites at the turn of the century were dismal – 33 years compared to 47.6 for whites – and there were only 878 African American men to every 1,000 African-American women, compared to 991 white men to every 1,000 white women.

In his 1906 edited publication, *The Health and Physique of the Negro American*, Du Bois used statistics from northern and southern cities to argue that health inequities facing African-Americans were a consequence of their poorer economic, social, and sanitary conditions, compared to whites. Du Bois (1906, p. 89) noted:

If the population were divided as to social and economic condition the matter of race would be almost entirely eliminated. Poverty's death rate in Russia shows a much greater divergence from the rate among the well-to-do than the difference between Negroes and white Americans... Even in consumption all the evidence goes to show that it is not a racial disease but a social disease. The rate in certain sections among whites in New York and Chicago is higher than the Negroes of some cities.

Du Bois would directly challenge Frederick Hoffman's widely read text *Race Traits and Tendencies of the American Negro*. Hoffman enlisted science to claim that 'it is not the conditions of life, but in race and heredity that we find the explanation of the fact to be observed in all parts of the globe, in all times and among all people, namely the superiority of one race over another, and of the Aryan race over all' (Hoffman, 2004 [1896], p. 312). Du Bois (1906, p. 89) replied directly to these claims:

The undeniable fact is, then, that in certain diseases the Negroes have a much higher rate than the whites, and especially in consumption, pneumonia and infantile diseases. The question is: Is this racial? Mr. Hoffman would lead us to say yes, and to infer that it means that Negroes are inherently inferior in physique to whites. But the difference in Philadelphia can be explained on other grounds than upon race. The high death rate of Philadelphia Negroes is yet lower than the whites of Savannah, Charleston, New Orleans and Atlanta.

While Eugenics was later widely discredited, the reification of socially-constructed racial categories as explanations for disease and premature death continues to be debated in twenty-first-century public health and medicine.

From Field Site to an Emerging Laboratory Science of the City

By the end of the nineteenth century modern city planning and public health were using physical interventions to respond to urban public health crises. While planning and public health both addressed sanitation and housing reforms during this time, the driving ideology was physical removal, of both 'environmental miasmas' – garbage, wastewater, slum housing, 'swamp' land, and so forth – and 'undesirable and sick' people. These interventions tended to be piecemeal, with the exception of the sanitary survey, and rarely addressed industrial or consumption practices that led to environmental waste. For sanitarians, the local solution to pollution was removal and dilution, but the downstream environmental health impacts were often ignored and unseen.

Five interrelated themes emerged from this field site view of the city era, including:

1. Removing and displacing physical blight;

2. Reliance on technical rationality;

3. Moral environmentalism;

4. Increased professionalization; and

5. Bureaucratic fragmentation.

These themes would remain encoded in the institutions of planning and public health as the laboratory view of the city era emerged at the turn of the twentieth century.

Chapter 3

The City as Laboratory

While the field site view of the city dominated much nineteenth-century urban health research and governance, a laboratory view of the city emerged in parallel to the rise of germ theory, bacteriology and laboratory science more generally. Laboratory science is credited with some of public health's greatest modern successes, such as vaccinations, immunizations and treatment of water and waste but, as I explore in this chapter, the laboratory view also had a great impact on the design and governance of cities which contributed to a perpetuation of urban health inequities in both rich and poor cities around the world.

Science is often viewed as a resource that influences how city planners, public health professionals and other urban policy administrators understand issues or apply its methods to problem solving. As we saw in Chapter 2, the field site view of cities employed science to justify interventions that without technical analyses might have been viewed as too political, for example providing services to the poor, or too expensive. Science then, can also act as a justification or rationalization for public decisions that inherently involve value judgments. In this chapter, I suggest planning and public health increasingly borrowed and actively sought to attach themselves to the increasingly social legitimacy of laboratory science. One implication was a more determined move towards professionalization and demarcating expertise in urban problem solving than had been the case when the field site view was more dominant. A second implication is the shift in urban administration so that it seemed more like a laboratory than a field site. A third influence was the desire to standardize instruments and nature, as happens inside the lab. Finally, the emergence of a set of urban betterment schemes that were exported around the world, much like laboratory findings, came for much of the twentieth century to define city planning aimed at promoting health.

The laboratory view of cities differs from the field view because laboratory science aims to be detached from the context where investigation is taking place, seeks to control and restrict the 'field', and relies on mechanical and standardized techniques. Research in the lab gains its legitimacy by restricting and controlling the experimental environment and those who participate. In the lab, mechanization and standardization create important distance between the researcher and the researched, and placelessness enables output from a lab located anywhere to apply to people, places and things everywhere. Even the artefacts of today's laboratory science are devoid of their context, since chemists buy purified reagents and cancer researchers depend on patented strains of mice, not those living in the wild.

Some of the earliest laboratory findings from bacteriology and germ theory led to non-specific policies intended to improve health for all, such as chlorination of drinking water and immunizations. Yet, as I highlighted in Chapter 2, the increased faith in universal truths also gave rise to the pseudo-science of Eugenics, where racism was couched as a scientific explanation for differences in health status, intelligence and a host of other factors between Europeans and non- Europeans. The laboratory was also where twentieth-century warfare was created, and war-like precision and discipline acted as driving metaphors for strategies aimed to 'defeat' twentieth-century urban epidemics of political unrest, poverty and illicit drug use. The laboratory view of cities helped generate important metaphors for urban policies that shaped and continue to shape the functions and identities of urban institutions.

As with the field site view, the laboratory view of cities was never absolute; place and context continued to influence urban health decisions and lay people and social movements continued to participate in some urban health research, policy-making and even delivering clinical services. Thus, the hybrid application of the field and laboratory views of the city is most important for drawing lessons from this history for healthy city planning. I will argue in this chapter that Community Health Centres have represented the hybridization of field and lab views of the city and, in doing so, can offer important insights for organizing twenty-first-century healthy city planning.

Germs, Labs and City Management

By the turn of the twentieth-century it was well known in public health that both miasma and contagion failed to explain certain aspects of urban health, such as why, with ubiquitous filth, epidemics only occurred sometimes and in some places. Contagion offered a theory of how disease travelled but not where disease came from. By this time the driving theory in public health shifted to germ theory, which stated that microbes were the specific agents that caused infectious disease (Susser and Stein, 2009). Germ theory hypothesized that each specific disease was caused by a unique germ and each germ had its own mode of transmission. In the decades leading up to and during the early twentieth-century, laboratory researchers such as Louis Pasteur, Robert Koch, Walter Reed and Charlos Chagas demonstrated that germs caused cholera, rabies, yellow fever, tuberculosis, typhoid, diphtheria, malaria and trypanosomiasis (now called Chagas disease).

Scientists used popular metaphors to communicate the concepts of germ theory widely (Krieger, 2011, p. 100). The first metaphor was 'seed and soil' which helped explain why exposure to a germ could be widespread but only some people would become ill. The metaphor also suggested that there is a latency period between exposure (planting) and symptoms (germination). Finally, the metaphor emphasized disease specificity, after all there was only one type of seed for each plant.

The second metaphor for germs was one of war. Germs became public 'enemy number 1'. Germs were ubiquitous and invaded the body, requiring sanitary defensive strategies and disinfectant offensive measures (Diamond, 1997). Battling germs also required an 'army' of experts and full support of the state. Science and the state, particularly in the US, would later enter into a 'social contract' where government would fund independent science that would serve the national interest (Bush, 1945).

Bacteriology stimulated laboratory research that developed vaccines to immunize the poor, rather than clean up their neighbourhoods, workplaces and improve their economic status. Laboratory public health research also treated drinking water, milk, and food for disease-carrying microbes. This research led to compulsory vaccinations for school-age children and the chlorination of municipal drinking water supplies (Leavitt, 1992).

As a direct response to disease specification and segmentation, municipal agencies for such services as garbage collection, water supply and sewerage, nuisance removal, school health, housing, and occupational safety were established (Duffy, 1990). Technical agencies like the *Corps des Ponts et Chaussées* in France helped establish and extend the professional bureaucracy. As new agencies were established and separate disciplinary 'silos' emerged for urban issues, professional specialization increased and collaborative work between the fields decreased, furthering separating public health from urban planning. The physicians that were now running public health agencies viewed the housing, playgrounds, and other environmental reforms of the early Progressive Era as expensive 'social experiments' (Kraut, 1988).

By the 1920s, there was a profound shift in urban disease distribution in cities of both America and Europe. For instance, C.E. Winslow (1926, p. 1077) showed that from 1875 to 1925 in New York City, communicable diseases had decreased and non-communicable had increased significantly. As Winslow reported, diseases such as scarlet fever, diphtheria and diarrhoea for children under five had declined by 99, 95 and 93 per cent respectively. Winslow also showed that in this same time period in New York City cancer, heart disease and diseases of the arteries had increased 176, 187 and 650 per cent respectively. Public health pioneers such as Wade Hampton Frost in the US and Major Greenwood in London would suggest that germs alone were an insufficient explanation for understanding these spatiotemporal shifts in population distributions of disease. The environment also mattered. For Greenwood (1935, p. 359) the actions of society mattered too, and he returned to the seed and soil metaphor, noting: 'The genesis of active tubercular disease involves three factors: (1) a seed; (2) a soil; and (3) some methods of husbandry'. The 'methods of husbandry' were the human shaping of the social, physical and geographic context where people lived but these were increasingly unspecified and routinely ignored in laboratory science.

Colonialism and Cities of the South as Labs

The laboratory view and the rise of germ theory also contributed to the emergence of what we might today call global health. Many early applications of laboratory science were in cities of the global South. The poor places and populations of the 'tropics' became the 'field laboratories' where discoveries in the West were applied (Anderson, 2006). The Rockefeller Foundation's International Health Commission in 1913 had a significant role in exporting emerging laboratory science to cities in the global South, particularly Latin America and the Caribbean. Focused on eradicating hookworm, the Rockefeller programme experimented with vaccines in British Guiana, Panama, Nicaragua, Honduras and a host of other nations (Palmer, 2010).

As Cueto (1994) and Anderson (2006) have noted, these and other similar programmes imposed emerging biomedical technologies on poor urban and rural subjects. The Rockefeller country programmes viewed cities and the local populations in the 'empire region' of the US as laboratories for discovery and testing. Yet, Steven Palmer, argues in *Launching Global Health* (2010) that the laboratory view was not an absolute. He shows that Rockefeller's International Hookworm Program used field workers that negotiated with local healers and politicians. The result, according to Palmer, was that many programmes in the Caribbean resulted in 'hybrid adaptations', or a synthesis of both the host countries' indigenous medical practices and the biomedical views dominant in the Rockefeller programme.

Colonial responses to urban outbreaks of disease also had lasting impacts on the form and function of cities across Africa (Curtain, 1985). In most cases, the colonial response to disease was rigid spatial segregation between colonists and indigenous populations. As outbreaks increased, so did segregation (Gandy, 1999). For example, in Dakar the French colonial authorities drove the African population out of the old neighbourhoods and into a new quarter they called 'Médina', which they surrounded by a 'sanitary cordon' following an outbreak of bubonic plague in 1914 (Betts, 1971). Using medical justifications, the city was radically transformed by the forced relocation of the African population and the destruction of their existing housing and communities. Their land was quickly developed as housing for Europeans. A decree was passed only allowing new housing that met French building standards. As Betts (1971, p. 148) notes, the creation of the Médina was a 'planned ghetto' with 'no proper sewage system, no electricity, no potable water'. It also concentrated the Lebou people whose culture and political activism would later influence Dakar.

The Vaccine Revolt in Rio de Janeiro

As we shall see in Chapter 4, the laboratory view would also stimulate popular resistance to overly narrow views of curing the city without accounting for local culture, tradition or history. In the early 1900s Rio de Janeiro adopted an urban 'beautification' policy. In addition to tearing down older housing, widening streets, expanding the ports and displacing large numbers of the urban poor (Nachman, 1977), pesticides were applied across the city – even in homes without the inhabitants' permission (Meade, 1997, p. 247) – and the government demanded that all Rio residents get the smallpox vaccination (Nachman, 1977).

The mandatory vaccinations combined with widespread displacement, raised suspicions among the poor that the programme was for their eradication not betterment (Needell, 1987). Rioting broke out on the streets of Rio in early November 1904 (*Ibid.*, p. 206) and lasted for six days when the government temporarily suspended the compulsory vaccination programme, but not before scores were dead or injured and hundreds arrested (Meade, 1989).[1]

Health and Social Justice in American Planning

The profession of American city planning was taking root in the early twentieth century around the same time as Rio's Vaccine Revolt. In America, conflict arose around the direction of the emerging profession. Benjamin Clarke Marsh and Frederick Law Olmsted Jr, son of the renowned landscape architect, publically disagreed over whether social justice or rational urban design should be the organizing principle for the profession. Marsh would assert in his book, *An Introduction to City Planning: Democracy's Challenge to the American City*, published in 1909 that to:

open the door of opportunity for health, we must close the door for exploitation of land. Charity in congested districts is exploitation's most powerful ally. A government must prevent what charity can only mitigate… Taxation is Democracy's most effective method of achieving social justice – including city planning.

Marsh, who dedicated his book to 'the increasing group of citizens in every American city who recognize that government is the most important factor in securing good living conditions and preserving the life, health and well-being of all citizens', used a review of national planning requirements in countries across Europe, along with pictures and data, to make his case that a 'city cannot secure healthful conditions without a city plan for the entire city'.

Block Boundaries	Population	Area Density per acre, 1905	Deaths under 5 Years of Age		All Ages	
			Deaths	Rate/1,000	Deaths	Rate/1,000
112th–113th, 1st Ave–2nd Ave.	4,325	958	164	87.03	231	24.5
Mott, Prince, Elizabeth & E. Houston Sts	3,468	1,107	106	92.2	151	24.9
Madison, Henry, Catherine & Market Sts	4,137	945	46	50.1	106	15.16
2–36 Jones, 1–37 Cornella, 164–174 W. 4th, 157–277 Bleecker Sts	1,739	975	20	59.5	70	23.2
301–399 E. 106th, 301–398 E. 107th St, 2064–2078 2nd Ave, 2051–2058 1st Ave	3,928	809	130	83.12	175	22.3

Figure 3.1. Urban health data for New York neighbourhoods from Marsh (1909).

The architects and engineers who dominated city planning during turn of the twentieth century America responded with disdain to Marsh's comments and his social welfare agenda. The most pointed and public response came from the younger Olmsted who used his keynote address to the Second National Conference on City Planning and the Problems of Congestion to argue for a radically different agenda for the planning profession, proclaiming:

The complex unity, the appalling breadth and ramification, of real city planning is being borne

Figure 3.2. Image from Marsh (1909). Note the caption where he related Berlin's housing to the future health of the city's children.

Anfiedelung Nord Ufer.

IN SOME BERLIN TENEMENTS, WHERE CHILDREN ARE WORTH AS MUCH AS LAND.—THE FUTURE BERLIN WILL SAFEGUARD THE HEALTH OF ITS CITIZENS SIMILARLY.

in upon us as never before, and one of the main purposes of such a conference as this, I take it, is to assist the workers in all the different parts of this complex field to understand these interrelationships more clearly. The ideal of city planning is one in which all these activities – all the plannings that shape each one of the fragments that go to make up the physical city – shall be so harmonized as to reduce the conflict of purposes and the waste of constructive effort to a minimum, and thus secure for the people of the city conditions adapted to their attaining the maximum of productive efficiency, of health and of enjoyment of life. (Olmsted, 1910, p. 3)

Capitalizing on his famous lineage and prominent position on the national stage, Olmsted advanced a vision of planning rooted in the City Beautiful ideal, where aesthetics, efficiency, and comprehensive physical plans were the goals of city planning, not social justice. He concluded his keynote address by outlining the three issues that uniquely defined city planning: circulation of transportation, the design of public spaces, and the development of private land. Strategies for improving the health and wellbeing of the urban poor were conspicuously absent.

According to Jon A. Petersen (2003, p. 245), the debate between Marsh and Olmsted 'ranks with the McMillan Plan for Washington as a definitive episode in the birth of city planning in the United States' and is crucial for understanding how and why city planning emerged as a novel discipline distinct from those concerned with social welfare in cities. While Marsh and Olmsted shared a faith in planning as a tool for change, Marsh wanted the field to tackle the inequities from 'population congestion' through new urban taxes, limits on private property rights, and increasing government regulations; Olmsted viewed the field as a new, technical extension of architecture and engineering. Olmsted and his supporters prevailed.

Like European urban public health reformers that emphasized poverty and economic inequalities as the pathway to health over the objections of sanitarians, it was Marsh's taxation and government regulatory reforms that were most controversial. Nelson Lewis, author of one of the first city planning texts, *The Planning of the Modern City*, would note:

There are many who believe that the chief purposes of city planning are social, that the problems of housing, the provision of recreation and amusement for the people, the control and even the ownership and operation of all public utilities, the establishment and conduct of public markets, the collection and disposal of wastes, the protection of public health, the building of hospitals, the care of paupers, criminals and the insane, and all of the other activities of the modern city are all a part of city planning. All of these, however, are matters of administration rather than of planning… (Lewis, 1916, pp.17–18)

Olmsted and his supporters had successfully defined the burgeoning field as technocratic, and professionals were debating how to incorporate new scientific and technical tools into their practice of analyzing and designing efficient cities (Fairfield, 1994; Petersen, 2003).

Partitioning the City for Health

Under pressure from private landowners to prevent noxious industries from locating in residential districts or near exclusive shopping areas where they had invested, American city planners extended Taylorist[2] notions of scientific efficiency in adopting a hierarchical ordering of land uses (Ford, 1915). American zoning ordinances borrowed from German ideas that divided cities by districts based on land use and housing type and built on nuisance laws used to protect public health by limiting odours, smoke, fumes, noises, and other noxious emissions from urban industries (Logan, 1976). New York City developed the first citywide zoning code in 1916 which specified building heights and setbacks and created residential, commercial, and industrial zones (Willis, 1992).

American urban zoning ordinances were regularly justified using public health arguments. The US Supreme Court would eventually weigh-in on the legality of regulating land use in the landmark 1926 Euclid v. Ambler ruling, stating:

The decisions enumerated in the first group cited above agree that the exclusion of buildings devoted to business, trade, etc., from residential districts, bears a rational relation to the health and safety of the community. Some of the grounds for this conclusion are promotion of the health and security from injury of children and others by separating dwelling houses from territory devoted to trade and industry; suppression and prevention of disorder; facilitating the extinguishment of fires, and the enforcement of street traffic regulations and other general welfare ordinances; aiding the health and safety of the community, by excluding from residential areas the confusion and danger of fire, contagion, and disorder, which in greater or less degree attach to the location of stores, shops, and factories. (272 US 365, p. 391)[3]

Mel Scott (1971, p. 192) stated that zoning 'was the heaven-sent nostrum for sick cities, the wonder drug of the planners, the balm sought by lending institutions and householders alike'. In practice, zoning tended to preserve the *status quo* through 'exclusionary' zoning and deed restrictions, or restrictive covenants, both acting to perpetuate Jim Crow segregation[4] (Babcock, 1966, p. 116). Zoning was also used by suburban planners to mandate minimum lot size, housing type, and house size in order to keep out lower income people, the majority of whom were immigrants and Southern African-Americans coming north during the Great Migration (Lemann, 1991). Extending Scott's (1971) use of health metaphors, zoning effectively 'immunized' wealthy and white populations from having the poor and African-Americans living in their neighbourhoods.

Laboratory-Like Healthy Urban Designs

At least two design schemes from the early twentieth century claimed to promote wellbeing no matter where they were applied, reflecting many of the characteristics of laboratory science. One was the Garden City and the other the Neighbourhood Unit. These two designs, still influential today, advocated for strict functional separation of land uses and were physically deterministic in suggesting that design alone could improve wellbeing.

In Britain, Ebenezer Howard aimed to integrate a regional perspective with principles from ecology to improve wellbeing in his Garden City design. The Garden City, he claimed, could create 'slumless and smokeless' cities and merge the best of the county into the city, while eliminating the features of each that were unhealthy (Howard, 1902). For Howard, the options were a town with foul air, high rents and slums, a country where one worked long hours for low wages, had little amusement and lacked spirit and society or the Town-County Garden City (figure 3.3) Howard's Garden City was organized on radial axes with central gardens surrounded by municipal buildings and grand boulevards that reached a ring road and railway. The central city and Garden Cities would have fixed populations to preserve their liveable qualities and agricultural land on the periphery. Each Garden city was to be networked to the others in a region (figure 3.4).

The Neighbourhood Unit was also couched as a way to improve the quality of urban life and bring more order to cities. Proposed by Clarence Perry in 1929, it was a design scheme centred around a primary school, where:

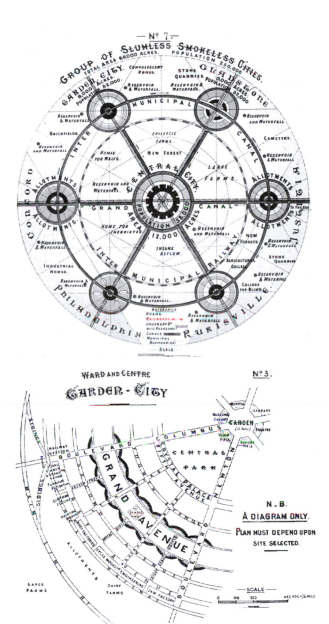

Figure 3.3 and 3.4.
Howard's Garden City
universal design concept.

A population of 5,000 to 6,000 people and 800 or 1,000 children of elementary school age …
[living] in single-family-per-lot sections requiring an area of about 160 acres … is a description
of the physical environment that is best adapted, in my opinion, for the growing of an urban
neighborhood community. (Perry, 1929, p. 98)

Reflecting an urban form similar to the Garden City ideal, the interior of the
Neighbourhood Unit consisted of a street pattern that encouraged pedestrian
circulation and reduced street congestion caused by automobiles, while the periphery

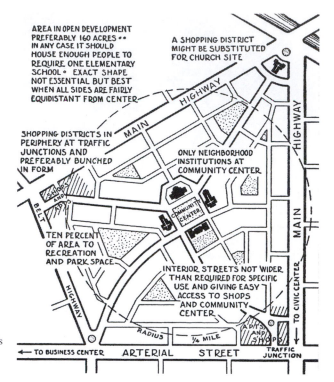

Figure 3.5. Clarence Perry's Neighbourhood Unit, 1922.

of the unit consisted of businesses located at traffic intersections (figure 3.5). While Perry's scheme was hailed as a design that might optimize space for the efficient delivery of services, provide for a safe residential environment, and encourage the social values of the day, the Neighbourhood Unit was also criticized by some for ignoring the social, economic, and political complexities of urban living and for being a plan that would ultimately promote economic residential segregation (Isaacs, 1948).

The Garden City and the Neighbourhood Unit offered a physical ideal that tended to ignore the often contested, gendered, variegated, and value-laden characteristics of cities. By leaving out the distinctive virtues of particular places in a bid for universal applicability, these representations of the city were intended to be credible and capable of being applied regardless of time and place, social and physical geography, or political and administrative organization – much like laboratory science.

Reflecting the rules for generating credible results in a lab, the Garden City and Neighbourhood Unit offered design schemes that aimed to gain exquisite control over the objects of their analysis by preselecting the healthy characteristics of community living while trying to segregate out potential 'contaminants' – both natural and human. The one-size-fits-all designs of the Garden City and Neighbourhood Unit models reflected common laboratory practices of mechanization and standardization in order to create distance between the researcher and the researched. Laboratory spaces, like the urban models, were designed similarly to allow other scientists at diverse locations to assume that the background ambient conditions were equivalent everywhere, removing suspicions that experimental results might be due to some peculiar and unannounced environmental factor (Gieryn, 1999; Latour, 1987).

Controlling the Colonial City with the Neighbourhood Unit

The Neighbourhood Unit concept was not limited to North American planning, as it and the Garden City 'travelled', imposing designs on cities around the world, particularly colonial cities. For example, in the 1948 *Nairobi Master Plan for a Colonial City*, both the Garden City and Neighbourhood Unit concepts dominate the plan (White *et al.*, 1948). A series of grand boulevards with radial roads and municipal buildings anchored the plan (figure 3.6). The planners rationalized that their proposal would situate Nairobi alongside other similarly designed global cities (figure 3.7).

Figure 3.6. 1948 Colonial Plan for Nairobi: Downtown Design. (*Source*: White *et al.*, 1948)

The planners used the model of the Neighbourhood Unit developed by Patrick Abercrombie in his Greater London Plan of 1944 (White *et al.*, 1948, p. 46) to 'ensure economy in development of roads and services and a healthier social life'. They proposed a Neighbourhood Unit, where about a thousand detached housing units surrounded a central green area with schools, churches, a health clinic, a community

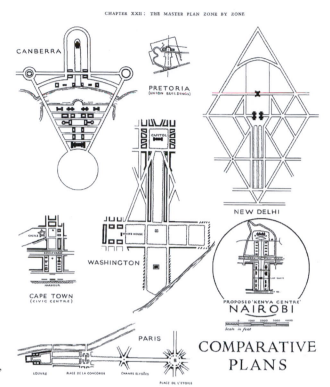

Figure 3.7. 1948 Colonial Plan for Nairobi: Nairobi compared to other world capitals. (*Source*: White *et al.*, 1948)

centre, and designated commercial areas (figure 3.8). The proposed scheme was specifically for a 'non-European population and its house plots are therefore small, but … the essential point is that the system is readily adaptable to any density standards' (*Ibid.*, p. 73). The Master Plan barely addressed the reality of state sponsored racial segregation and ultimately the planners defined their task as purely technical (see Chapter 5).

By defining planning as pure reason and separate from politics, the Nairobi Master Plan of 1948 was perpetuating the colonial vision of the African city as needing curing.

Planning the Healthy Neighbourhood

Clarence Perry's Neighbourhood Unit idea also took hold with planners, developers, and the American Public Health Association's Committee on the Hygiene of Housing. The APHA committee adopted the Neighbourhood Unit design scheme as the basis for two reports; one, in 1938, *Basic Principles of Healthful Housing*, and a second in 1948, *Planning the Neighborhood* (figure 3.10). The earlier housing guide detailed thirty essential health aims that were believed to be the minimum required for the 'promotion of physical, mental, and social health, essential in low-rent as well as high-cost housing, on the farm as well as in the city dwelling'. The latter document set

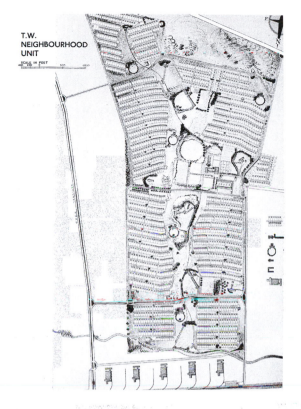

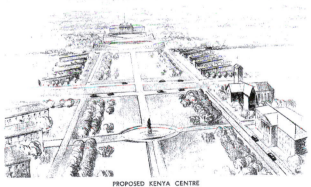

Figure 3.8. 1948 Colonial Plan for Nairobi: Neighbourhood Unit Concept. (*Source*: White *et al.*, 1948)

Figure 3.9. 1948 Colonial Plan for Nairobi: Grand Boulevard Design Scheme. (*Source*: White *et al.*, 1948)

Figure 3.10. Planning the
Neighbourhood, American
Public Health Association, 1948.

standards for the 'environment of residential areas', defined as 'the area served by an elementary school', and emphasized that:

No perfection in the building or equipment of the home can compensate for an environment which lacks the amenities essential for decent living. We must build not merely homes but neighborhoods if we are to build wisely for the future of America... [T]he effects of substandard environment extends beyond direct threats to physiological health, and involves . . . significant detriments to mental and emotional well-being. (APHA, 1948, pp. vi–vii)

Significantly both the 1938 and 1948 documents recognized the existence and persistence of health disparities in poor neighbourhoods and how stigma might influence health status:

[T]he mere elimination of specific hazards in poor neighborhoods falls short of the real goal of planning an environment which will foster a healthy and normal family life ... a sense of inferiority due to living in a substandard home may often be a more serious health menace then any unsanitary condition associated with housing. (*Ibid.*, p. vii)

The APHA committee stopped short of recognizing that widespread residential segregation might contribute to poor health, stating: 'Further research is needed to determine to what extent housing segregation or housing aggregation of differing population groups may create mental tensions or otherwise affect health' (*Ibid.*, p. 2).

Banerjee and Baer (1984), in a detailed review of *Planning the Neighborhood*, observed that the APHA guidelines were instantly influential because most practitioners presumed that the design standards it offered linked the built environment with health concerns at a time when no other similar standards existed. However, they also note that since most of the 'neighbourhood effects' described with numerical precision in the APHA report could not be, nor had yet been, empirically measured, the precision of the recommendations were artificial at best and tended to reflect the opinions of a select group of experts (Banerjee and Baer, 1984, pp. 24–25). Other critics of *Planning the Neighborhood* challenged its physical deterministic orientation, suggesting that the social health of a place may not match up neatly with the confines of the Neighbourhood Unit. Yet, as Fischler (1998, p. 390) has noted, the APHA adoption of the Neighbourhood Unit and publication of specific healthy design standards 'represent the culmination of a search for scientific methods to secure collective wellbeing. They are the fullest expressions of the welfare state in the field of urban development'.

The idea that urban planning could be underwritten by notions of universal hygienic spatial planning standards applied anywhere was not unique to American city planning. In the UK, the Central Housing Advisory Committee, would publish in 1944 Guidelines on the Design of Dwellings (commonly referred to as the 'Dudley Report') to guide post-war reconstruction both of which were based the design standards of the neighbourhood unit and Garden City.[5] Kristin Ross's study of French cultural development, *Fast Cars, Clean Bodies* (1995), argues that hygienic city planning in the 1940s forced the poor and North African workers from central Paris to the suburbs. According to Ross, policies and discourses of urban hygiene served to justify the demolition of entire *quartiers* or neighbourhoods in Paris between 1954 and 1974. One result was a shift in population to the outlying suburbs, especially Algerian immigrant workers, a population that was 'resettled' in *bidonvilles* – or peri-urban shantytowns. These same populations were also forced into *îlots insalubres*, or unhealthy blocks, within the city that were planned in the 1960s and 1970s (Ross, 1995).

Housing, Health and Urban Renewal

In America, the *Planning the Neighborhood* guidelines were increasingly used to justify state-sponsored slum clearance, with municipal public health agencies leading the way. By 1931 a group of influential women aimed to reignite the American public housing debate in response, in part, to the lack of a national housing movement and increasing slum populations (Wood, 1931). Led by Catherine Bauer, the Director of the Labor Housing Conference, and Mary Simkhovitch, these women organized the National Public Housing Conference (Bauer, 1945) and argued for a greater federal government role in building housing for the poor that was safe, affordable, and constructed in modernist, high-rise buildings on super-blocks (Pluntz, 1990). A key aspect of this group's public housing programme was using public health justification for the clearance of existing slums, followed by the construction of government-subsidized low-cost housing.

THE DEAD HAND OF BLIGHT

Figure 3.11. Dead Hand of Blight 1947. (*Source*: Cartoon by John W. Moreley, published in Tomorrow's Town, 1947, *Slums and the Taxpayer*, volume 5, no. 2)

Urban renewal was a programme and theory that aimed to remove downtown blight – viewed as the cause of moral evil and the breeding ground for disease – and rebuild whole sections of the city using the best of modern technology and scientifically rational design. Yet urban renewal tended only to increase poverty for residents of poor neighbourhoods because their homes were replaced with either inadequate public housing or, as was more often the case, private real estate developers acquired the downtown land cheaply and opted not to build new housing but expensive high-rise office towers (Weiss, 1980). Not only were neighbourhoods physically fractured, but social and emotional ties, trust, and notions of collective efficacy were also severed by urban renewal, further diminishing the health-promoting resources available for African-Americans (Fullilove, 2004).

Yet some public health officials denounced the narrow 'hygiene of housing' view that was increasingly used to justify 'negro removal' (*Ibid*.), another name for urban renewal. For example, E.R. Krumbiegel, the Commissioner of Health in the City of Milwaukee, criticized urban health professionals and engineers in 1951 for taking a 'traditional physical and disease approach to the hygiene of housing', and pointed out that health departments are called upon to fix 'the planning mistakes of the past' (Krumbiegel, 1951, p. 500). Krumbiegel also noted that by concerning themselves with 'the elimination of rodent infestations, the provision of a potable water supply on the dwelling premises, and the construction of suitable facilities for the disposal of sewage', health officers had not taken a 'truly comprehensive' approach to improving housing that should include a 'broader sociological viewpoint' (*Ibid.*, p. 499).

The commissioner of public health in Springfield, Massachusetts, noted:

Objectively speaking, health departments in many cities have found themselves in the hideous role of persecuting and harassing the poor. A health department that vigorously enforces housing and sanitary code regulations frequently compels an identical family to move, and then move, and then move again, sometimes within a few months of each move, and the poor family repeatedly and successively takes refuge in substandard housing ... the sociopsychological cost of repeated moving to adults and children of the family are formidable and inhumane. The negative approach of condemnation must go hand-in-hand with the positive task of rebuilding our cities. (Bellin, 1966, p. 778)

The US Federal Housing Acts that contained urban renewal also insured mortgages for new homes, but not for older houses, effectively 'redlining' inner-city neighbourhoods out of the programme (Hirsh, 1983). White racism in housing was perpetuated by the planning field's acceptance and perpetuation of this *de facto* policy of segregation (Abrams, 1955). Federally subsidized mortgages often required that property owners incorporate restrictive racial covenants into their deeds. According to Massey and Denton (1993, p. 52):

builders ... adopted the [racially restrictive] covenant so their property would be eligible for [federal] insurance, and private banks relied heavily on the federal system to make their own loan decisions... Thus the federal government not only channeled federal funds away from black neighborhoods but was also responsible for a much larger and more significant disinvestment in black areas by private institutions.

Although the federal government ended these discriminatory practices after 1950, it did nothing to remedy the damage it had done or to prevent private actors from perpetuating segregation until much later.

With the 1956 passage of the Federal Aid Highway Act and perpetuation of urban renewal, residents of many urban communities of colour were also shut out from the health-promoting benefits of suburban living, such as home ownership, capital accumulation, access to better funded schools, and participation in the growing suburban economy. By the 1960s and 1970s there were two Americas; one increasingly middle to upper class white, living in suburbs and another working class and poor African-American, living in inner cities.

Social Movements and Medicine

By the 1960s planning and public health were grappling with widespread social unrest and were hard-pressed to respond to activists' claims that large-scale public development projects and modernist designs were not any better than piecemeal changes that built on the existing fabric of older neighbourhoods (Goodman, 1971). Activists also challenged public health professionals to address why, in the face of rising economic prosperity and improvements in medical technology, inequalities in health persisted particularly for the urban poor and people of colour? Activists in Latin America, inspired by leaders such as social medicine advocate and Chile President Salvador Allende, pushed for governmental reforms that linked economic and social inequalities to health inequities (Waitzkin et al., 2001).

Puerto Rican activists in New York City's 'El Barrio', or East Harlem, organized street cleanups after the sanitation department refused to collect neighbourhood rubbish for weeks. The group convinced local health professionals to train lay residents in the techniques of door-to-door lead-poisoning screening and tuberculosis testing (Abramson et al., 1971). Borrowing from Social Medicine in Latin America, these activists were part of a social movement called the Young Lords[6] and started day care programmes in local churches, provided breakfast in neighbourhood schools, organized tenants to demand housing improvements, and occupied a neighbourhood hospital to highlight its inadequate service to the local population (Melendez, 2003).

Resisting the Lab

In America, the public dissatisfaction with planning was captured in the now classic critique, Jane Jacobs's (1961) *The Death and Life of Great American Cities*. According to Jacobs, the mega-block projects of urban renewal were destroying the aspects of neighbourhoods that made them liveable, such as human-scale streets that encouraged connection to and contact with one's neighbours. For Jacobs, a healthy community was as much determined by social characteristics as physical, where neighbours and strangers constantly interacted in an 'urban ballet' of familiarity and chance encounters (Jacobs, 1961, p. 65).

Environmental health was met with an equally influential book, the 1962 publication of Rachel Carson's *Silent Spring*. Carson challenged the 'better living through chemistry' ideal of the time that viewed industrial chemicals as largely benign. Writing about the harmful effects that chemicals such as DDT were having on ecosystems – 'silencing the songbirds' – Carson re-popularized nineteenth-century themes linking industrial pollution and environmental health (Gottlieb, 1993). Perhaps as important, Carson's work challenged the dominant idea in planning and public health that advances in science and technology were unquestionable signs of progress, in the public interest, and would improve human health. Yet some have noted that Carson's consumer-oriented focus on the ecology of suburban spaces and federal wildlife refugees made the bodies of farm workers and inner-city residents relatively invisible to the growing environmental movement (Lear, 1997).

Carson was also challenged by industry which, in the shape of Monsanto, published a rebuttal to her book called *The Desolate Year* (figure 3.12). The Monsanto report claimed that chemicals like DDT had saved thousands of lives by eliminated pests. Life without chemicals, they argued, would be catastrophic, as food supplies would be threatened, diseases would return and the overall quality of life on the planet would be reduced. Carson's work, they argued, was advocating regulations that would be disastrous for human life (Monsanto, 1962).

Figure 3.12. Desolate Year, Monsanto Corp.

Environmental Health, Justice and Cities

While national governments divested from cities this era saw new environmental regulations that worked to protect human health and the 1960s and 1970s saw a resurgence of the American environmental movement. This movement's achievements were significant and remain as some of the most important institutional and legislative changes for promoting health and equitable city planning in twenty-first-century American cities. In addition to creating the US Environmental Protection Agency and Occupational Health and Safety Administration, Congress would adopt the National Environmental Policy, Clean Air, and Clean Water Acts and begin to phase out lead in gasoline all during the first years of the 1970s.

The National Environmental Policy Act established for the first time that protecting human health was a national priority, not just ecological preservation and conservation. An executive-level environmental agency, the Council on Environmental Quality, was created and environmental impact assessment was required for projects, policies, programmes and plans. Importantly, the 'environment' under NEPA was defined broadly, and included such domains as housing, population, cultural and historic resources. Yet, over time, the scope of environmental analyses narrowed and risk assessment, which defines environment and human health much more narrowly, became standard procedure. Concern of researchers and activists that the limited scope of environmental reviews was not addressing the broad determinants of health gave rise to health impact assessment (HIA) and environmental justice analyses, both practices that aim to capture the cumulative biological, physical and social exposures that can make already vulnerable populations more susceptible to illness, whether at home, school, work or play (Payne Sturges *et al.*, 2004; Corburn, 2005).

By the early 1980s academics and activists around the world began to push for the reconnection of city planning with public health and in 1986 the World Health Organization, Office for Europe, created the Healthy Cities Project (Hancock and Duhl, 1988). The movement aimed to get cities to commit to developing a healthy city plan and to build networks of cities and towns committed to health (Tsouros, 1995). In the United States, the Coalition for Healthier Cities and Communities was started in the 1990s and aimed to get city and county health departments to embrace the broad

Table 3.1. Key historical events in city planning and public health.

Years	Public Health Events	City Planning and Health Events	Health Equity Issues/Questions
1840s–1890s	• Infectious disease epidemics in cities, such as yellow fever, typhoid and cholera • Mortality differences documented by economic, social and physical conditions of city wards • Miasma – filth – and Contagion – direct passage of poison from one person to another – leading theories of disease • Sanitary Surveys	• Metropolitan sanitary commissions and boards of health created • Water and waste removal infrastructure but industrial pollution seen as progress • Housing reform – ventilation, bathrooms and fire escapes • Settlement Houses – linked social, occupational and neighbourhood conditions • Parks, playground and bathhouse movements	• Filth was everywhere, but why did epidemics only occur sometimes and impact the poor most? • Not clear where disease came from • Eugenics blamed disease and death rates for African-Americans on inherent physical and biologic inferiority
1900s–1940s	• Germ theory- specific microbes lead to specific diseases – replaces miasma • Doctors and laboratory research replace sanitarians and engineers • Vaccinations and chemicals treat individuals and bacteria; environment and prevention moves to background • Neighbourhood health centres combined health and social planning	• 'City Beautiful' aesthetic • Scientific and efficient plans based on laboratory principles and Taylorism • Zoning legitimized, in part, as protecting public health • Universal models to promote well-being, such as Neighbourhood Unit, Garden City and concentric zone • APHA publishes guidelines for healthy housing and neighbourhoods	• Laboratory research seeks universal interventions inattentive to living conditions of poor and people of colour • Du Bois argues that social factors, not inherent inferiority, explains racial differences in health
1950s–1990s	• Biomedical model leading framework = health determined by individual biology, behaviour and genetics • Interventions aim to alter lifestyles and 'risk' factors, such as smoking, • Hygiene of housing reconsidered • Chronic disease focus of profession; HIV/AIDS afflicts people of colour greatest • Healthy Cities Movement & social epidemiology	• Federal housing policies physically and socially fracture poor urban communities of colour • 'Planned shrinkage' removes services in low income neighbourhoods • Social movements resist elitist, top-down planning • Federal environmental legislation, including NEPA • Suburban sprawl and health links explored	• Urban divestment, deindustrialization and racial residential segregation • Place inequities become concern of social epidemiologists to explain distribution of health inequities • Social epidemiology asks how society and aspects of place 'get into the body?'

view of health reflected in the European Healthy Cities Project (Norris and Pittman, 2000). In 1993 the International Society of City and Regional Planners (ISOCARP) congress focused on reconnecting planning and public health, and was entitled, 'City-Regions and Well-Being: What Can Planners Do to Promote the Health and Well-being of People in the City-Regions?'.

The Healthy Cities Project is part of a series of international efforts to promote health equity. The 1980 publication in Britain of the Inequalities in Health report (DHSS, 1980) (commonly referred to, after the chairman's name, as the Black report) ignited international debate over the social and economic determinants of health inequities (Townsend and Davidson, 1982). After the 1988 release of the US Institute of Medicine's Committee for the Study of the Future of Public Health report, leaders in the field agreed that the nation's public health activities were in disarray and that the field needed to refocus its efforts to address the growing inequalities in health across population groups (IOM, 1988). A 1998 publication in Britain, the Acheson Report, again highlighted that action was urgently needed across sectors of government and society to address rising health inequities and that medical care alone was insufficient to reverse this alarming global trend (Acheson *et al.*, 1998).

Merging Field and Laboratory through Community Health Centres

This chapter has suggested that the laboratory view of cities moved research and action in city planning and public health towards a focus on non-specific, universally applicable interventions (i.e. chlorination of drinking water, urban renewal) and bureaucratic institutions that were increasingly narrowly specialized, fragmented from one another, and the domain of a select set of professional experts. However, there was resistance to the laboratory view and instances where the laboratory and field views of the city were brought together to improve urban health. One such merging of the laboratory and field view was the Community Health Centre movement.

In the US, neighbourhood health centres emerged during the late nineteenth century as a one-stop location in poor, often immigrant urban areas, where ambulatory health services were combined with community participation in development and planning decisions (Rosen, 1971). A federal policy, the Sheppard-Towner Maternity and Infancy Protection Act of 1921, funded a network of community health centres in urban and rural areas. These centres attempted to bring clinical and social services to the poor, instead of forcing needy residents to travel to faraway central offices. Health centres were started in predominantly immigrant neighbourhoods of Milwaukee and Philadelphia, the Mohawk-Brighton district of Cincinnati, New York's Lower East Side, and the West End of Boston (Nelson, 1919). One of the only community health centres to serve African-Americans was started in Atlanta by a women's club, the Neighborhood Union (Smith, 1995).

J.L. Pomeroy, the County Health Officer of Los Angeles, launched a network of health centres throughout the city in 1919 staffed by physicians, nurses and social workers focused on combining preventive and curative services (Pomeroy, 1929). By 1916 over fifty-six milk stations in New York City supplied clean dairy products, were staffed with visiting nurses, and acted as maternal, infant, and child care centres (Duffy, 1990). In a radical move for the time, a Jewish physician was appointed to the health centre in New York's Lower East Side because he was seen as someone who could best relate to the local culture (Rosen, 1971). C.E. Winslow would note in his 1926 article, 'Public Health at the Crossroads', that the most striking development of the public health movement of the time was the community health centre.

A central feature of the health centre was the creation of block committees with community representatives. These committees met regularly and provided an opportunity for residents to participate directly in community affairs, while also using the professional skills of the health centre's physicians and nurses (Sparer and Johnson, 1971). Block workers represented residents and visited families, keeping them in touch with centre programmes and raising their concerns at meetings (Kreidler, 1919). Another committee run by the health centre, the occupational council, organized local business and professional groups and gathered their input and support for the work of the centre. Both committees acted as neighbourhood planning bodies, since no new activities were undertaken in the neighbourhood until they had the support of the two councils (Gillette, 1983). Neighbourhood health centres were a one-stop location for clinical care, community resources, and intensive participation by and involvement of local residents (Bamberger, 1966).

The creation of health centres had a significant influence on city management, since new health administrative districts were created to define the catchment areas for the centres and new bureaucratic staff were required that could bridge health research, clinical services and community participation. In 1932 Baltimore, the Eastern Health District was created as a collaborative between the Baltimore City Health Department, the Johns Hopkins School of Hygiene and Public Health, and a number of community-based voluntary organizations. According to Rosen (1971, p. 1631), the district made it possible for these partners to come together for the first time to conduct 'intensive study of public health problems and has provided a field laboratory for the testing of new administrative procedures and for the training of personnel'.

While merging social and physical planning with health services for the poor, neighbourhood health centres declined rapidly after World War I. Criticism by physicians and the powerful American Medical Association, who accused the centres of practicing 'socialized medicine', reduced their political and financial support (Rosen, 1971). Federal matching funding for neighbourhood health centres ended when the Sheppard-Towner Act was allowed to expire in 1929.

Neighbourhood health centres would return in the 1960s, again with federal support through the Office of Economic Opportunity (OEO) (Lefkowitz, 2007; Sardell, 1988). This time they were based on the model of community-oriented primary care developed by Sidney and Emily Kark, which embraced social medicine ideas and linked economic and social conditions to prevention and treatment (Kark and Kark, 1983; Susser, 1993). The first two OEO health centres were in Boston's

Columbia Point neighbourhood and rural Mound Bayou, Mississippi. According to Jack Geiger, a leader of the 1960s health centre movement, the centres:

were designed to reduce or eliminate health disparities that affected racial and ethnic minority groups, the poor, and the uninsured. The CHCs were to constitute a key component of the national public safety net, focused simultaneously on the care of individual patients and on the health status of their overall target populations. With their host communities involved in their governance, the centers were to be 'of the people, by the people, for the people'. (Adashi et al., 2010, p. 2047)

Describing his work in a health centre in 1960s Mississippi, Geiger noted that malnutrition was the leading problem facing children, but the centre only had a pharmacy that distributed prescription drugs. So, doctors were instructed to write prescriptions for food that could be used at local shops and paid for out of the clinic's pharmacy budget. Geiger (2005, pp. 7–8) went on to describe the broad social determinants and community resilience work of one community health centre in the 1960s:

And so, in addition to the medical care we provided, we had food and other models of activism. We repaired housing. We dug protected wells and sanitary privies. We urged people to start vegetable gardens, and a thousand families raised their hands, and that gave us a better idea. With a grant from a foundation as a start-up, we rented 600 acres of land that was sitting empty nearby in the Delta, and organized what we called the North Bolivar County Cooperative Farm … families pooled their labor to grow vegetables instead of cotton… We invented a new occupation: nutritional sharecropping. And in the first two years the Farm Co-op produced literally tons – scores of tons – of vegetables for people to eat, enough so that people were solving the problems of hunger and malnutrition through their own efforts.

Despite their success in addressing broad social determinants of health, federal funding for community health centres declined in the 1970s. Financing was increasingly tied to clinical services and specific disease outcomes, and the ability of health centres to work on the social and economic drivers of health inequities was constrained (Lefkowitz, 2007).

Conclusions

The hybridization of the lab and field views for urban health was the exception not the rule for much of the twentieth century. The laboratory model helped give rise to the individualistic biomedical model that remains a powerful force in medicine and public health in the twenty-first century. The legacy of the laboratory view also continues to impact city administration, as most public health departments are organized around specific diseases and behaviours, not communities or social determinants of health. Yet, re-emergence of social epidemiology in the 1980s would question the efficacy of one view of health promotion, either the field or laboratory view, and instead advanced the idea that social context and biology and behaviours must be considered together for changing inequitable distributions of disease and death. As the social context of health reconnects with urban policy making in the twenty-first century, this chapter has provided examples of strategies to avoid and those to consider as models for research and practice. The next three chapters offer detailed cases of contemporary experiments aimed at healthy and equitable city planning.

Notes

1. The vaccination process was eventually restarted and credited with eradicating smallpox from Rio de Janeiro. In 1907, the 14th International Congress on Hygiene and Demography in Berlin awarded Cruz their gold medal for his efforts.
2. Frederick Winslow Taylor (1856–1915) is regarded as the father of scientific management and one of the first management consultants.
3. See http://supreme.justia.com/cases/federal/us/272/365/case.html.
4. Jim Crow Laws were first passed in the South in the aftermath of Reconstruction (1865–1877) after the Civil War (1861–1865) and continued through the passage of the Civil Rights Act (1964) and even beyond. In the South, the Jim Crow Laws ultimately created a *de jure* separation of the races, while in the North, although few formal laws were enacted, *de facto* segregation of the races prevailed through the practices of everyday life.
5. Importantly, the UK housing standards based on the neighbourhood unit were not viewed as unquestionably health promoting. In 1948, Lord Silkin (1948), then Minister of Town and Country Planning, addressing the Town Planning Institute, noted: 'In every plan now it is fashionable to provide neighbourhoods. The assumption is that by dividing up your population into groups of 10,000 to 20,000 and surrounding them by open spaces, railways and main roads you will get nice little communities living happily and sociably together. On what evidence is that based? … do we really get a good life that way? What steps do you take to ensure that people inside these little areas do mix freely together and do all the things one thinks it good for them to do? I would like more thought to be given to the question of neighbourhoods, even to the whole conception of the idea. I have fallen for it myself, but I would like to think it out again'.
6. See http://en.wikipedia.org/wiki/Young_Lords

Chapter 4

Favela Health in Rio de Janeiro, Brazil

Navigating for Health on the 'Hill of Vultures'

In Morro do Urubu *favela* in Rio de Janeiro, Gloria is leading a community meeting about engaging youth to map the neighbourhood in order to document both assets and dangers in this *favela* in the northern part of the city. A section of the *favela* was washed away in torrential rains in April 2010 and the land was condemned by the city as unsafe for reconstruction. The young people had ideas for how the new 'open space' might be used and what else in the community had been damaged by the rains and needed repair. But, dominating the meeting was the roar of a motorcycle racing up and down the street outside the Posto de Saúde, or community health centre, where we are meeting. Gloria tried to bring us back to the core issues:

Look, the city came in here and people were forced to leave their homes. They said our health was at risk from slides and disease. But the broken sewers, garbage and washed-out stairs remain. These are the risks I face everyday. The city officials don't look like us and we must set the agenda for improving our own community.

I keep noticing Gloria's eyes glancing out to the street through the open door behind her. She is a dynamic community leader, full of energy and there is a warmness to her spirit suggesting she is much younger than her fifty-something years. Yet, even she cannot hide that her concern at the moment is more than promoting community well-being as a leader of *Assoçiãcao de Mulheres e Amigos do Morro do Urubu* (AMAMU), a partner organization of the Rio Healthy Cities network organized by the Rio-based non-governmental organization, *Centro de Promoção da Saúde*, or Centre for Health Promotion (CEDAPS).

The young boy on the motorcycle, shirtless and shoeless, cannot be more than 12 or 13 years old. He is hardly an intimidating figure, unable to touch the ground while sitting on the bike, but the young people in the health centre with me know better. One teen turns to me and describes the ritual happening outside:

That kid on the bike is a lookout for a local drug dealer and his gang in this place. That's his job. Up and down the street. He may not do anything, but it is a sign that others are waiting, watching, and something is going to go down. These guys are in a war with another neighbouring gang. They can close schools, shut down the street, just control your life. Always present, like vultures.

Gloria's organization is part of a CEDAPS programme linking improvements to *favelas* in the city to health promotion and prevention, called *Plataforma dos Centros Urbanos no Rio de Janeiro*, or the Platform for Urban Centres in Rio de Janeiro. CEDAPS is leading the *Plataformas* programme in Rio, with support from UNICEF, but it is a national urban programme focused on bringing together young people from the community to work on health promotion activities.

Maria, a CEDAPS community action group leader from the Complexo do Alemão *favela*, spoke up and described the importance and power of planning and sharing ideas. She recounted how a community coalition wanted to work with a local Family Health Unit – a team of lay health outreach workers, nurses and a physician that staff a neighbourhood health centre. Despite the directive of the national health system (*Sistema Único de Saúde* – SUS) to prioritize community health promotion, the Family Health Units were still largely focused on delivering curative services. She noted:

Our network with CEDAPS came up with five participatory councils that worked with the units to define what we thought the health promotion agenda should be. We came up with things such as cultural and after-school activities, creation of a walking group, a focus on mental health, and regular dialogues between Family Health Unit professionals and residents. We developed a web site, organized trips for our youth to visit other areas of Rio, and created a group of local small businesses. We have all participated in the design, and soon construction, of a new Favela-Bairro funded community centre.

Gloria reminded the group that they were still working to understand fully the health conditions their community faced, and that no matter the threats, their community would learn from other groups in the network like Maria's. Some of the group stood up and began hanging maps and charts on the walls of the community centre. The meeting proceeded, but with the sound of the motorcycle still ever present in the distance.

In Morro do Urubu, as in Complexo do Alemão and other *favelas*, CEDAPS is building networks of community groups to promote greater health equity through participatory research, planning and advocacy. CEDAPS founded and coordinated the Rio Healthy Cities Network, in which over 180 different *favela* communities work together on issues ranging from AIDS, violence reduction, education, improving housing and infrastructure, job training, youth leadership and a host of other planning related issues. Much of their work is targeted at existing policies and programmes intended to improve health, wellbeing and racial justice. In some cases CEDAPS organizes community planning processes[1] as part of these state-sponsored interventions while in others it works to ensure the programmes are serving the needs of the *favela* population, such as the community health outreach workers employed by Brazil's *Programa Saúde da Família*, or Family Health Programme. In still other projects, CEDAPS is working with organizations that support families receiving benefits under Brazil's *Bolsa Família*, poverty and hunger elimination programme. In each case, CEDAPS uses community organizing, sharing of information and strategies across their network of *favela*-based organizations and action-oriented research to help ensure government policies are working in the places where they are most needed.

According to Katia Edmundo, Director of CEDAPS, coordinating activities through their networks is intended to 'make structural changes by building from the neighbourhood while realizing that change from below needs to be supported by change at the top'. This is the essence of the neighbourhood to nation links that are necessary for healthy and equitable city planning.

Despite its long history of vast inequalities in both rural and urban areas, Brazil's absolute poverty rate between 2003 and 2008 dropped from 39 to 25 per cent, while extreme poverty declined during the same period from 17.5 to 8.8 per cent of the population. Some of these improvements have been tied to the national *Bolsa Família* programme, which supports nearly 22 per cent of the Brazilian population through conditional cash transfers (Soares *et al.*, 2010). These are only limited measures, but they are an indication that social policies are having an impact on the wellbeing of the poor across Brazil.[2]

As this chapter highlights, public policies at the national, state and municipal scale are only successful if they have community-based accountability and on-going monitoring. I suggest that CEDAPS is a crucial intermediary organization that ensures communities of the urban poor in *favelas* are able to participate in planning for their own health and wellbeing while also working to ensure that government interventions are accountable on-the ground. The informal settlements of Rio de Janeiro are infamous, and have been omnipresent as the city has grown and developed over the past century or more. Since at least 2010, Rio has developed a multi-issue, multi-sector strategy for improving the lives and living conditions of *favela* residents. The recent strategies from *Favela-Bairro* to the Social Police Pacification Units (Unidade de Polícia Pacificadora – Social UPP) to *Bolsa Família*, among others, are being watched around the world to see how a city and country can address chronic urban inequality. Here I explore some of these processes and the role of CEDAPS in their design and implementation, in order to analyse how together they can inform the practice of healthy city planning.

A Planning and Health History of Rio's *Favelas*

In 2010, Brazil's census bureau, the *Instituto Brasileiro de Geografia e Estatística* (IBGE), reported that more than 22 per cent of Rio de Janeiro's over 6.3 million residents live in *favelas* and/or 'substandard' and 'irregular' communities. The 2010 census reports that there are 1,393,314 people in 763 *favelas* in Rio, ahead of São Paulo, whose *favela* population is closer to 1.2 million (IBGE, 2011). The 2000 Census reported 1,092,283 residents in Rio *favelas*, or 18.65 per cent of residents. Thus, in 10 years the *favela* population in Rio has grown approximately 27 per cent,[3] during a time of national economic growth and concerted strategies to improve the lives and living conditions of *favela* residents. Further, more than two-thirds of the urban poor are of Afro-Brazilian decent, more commonly referred to as *pretos* (black) and *pardos* (brown or multi-racial) – based on skin colour. Understanding why *favela* populations continue to grow and the effectiveness of policies aimed at improving the health of the urban poor, demands a review of how they came to be and what policies influenced their wellbeing throughout Rio's and Brazil's history.

The name Rio de Janeiro comes from the Portuguese who, in 1567, sailed into a bay they thought was the mouth of a river (Rio de Janeiro or January River). Portuguese colonialists made Rio their capital in 1763 and turned to slave labour to build their empire. Over the next 125 years, Rio would become an international centre of commerce. The abolition of slavery occurred in Brazil in 1888 and the declaration of the Brazilian republic in 1889 (Baer, 2001). During the early years of the republic, soldiers returning to Rio in 1897 from the War of Canudos, a civil conflict in an area in the Northeast state of Bahia, settled on a hill in the city. The community resembled an area where the soldiers lived in Bahia named 'Morro da favella', which was also the name (*favella*) of a thorny plant indigenous to the Bahia area (Abreu, 2008). Thus, as recounted by Euclides da Cunha in his classic, *Rebellion of the Backlands*, the conflict in Canudos also contributed to the origins of a name now associated with urban segregation and poverty (Da Cunha, 1944).

The Vaccine Revolt and Urban Health in Rio's *Favelas*

Public Health was soon enlisted to arrest epidemics of infectious disease and justify the razing of communities of the urban poor where disease was suspected of breeding. As mentioned in Chapter 3 an urban 'beautification' policy was introduced in Rio in the early 1900s. The Public Health Director, Gonçalves Oswaldo Cruz, was charged with implementation. As part of this policy, older housing was torn down, streets widened and ports expanded. A newly widened, Parisian-style boulevard, Avenida Central (today Rio Branco) lined with banks, cultural institutions and businesses was completed 1904. Thousands of urban poor residents were displaced from the central zone of the city to Rio's northern area and forced to resettle on steep hillsides and other undeveloped land (Nachman, 1977).

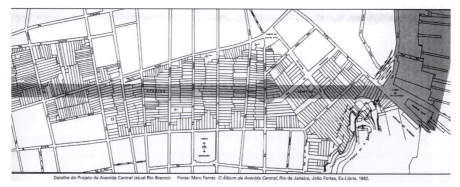

Detalhe do Projeto da Avenida Central (atual Rio Branco)   Fonte: Marc Ferrez. *O Álbum da Avenida Central*, Rio de Janeiro, João Fortes, Ex-Libris, 1982.

Figure 4.1. Central Avenue in Rio de Janeiro: 1905 Hygienic Policy teardown areas shaded in grey. (*Source*: Ferrez et al., 1982)

Figure 4.2. Av. Presidente Vargas; before (*top*) and after urban renewal 1944 (*bottom*), Rio de Janeiro. (*Source*: Arquivo Municipal da Cidade do Rio de Janeiro)

The beautification policy included mosquito inspectors ordered to spray pesticides across the city, including within people's homes (Meade, 1997, p. 247). The inspectors were also authorized to declare a building unsanitary and subject to demolition. Yet it was a requirement within the beautification law that all Rio residents get the smallpox vaccination that stimulated widespread protest (Nachman, 1977). Almost immediately, the poor and others in Rio were sceptical of the programme and whether its real intentions were to drive them out of the city (*Ibid.*).

One group of protesters was from the Positivist church. The Positivists followed the philosophy of Auguste Comte, who claimed that science was capable of providing evidence and answers that should to be applied to society, politics and all aspects of life (Nachman, 1977, p. 22). Since the claims of science were undeniable, according to the Positivists, science was the only legitimate justification for state intervention over society. The Positivist Church in Rio took issue with the smallpox vaccination programme because they claimed there was no published, verifiable scientific evidence that the policy would be effective and therefore was unjustified.

An increasingly popular labour movement, *Centro das Classes Operárias*, also began to oppose the mandatory vaccinations, but on political rather than scientific grounds. The labour union leaders saw the controversy as an opportunity to oust the existing Brazilian president (Meade, 1989, p. 249). The labour movement's leader, Vicente Ferreira de Souza, was of mixed-race heritage, had trained as a doctor, and was highly respected among the working class and black Brazilian urban population (Nachman, 1977, p. 24). The movement described the vaccine law as a battle between a white, elite Congress and the poor, darker skinned residents of Rio.

For six days, from 10 to 16 November 1904, rioting broke out in the streets of Rio over the programme (Needell, 1987, p. 206). On 14 November, military cadets tried to overthrow the government. Two days later the government temporarily suspended the compulsory vaccination programme, but not before scores were dead or injured and hundreds arrested (Meade 1989). The impact on the city was also long lasting. As Stepan (1976) has argued, the hygiene programme used the emerging and still relatively unknown science of bacteriology to reshape radically the physical landscape of Rio by removing low-cost housing from the urban core where jobs and other amenities were located. According to Meade (1997), the riot and public-health clearance programme also resulted in the social fragmentation of Rio that continued for the next century, weakening cross-class political alliances that would help the Vargas dictatorship rise to power (Baer, 2001).

The Impacts of Early Twentieth-Century Urban Planning on the Health of the Poor

By the 1920s, Rio's city government, or the *Prefeitura*, hired a French planner, Alfred Agache to design a new plan for city development. The plan became known as the Agache Plan, and according to Abreu (2008, p. 143), perpetuated the formal separation of social classes in Rio. Under the Agache plan, sections of the city were divided into functional use zones that limited land uses. For example, Central Rio was to have six distinct geographic centres; business, administrative, monuments, financial, embassies, and gardens (Agache, 1930). The Agache plan also borrowed from the radial street, grand boulevards and green space designs of the Garden City model popularized by Ebenezer Howard in England. The Agache Plan offered Rio a strategy of continued segregation of land uses and rich from poor (Abreu, 2008).

In part a response to the lack of affordable housing in Rio de Janeiro at the time, the *Instituto de Aposentadoria e Pensões dos Industriários* (IAP) or the Institute for

Figure 4.3. The Agache Plan for Rio de Janeiro, 1930.

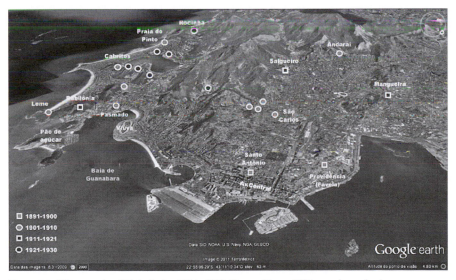

Figure 4.4. The growth of Rio's *favelas*, 1891–1930 (*Source*: Abreu, 1994, map by author).

Industrial Workers' Retirement and Pensions was created in 1936. For the first time, the IAP linked social security with medical care, which was only accessible to those who were employed. Under this plan, the services a person received and the level of coverage of health care depended on occupational class; bankers received much more care than railroad workers (Paim *et al.*, 2011). Under the IAP, casual workers and the unemployed were either forced to pay for services out-of-pocket or, as was more often the case, received no formal health care at all. The IAP also offered housing financing to its working members, which helped to develop a middle-class housing market in Rio (Silva, 2005). The social security system reinforced the notion that the benefits of citizenship and city living were linked to social class (Santos, 1979, pp. 75–76).

Table 4.1. Rio de Janeiro's *favela* population growth, 1950–2010.

	Rio de Janeiro population (total)	% growth	Favela population (estimated total)	% growth	Favelas % of total Rio de Janeiro population*
1950	2,377,451		169,305		7
1960	3,281,908	38	335,063	98	10
1970	4,251,918	30	565,135	69	13
1980	5,090,790	20	722,424	28	14
1991	5,480,778	8	882,667	22	16
2000	5,857,904	7	1,092,959	24	19
2010	6,323,037	8	1,393,314	27	22

These data are from the government bureau of statistics which conducts the decennial census and capturing accurate population counts in *favelas* and urban poor communities is challenging and, as a result, official data tend to under-count. In addition, in 2010 the IBGE used different methodologies from previous censuses to count *favela* residents, including satellite images. Also notable for the total Rio statistics is that IBGE did not include favelas in the outer regions of the city, such as Vila do João, Maré, Vila Kennedy or Cidade de Deus which would significantly increase the overall population numbers.
Sources: Abreu, 2008; IPLANRIO, 1993; IBGE, 1980, 1991, 2000, 2010; Armazém de Dados, 2003.

Shifting Governance and the Growth of *Favelas*

By the 1940s, Brazil was in the grip of Getúlio Vargas's dictatorship and he appointed Henrique Dodsworth's as Rio's Mayor. Dodsworth enlisted Victor Taveres de Moura to document the health and living conditions of the urban poor in Rio and published a report entitled, *Favelas of the Federal District*, in 1943. Emerging from this research was a policy of trying to appease *favela* residents through the development of what were called 'proletarian parks' (Parisse, 1969; Valladares and Ribeiro, 1994). The first three 'proletarian parks' were in the Rio neighbourhoods of Gávea, Leblon, and Caju, and thousands of *favela* residents were resettled in what were intended to be temporary settlement areas. According to Zalvar and Alvito (1999) the state increasingly feared a political backlash and uprising of the urban poor during this time, so the Archdiocese of Rio de Janeiro was enlisted to help the development of the parks and provide health and education services to the poor. Between 1947 and 1954, this state-church partnership brought water, sanitation and electricity service to over thirty of Rio's *favelas*.

Between 1945 and 1964 Brazilian governance shifted to democratic instability from dictatorship (Donnangelo, 1975). Rapid urbanization, migration and the penetration of international capital into Rio placed new pressures on the urban poor and demanded new state policy responses (Burgos, 1999). Brazil's first Ministry of Health was created in 1953. A new *favela* policy, *Aliança para o Progresso*, or the Alliance for Progress, was created during the Cold War and received funding from the US (Avila de Matos, 2008, p. 359). The Alliance for Progress built urban public housing, such as Vila Kennedy in Senador Camará, Vila Aliança in Bangu and Vila Esperança in Vigário Geral. These developments consisted of almost 8,000 housing units on the outskirts of the city in areas that lacked infrastructure, transportation and employment. As a Cold War programme supported by foreign interests, the Rio municipality largely withdrew from these areas once the housing was complete, leaving a vacuum that gangs quickly filled (Zalvar and Alvito, 1999). Violence in Rio's *favelas* escalated just as the military dictatorship came to power in 1964.

The military dictatorship increased state-sponsored violence in Rio's *favelas*. The regime often viewed *favelas* as safe houses for communist activity and regularly carried out mass evictions. Violent evictions and the razing of entire *favelas* in Rio were common (Baer, 2001).

Yet, the dictatorship also promoted development in some *favelas*. One programme launched by the State of Rio de Janeiro during this time was the Centre for Community Development (*Companhia de Desenvolvimento de Comunidades*, CODESCO). While previous programmes had been largely about removing and relocating, CODESCO aimed to integrate the '*aglomerados subnormais*' (or 'subnormal conglomerations' in other words *favelas*) with the 'normal' surrounding community (Santos, 1981). CODESCO was organized by a group called *Quadra*, a multi-disciplinary team of architects, urban planners, sociologists and economists, and together they devised a policy where low-interest, long-term loans would be offered to residents to build their own houses. The programme was piloted in three *favelas*; Brás de Pina; Mata Machado and Morro Uniao. Under this programme, the state committed to provide basic infrastructure, and would widen the main access roads, install water, sanitation and electricity infrastructure, and secure land for community facilities such as schools, clinics and recreation (*Ibid.*). CODESCO only completed the three pilot projects and was discontinued in 1969. Yet, it developed a new model for community-driven *favela* upgrading that integrated different sectors and services with local and professional expertise, and helped galvanize the emergence of a social movement focused on the needs of the urban poor: *Movimento Nacional pela Reforma Urbana* (MNRU), or the National Movement for Urban Reform (Perlman, 2010).

Democratic Transition and Integrated Urban Health Policies

As democracy re-emerged in 1985, new leadership in Rio launched *Projeto Mutirão* (Project Task Force), which aimed to integrate *favelas* both physically and socially into the fabric of the city (*Ibid.*). This policy combined community development with employment and was later renamed, *Projeto Urbanização Comunitária/Mutirão Remunerado* (Project for Community Urban Reform/Paid Task Force) (Fernandes and Valencia, 2004). The state government launched a parallel policy, *Cada Família Um Lote* (CFUL) – 'A Plot for Each Family', which aimed to initiate a process for issuing titles to *favela* residents (Perlman, 2010). While this programme was seen as clientelistic and failed to deliver titles to a large number of *favela* residents, it would later give rise to a community driven, collaborative land titling programme called *Morar Legal* that continues today (Perlman, 2010).

Municipal Health for All

From the formation of the old Brazilian republic in 1889 to the military dictatorship that ended in 1985, health was a centralized function of the federal government and focused largely on curing infectious diseases. Access to medical care and the quality of that care was often determined by one's occupational status, and during the military dictatorship a private health care system emerged for the rich (Paim *et al.*, 2011). The transition to democracy in the 1980s gave rise to health social movements that helped create a new national health system that focused on health promotion and care for all (Baer, 2001, p. 430).

As a participant in the early reform movements, Daniel Becker of CEDAPS recalled that the approach was to shift away from viewing health as exclusively biological and the domain of medical services, but rather as a social and political issue:

The movement of activists, researchers and academics was informed by and had been practicing social medicine very much aligned with other Latin American countries. The Alta Alma Declaration in the late 1970s reinforced to the global community that social equity, economic policy and human rights, should be viewed as part of primary care. This was also an embrace of citizen democracy; participation by the people to hold their government accountable for what they needed. (Becker, 2011)

Social movements succeeded in integrating health reform into the 1988 Constitution. Today, Brazil has a national Unified Health System (SUS) that is managed at the municipal level. To understand better the emergence of this policy and its cascading impacts on urban planning and health equity in cities, I trace Brazil's approach to the AIDS epidemic starting in the early 1980s.

The Brazilian Fight against AIDS: Relational Policy-Making for Health Equity

Brazilian health reform in the 1980s took place in the shadow of a growing national HIV/AIDS epidemic.[4] The first national AIDS programme was established in the country in 1986, but received little funding (Levi and Vitória, 2002). However the Brazilian government's response to AIDS in the 1980s was largely driven by mobilized civil society groups in cities (BMH, 2001; Parker, 2003, 2009). A linked movement for civil rights, urban policy and health reform – referred to as the *Movimento Sanitário* – emerged in São Paulo and grew to include Rio (Parker, 2003). One of the movement's first demands was to establish municipal AIDS programmes rather than leaving the responsibility with the national health ministry. Decentralization of HIV/AIDS prevention meant that municipalities had to find creative and cost effective ways to prevent the spread of the disease, since they would be burdened with the responsibility of care.

The growing movement also set out to challenge the federal government about patent rights for emerging antiretroviral (ARV) drug therapies that were under the control of American and European pharmaceutical corporations. The activists demanded that the Brazilian government invoke a clause in international trade and patent law that allows developing countries to break patents for emergency health reasons without sanctions. Brazil agreed and sought what are called *compulsory licences* to produce generic versions of patented drugs for domestic use.[5] No other country in the world had invoked this clause. By 1996, Brazil had passed a law granting all Brazilians' free access to antiretroviral drugs through the National Health System and cheap ARVs were the only way to make this a reality (Nunn *et al.*, 2009). Brazil issued the compulsory licenses, stimulating a large domestic pharmaceutical industry of ARVs producers, among other drugs (Parker, 2003).[6] By 2011, Brazil was producing at least eight different ARVs that are part of today's AIDS drug cocktail (Paim *et al.*, 2011). While pharmaceutical companies and the US challenged Brazil's decision, social movements pressured the government to persist and continue with the programme (Galvao, 2005). Today, Brazil's drug industry is the eighth largest in the world, and continues to be supported by the Ministry of Health's policy of reducing the importation of drugs and the promotion of generic drugs (Paim *et al.*, 2011).

Another feature of the AIDS programme was to de-stigmatize the disease, testing and prevention. This was particularly challenging in a country with a strong Catholic tradition (Parker, 2003). However, activists took on the rhetoric of the church early in their campaigns and worked with municipal governments to develop campaigns focused on condom distribution and use and sex education. In addition, activists worked to pass legislation recognizing and protecting homosexual and transsexual rights and legalizing commercial sex work. Policies and programmes followed that distributed clean needles for intravenous drug users, targeted prison health and made blood screening mandatory.

The Brazilian AIDS programme, for which the country won the 'Human Rights and Culture of Peace' prize from the United Nations Educational, Scientific and Cultural Organization (UNESCO) in 2001, is recognized around the world as a monumental success. The early AIDS activism spilled over into the drafting of health and urban policies within Brazil's new Constitution.

Constitutional Guarantees of Health and the 'Right to the City'

Brazil's 1988 Constitution declared a right to universal and equal access to health services irrespective of a person's economic status or occupation. The constitution also

included a chapter on urban policy that articulated the social function of property, the city, and the rights of urban squatters – mostly *favela* residents – to obtain title to land (Fernandes, 2007). The 'urban chapters' (Articles 182 and 183) in the Constitution codified the social functions of a city as 'ensuring the well-being of its inhabitants'. The Constitution also gave formal property rights to those living in informal areas for 5 years or more.

The constitutional urban framework set in motion more detailed work by civil society groups to define the characteristics and process behind a 'right to the city'. On 10 July 2001 Brazil adopted Federal Law no. 10.257, the 'City Statute', which provided more details for implementing the urban chapter in the Constitution. The City Statue expanded and defined the role of municipalities in urban planning, urban development and management, and stated that a city itself must fulfil a social, not just economic, function. City governments were charged with drafting new land-use policies where individual property rights needed to co-exist with the social, cultural, and environmental interests of the city and the needs of its population (*Ibid.*). The main mechanism to accomplish this was through the drafting and adoption of Master Plans that were required to include mechanisms for public participation.

Specific public participation processes defined in the City Statue included a right for citizen consultations, the creation of urban management councils, popular referenda, and ongoing reporting of neighbourhood environmental and social impacts. Participatory budgeting was also recognized as an essential aspect of citizen participation in city governance (*Ibid.*). The City Statue also encouraged more explicit debates about structural racism in Brazil, since urban poverty and *favela*-like living conditions disproportionately impact Afro-Brazilians. This culminated in the 2010 passage of the Statue of Racial Equality (Gasnier, 2010).

The Brazilian Constitution included a new right to health and this led to the creation of the Sistema Único de Saúde (SUS) – a national health care and prevention programme (Baer, 2001; Gouveia *et al.*, 2005).[7] The SUS decentralized health promotion and care to municipalities and required community participation in planning and implementation. Municipal Health Councils were established to define health priori-ties and oversee implementation. These consist of government officials, health service providers, professionals and citizens. The councils have veto power over the annual plan and budget put forward by the health secretariat and if this happens, the Ministry of Health does not transfer funds to the municipality (Coehlo *et al.*, 2005, p. 176).

Community Health Centres and Health Agents

Almost all health promotion aspects of SUS are implemented at the community level through the *Programa Agente Comunitário de Saúde* (PACS), or Community Health Agent Programme, and linked to the *Programa Saúde da Família* (PSF), or Family Health Programme, which are community-based clinics. The Community Health Agents are lay people from the community who help link families to services and engage them in planning activities, such as those described by CEDAPS in the opening of this chapter. Each Family Health Unit has one doctor and nurse and a team of six or more community health agents. The team works in a geographic area serving the local population.

CEDAPS plays a crucial role in the health agent and family health clinics programmes. According to Daniel Becker (2011) of CEDAPS:

We started by developing community-based clinics in Vila Canoas and Parque da Cidade, and the Ministry followed our model. Now, we are helping to train a lay health workforce that can get a salary for doing community organizing and mobilization work. This is in essence what the health agents do.

CEDAPS has developed Community Prevention Centres and trained prevention agents who work directly with the SUS-led programme. The federal system has been under-funded, and *favelas* are most frequently the places that do not see a health agent when funding is cut. According to Katia Edmundo (2011), CEDAPS fills a crucial gap in these cases:

Our agents also come from the community, so the residents rarely see a difference. The PACS is limited because they do not have a clinic in every community and agents are spread across many *favela* neighbourhoods. We are able to have people work with them who are from the community and live there, in many more places than they can reach.

CEDAPS helps to strengthen and expand the health outreach worker networks in *favelas* and keep residents connected to the Family Health Clinics.

By 2010, only 15 years after the launch of the Family Health Programme, infant mortality has dropped from 48 per 1,000 to 17 per 1,000; diabetes and stroke hospitalizations have decreased more than 25 per cent, and the percentage of children under 5 who are underweight has fallen by 67 per cent (WHO, 2010). Life expectancy at birth, for both sexes, had also risen from 67 years in 1990 to around 73 years in 2008. By some estimates, over 250,000 community health workers – all from poor communities – are employed through the Family Health Programme (Harris and Haines, 2010). While the programme has serious challenges, including recruiting and retaining doctors and maintaining adequate funding, it remains, according to the World Health Organization, the 'best example in the world of scaling up comprehensive health promotion from *neighborhoods to the nation*' (WHO, 2010, emphasis added). Cities and countries across the global South aim to replicate the programme innovations, such as its network of breast milk banks, which collect and distribute donated breast milk to newborn babies whose mothers cannot supply the milk to meet their needs (Boccolini, 2011).

Favela-Bairro

Building on national health and urban reforms, along with support from international donors, in 1994 the municipality of Rio launched the Urbanization of

Popular Settlements of Rio de Janeiro Programme (Programa de Urbanização de Assentamentos Populares, PROAP), better known as *Favela-Bairro*. While *Favela-Bairro* is still ongoing, having entered its third stage in 2010, it is widely viewed as one of the most successful and effective programmes for addressing chronic inequality in urban informal settlements in the world (Soares and Soares, 2005; Perlman, 2010, p. 276; IDB, 2010).[8]

The objectives of *Favela-Bairro* Phase I were to integrate *favelas* into their surrounding neighbourhoods through infrastructure and urban design and to include social and economic development programs in these same places. According to Soares and Soares (2005), *Favela-Bairro* focused on improving four aspects of the informal settlements:

1. Basic infrastructure (water, sewerage, drainage, street lighting, street paving, parks and sport areas, reforestation);

2. Social services (childcare centres; social-service centres with an emphasis on families, children and adolescents; income and work-generating activities);

3. Community organization and development; and

4. Land titling.

The Housing Department of the Municipal government (SMH) runs the programme with support from the Inter-American Development Bank (IDB). Fifteen different *favelas* were selected for the first round of implementation (Cardoso, 2007). Competitive bids were sought from private firms to design and implement the projects while the government performed oversight and management (Soares and Soares 2005).

The approach behind *Favela-Bairro* was very much aligned with the health promotion strategies of SUS. The project started by focusing on ensuring *favela* residents had access to quality and affordable physical infrastructure, including what were seen, according to Rio Municipal planner Fernando Cavallieri (2010), as:

the basic 'circulatory systems' of a neighbourhood – water and sewer, roads and pathways, waste collection – and these were combined with the 'bones' of a healthy community, such as secure housing, schools, day care, employment and community centres.

A second aspect of this integrated strategy was widespread and on-going community participation, including a management plan to maintain services and training and employment of residents to construct and maintain facilities in their own neighbourhoods. Finally, the programme used community outreach workers to engage residents and brought offices and services of the municipal government into the neighbourhoods to ensure that residents received social, economic and health services to improve their lives. According to Cavallieri (2010):

This was an ambitious programme with many parts. We knew from past interventions, and community members reminded us, that we were likely to get things wrong in terms of what the community needed more often than getting it right. So, we monitored and adjusted projects.

Having planners and health promoters from the community as active participants allowed projects to get accurate feedback. Stairways were redesigned, streets formalized, recreation spaced moved.

While this seemingly adaptive and learning-based strategy worked for some aspects of the project, *Favela-Bairro* has not delivered on the security of land rights or consistent employment for residents (Perlman, 2010).

One of the most successful features of *Favela-Bairro* are the Urban and Social Guidance Centres (*Posto de Orientação Urbanística e Social*, POUSOs). The POUSOs are physical locations in the community which house a team of architects, planners, engineers, and social workers. This team remains in the community for the entire length of project design, development and post-implementation. Community members are hired as outreach workers to engage residents in the projects and in monitoring implementation. Residents can use the professionals for other services as well, such as accessing social programmes, helping with housing construction and fixing broken infrastructure. The POUSOs also act as a local land-use and building code enforcement unit, but one that is instructed to work with the community to improve structures to meet safety codes (Soares and Soares, 2005). Another key function of POUSOs is to provide *favela* residents with certificates of occupancy, called *Habite-se*, which certify that the home meets applicable laws and codes. This is a crucial first-step toward official title. The certificates can provide residents with an increased sense of housing security, leading many to invest in their home and community before legal titling takes place (Perlman, 2010). Under Phase III of *Favela-Bairro*, every project site will have a permanent POUSO, ensuring ongoing monitoring and government-community participation in physical, social and economic development projects (IDB, 2010).

Bolsa Família: From Treetops to Grassroots

In both the nation health system and the *Favela-Bairro* programme, decentralization from central government to the municipality is a central feature of the each policy. National policies also include provisions for decentralization, recognizing that no matter the scale of the social policy, community accountability is crucial. *Bolsa Família*, the largest national poverty alleviation programme in Brazil, also includes decentralized implementation.

Bolsa Família gives poor people money on condition that they undertake certain socially beneficial behaviours. The concept is called a conditional cash-transfer; the participant gets the cash on the condition that he or she abides by the government's rules. Yet, the rules are all behaviours that are understood to have individual, family and broader community benefits. For example, families receive a monthly cash payment for having their children immunized and enrolled in school. Prior to *Bolsa Família*, Brazil had a number of different safety net programmes that paid families for social goods, such as *Bolsa Escola* (schooling), *Bolsa Alimentação* (reducing nutritional deficiency), *Cartão Alimentação* (food stamps), and *Auxilio Gas* (compensating for adjustments in fuel costs), but each was managed by different bureaucracies, used different criteria to select beneficiaries and had different arrangements with banks for issuing payments (World Bank, 2010). A new ministry, the Ministério do Desenvolvimento Social e Combate à Fome (Ministry of Social Development and Hunger Combat) now manages all these programmes under *Bolsa Família* and *Caixa Econômica Federal*, the federal bank, manages all the cash transfers through a debit card.

In 2010, cash transfers reached nearly a quarter of Brazil's 200 million people and according to the World Bank, 23 million Brazilians had been lifted out of poverty since 2003 due to *Bolsa Família* (*Ibid.*). According to the University, Fundaçao Getulio Vargas (FGV), the number of Brazilians with incomes below 800 Reais ($440) a month had fallen more than 8 per cent every year since 2003. The Gini index, a measure of income inequality,[9] fell from 0.58 in 2003 to a 50 year low of 0.519 in 2011. Yet, *Bolsa Família* payments average about 22 Reais ($12) per month per child, with a maximum payment of 200 Reais and the programme costs the Brazilian government just 0.5 per cent of GDP (*Ibid.*). The initial years of the programme were so successful that the Brazilian government changed some categories and criteria for benefits.[10] For instance, the original programme paid families to keep their children in school to complete primary education, but this was extended to include secondary education, while expanding the age requirements for school attendance from 15 to 17 and adding a new, higher payment for in-school 16 and 17 year olds (*Ibid.*, p. 10).

The World Bank's 2010 evaluation of *Bolsa Família* focused on health and sampled 11,000 families in 269 municipalities and twenty-four states across Brazil. Some select health outcome findings from the evaluation included:

◆   Immunization coverage in *Bolsa Família* (BF) participant families was 15 per cent higher than a control group.

◆   Over 62 per cent of BF children were breast-feed for the first 6 months of their lives compared to 54 per cent of a control group.

◆   Premature births were 14 per cent less in BF women than women in a control group.

◆   Under nutrition was 39 per cent less in children in BF than those in a control group (*Ibid.*).

A key aspect of *Bolsa Família* was to eradicate hunger (*Fome Zero* or Zero Hunger) for the poor. It made food a national human right and stated that government had a responsibility to offer healthy, inexpensive food to anyone. The programme borrowed from a similar one started by the Mayor of Belo Horizonte in 1993. The new national Ministry of Social Development and Hunger Combat (Ministério do Desenvolvimento Social e Combate à Fome) supports local programmes that not only include direct financial aid to poor families but also financial and development support for the growth and distribution of food (including subsistence farming), facilitating the development and siting of low-cost restaurants, educating people about healthy eating habits, and distributing vitamins and iron supplements (*Ibid.*).

The Brazilian Ministry of Health reports that for each Real received through the gramme, 62 cents were spent on food, as opposed to only 24 cents for those not participating. An estimated 75–85 per cent of families have increased their overall consumption of healthier foods, diversity of food types, the number of meals they eat per day, and the quantity of children's food. Some of these gains are impacting gender equity issues, as women report an improved ability to make choices for themselves and their families, a reduction of domestic insecurity, and an almost 43 per cent reduction in the incidence of domestic violence among recipient households (*Ibid.*, p. 23).

The Ministry of Health evaluation of *Bolsa Família* concluded that the social and health gains from the policy were not due to an increase in the number of people receiving benefits but rather were due to closer coordination between *Bolsa Família* and other *place-based interventions* in poor communities. The Ministry report cited the family health programme's new community health centres, the hiring of community health agents, and the implementation of community-based health promotion and prevention programmes as the key factors behind the positive health impacts of *Bolsa Família* (Soares, 2012). For example, the study found that when programme participants were asked what enabled them to meet the conditions for the payment:

◆   67.5 per cent of respondents reported that a school closer to home was the most significant reason their children were able to regularly attend.

◆   67 per cent of *Bolsa Família* beneficiaries reported that close proximity to a functioning health centre was the most significant reason behind vaccine compliance, and increased pre-natal, new born and maternal care.

◆   38 per cent reported that the ease of getting care at their local health centre was the most significant factor behind improved adult care (Soares, 2012).

These results suggest that integrating programmes and place-based institutions is a key factor for success. This is the crux of the work of CEDAPS in Rio's *favelas*.

CEDAPS: Networked Solutions for *Favela* Health Equity

In all their organizing, planning and health promotion work, CEDAPS is guided by a methodology they call *Construção Compartilhada de Soluções em Saúde*, or Shared Construction of Solutions in Health (figure 4.5). This model is adopted from one of their sponsors, the Dryfus Foundation Problem Solving for Better Health approach. For CEDAPS, the shared construction method is rooted in Latin American social medicine and Paulo Freire's *Pedagogy of the Oppressed* (1972), as well as the International Healthy Cities movement (Becker *et al.*, 2004, 2007; Edmundo *et al.*, 2005). Practically, this means that social rather than medical solutions are the starting point and promoting greater equity for the poor is the guiding principle.

Table 4.2. Public policies for health and informal settlements in Rio de Janeiro.

Period	Political Context	Health Policies (Select)	Informal Settlement Approach	Informal Settlement Policies (Select)
Old Republic 1889–1930	Liberal Oligarchic State Agro-exporting economy	General Directorate of Public Health. Social security health care. Dichotomy between public health and social security. Focus on infectious diseases.	Eradication	Passos Reform (1902–1906). Eradicated informal settlements and *cortiços*. Plano Agache (1927). transform Rio into a 'modern, functional city'.
Vargas dictatorship 1930–1945	Authoritarian state Industrialization and urbanization	Ministry of Education and Public Health Infectious diseases in urban areas: Yellow fever, syphilis and TB campaigns	Eradication (some urbanization)	Parques Proletários (1941–1942). Leão XIII Foundation (1946).
Democratic instability 1945-1964	Liberal, populist governments Rapid urbanization, migration, import substitution	First Ministry of Health (1953) Law unifies social security for urban workers. Private health sector emerges.	Eradication and Urbanization	SERFHA (1956). Governmental agency focused on *favela* improvement. Federal Council on Housing (1960), COHAB.
Military Dictatorship 1964–1985	Military dictatorship; economic boom (1968–1973); administrative reforms	Social Security Organizations (IAPs) Privatized medical care model Chronic diseases & violence in cities	Eradication (with urbanization in 1980s)	CODESCO (1967). *Projeto Mutirão* (1981). *Proface* (1983): water & sewerage to *favelas*. *Cada Família Um Lote* programme (1983), land tenure initiative.
New Democracy (1988–2003)	Recession & economic stabilization Rise in democratic social movements	Health drives national reform agenda, e.g. AIDS policies. New Constitution (1988). Unified Health System (SUS) prevention & decentralized to municipalities	Urbanization and integration	*Plano Diretor* (1992), the new city plan. *Favela-Bairro I* (1994), urban upgrading programme implemented in thirty-eight *favelas*. City Statue (2001).
Luiz Inacio Lula da Silva governments (2003–2006, 2007–2010)	Economic stability Poverty (US$ 2 per day) fell from 21% of the population in 2009. Extreme poverty ($1.25 per day) declined from 10% in 2004 to 2.2% in 2009.	National Commission on Social Determinants of Health (2006) Family Health Support teams for Family Health Programme (2008)	Integration and inclusion	*Favela-Bairro II* (2000). Morar Carioca UPP & Social UPP (2008). *Bolsa Família*. Growth Acceleration Programme (PAC) (2007). Racial Equity Statue (2010).

In *favelas* like Morro do Urubu, CEDAPS partners with an existing group and works with them to learn about the issues the community faces and the needs they might have. The process of reconstruction after a devastating mud slide in Morro do Urubu highlights some aspects of this approach, as described to me in 2011 by Ives Rocha, a CEDAPS planner who performs monitoring and evaluation:

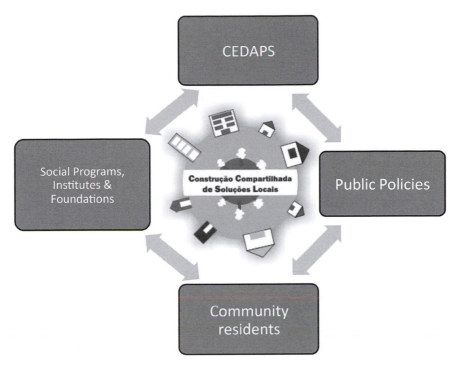

Figure 4.5. CEDAPS' Shared Construction of Solution in Health model (*Source*: CEDAPS, 2011)

The process began with listening and issue and stakeholder mapping. The community identified a number of desires for the space, from recreation to idle open space. We then did a stakeholder mapping process to identify the organizations and policies that could address the community needs. The POUSO and *Favela-Bairro* programmes were important ones, but there were others. Our Youth Build and Platform for Urban Centres were also important programmes. Since the idea is always to build leadership, a youth leadership group emerged from the process.

The youth group met and discussed ideas for the site. A physical mapping project was launched to document other changes that had occurred in the community since the slide. Youth teams used paper maps to document changes in the community and these were entered onto aerial photos of the community for all to review. Through CEDAPS's *Plataformas Program* – where they are developing urban centres with youth throughout the city – the maps are posted online so all community residents could comment on them and add text and images.

Community Prevention and Planning

The planning strategy in Morro do Urubu organized residents around a place-based issue, and CEDAPS helped the group connect the place issues to larger themes the community was interested in addressing. A consistent theme is HIV/AIDS prevention in all the work of CEDAPS. Yet, among the youth in Morro do Urubu, jobs, safety and housing are their priorities. According to Katia Edmundo of CEDAPS:

The AIDS work continues and helps anchor much that we do. However, the more our prevention work expanded, the more our members made the connections between HIV and other economic, racial justice and environmental issues. Women might get free drugs, but they needed food to take the medications. Racism in the work force and education plays a big part. Sometimes this was due to lack of employment. Sometimes it was because of a required payment to a gang for security. Some health benefits required an address, but they don't exist in an informal settlement. So these were issues of community development, institutional change and planning that expanded our AIDS prevention work. (Edmundo, 2011)

The AIDS prevention work is organized around networks of community prevention centres and prevention agents that implement local health action plans drafted through a participatory process in the community. The Community Prevention Centres act as places in a neighbourhood for planning and education, as well as sites for distributing safe-sex educational materials, free condoms and other sexually transmitted disease prevention strategies. Community prevention agents staff the centres and regularly refer residents to local clinics for services the prevention centre cannot provide.

The Prevention Centre in Morro do Urubu is located on a busy street next to stores frequented by residents. A table outside has educational material and condoms, while signs posted announce community meetings, computer trainings and services offered. A wall of computers inside acts as a training site and a cyber café. According to Rocha, the prevention centre and agents keep the young people and residents engaged:

There are lots of reasons why residents would just stop participating. What we try to do is to give them resources and incentives to stay engaged, from jobs to social activities. The planning process can become an alternative to a harder life. Some of these young people rarely get a chance to leave their community. (Rocha, 2011)

In order to keep youth engaged, CEDAPS developed the *Network of Young Health Promoters*. Here too, the network organizes residents and connects them to state-sponsored projects and services. The Young Health Promoters Network has trained over sixty young people to work with the Family Health Units in Maré, Complexo do Alemão and Rocinha, some of Rio de Janeiro's largest *favelas* (Edmundo, 2011). The youth network is integrated into a project called Health Promoting Schools, which partnered with the Municipal Secretaries of Health and Education of Rio de Janeiro. The project worked to improve health and the quality of life for youth and adults in *favelas* using in-school and out-of-school projects. Over eighty schools and eleven family health units participated and the project has reached over 10,000 students, 860 teachers and 4,700 families (CEDAPS 2010). The health promotion activities included reading, self-esteem, violence reduction training, teacher capacity building around health promotion, and the planning and design of community clinics built under *Favela-Bairro*.

In the *Plataformas dos Centros Urbanos* project, young people are reframing city and

Figure 4.6. Map of local groups in Rio de Janeiro participating in the Platform of Urban Centers, coordinated by CEDAPS. (*Source*: CEDAPS, used with permission)

state policies through community mapping. CEDAPS has linked the local youth work to policy through *Grupos Articuladores Locais* (GAL) or local organizing groups that bring together youth, community based organizations, and representatives from government agencies, such as professionals in urban planning and public health (Rocha, 2011). According to Lauren Valdez (2011), an intern with CEDAPS:

The youth work often expanded the consideration of policy approaches for the professionals. They also connected safety and lack of opportunities to experiences of racism. When the issue was violence, the solutions from youth included employment and musical performances. When the issue was dengue, the youth identified places where mosquitoes could breed. Then the issue was stress and mental health, the GALs connected to *Favela-Bairro* and other initiatives that were focused on new public transportation options. Many professionals did not make the issue connections in the same way as the youth.

With a network of over fifty GALs spread across Rio, the *Plataformas* programme is a forum for urban innovations. While many of CEDAPS's programmes seem overlapping, Katia Edmundo explained the rationale to me:

The more networks and connections in *favelas*, the greater the likelihood of support for individuals, families and the entire community. No one network can deliver equity, so we try to integrate the networks and find ways that they can relate their work with the others. Its about 'building people infrastructure' to change living conditions and public policies. (Edmundo, 2011)

Yet, tracking the impacts of these networks on population health is challenging. CEDAPS constantly confronts requests for evidence that building networks of the urban poor promotes health. As Becker described to me:

The work of CEDAPS and our impact on policies and people are hard to measure. Some of this has to do with public health's obsession with individual data. But we focus on social systems and change, with people as agents of change. Our 'outcome' variable is social not individuals. Measuring social change is challenging and we could do a better job in this area. (Becker, 2011)

As Francisco Inácio P.M. Bastos, a senior researcher with the Oswaldo Cruz Foundation – FIOCRUZ, in Rio, reflected on the work of CEDAPS:

The organizing work of CEDAPS makes health policies work. They coordinate the local democratic accountability that we as scientists and government can't. Or we just don't do it as well as they do. It's not about one or the other. I think we do other things well. They recognize, as do we, that *favela* health is not one thing, not one approach, not one policy or intervention. Today its crack, yesterday it was gangs, before that HIV. These don't go away, so we have developed processes to improve health in an ongoing way. We measure success if an indicator is moving in a desired direction. This may or may not indicate that life in *favelas* is getting better or that we are eliminating the need for *favelas*. The success of CEDAPS is from ensuring we are not narrowing our vision of health equity.

Figure 4.7. Relational mode of *favela* health in Rio. (*Source*: Author)

From Neighbourhood to Nation for *Favela* Health

This chapter has highlighted some of the factors that are contributing to healthy city planning in the *favelas* of Rio. The processes are ongoing, but some of the measures of success described here suggest that lives and living conditions are improving. However, the work in Rio also suggests that the combination of networked community participation, municipal policies and federal commitments, are essential elements for *favela* health (figure 4.7).

First, broad community based participation acts as the foundation for healthy planning. This is central to the work of CEDAPS but the commitment to citizen democracy was also legislated through the Constitution, through the national health licy and other policies. A national commitment to deliberative democracy is combined with neighbourhood institutions to put this into practice.

Second, networks build capacity locally, connecting *favela* residents to others, but also connecting across policy scales from municipal to federal. The creation of the Healthy City Network and other networks by CEDAPS highlights how to connect people and ideas with institutions and services. The policies themselves included networked features, such as the Family Health Units and the POUSOs of *Favela-Bairro*.

Third, issue integration is an equity strategy. From the AIDS programme to *Favela-Bairro* to *Bolsa Família*, many of the policies integrated different planning sectors and dimensions of public health. The early success of *Bolsa Família* suggests that a key reason is its intentional integration with other place-based policies. Even the function of the city itself, defined in the City Statue, was recognized as needing to be integrated into the social needs of its population.

Fourth, physical centres anchor social policies. The family health centres, POUSOs and health promotion centres of CEDAPS all acted as sites in a community that helped organize resident attention while providing essential short-term service needs. This approach directly challenges the idea that social policy is either people- or place-based. In Brazil success seems to come from both.

Fifth, decentralization to the municipality for matters of health promotion, planning and development seem to be contributing to the success in Rio. From health promotion and services to infrastructure planning, decentralization seemed to generate new city leadership for healthy and equitable planning. Yet, the municipal decentralization was only possible with federal support, particularly financial. Similarly, community-based planning was able to scale-up or have a wider impact when combined with municipal government support, thus improving the lives and living conditions for many more *favela* residents than neighbourhood-based initiatives could have done on their own.

The healthy planning work in Rio is imperfect and I will discuss some additional challenges in Chapter 7. However, its integrated, networked, community and state approach holds promise for healthy city planning everywhere.

Notes

1.   In a community planning process CEDAPS brings together residents to discuss issues, prioritize and plan for actions, and implement actions.
2.   One indicator of the success of Rio and why it is an interesting case for understanding healthy city planning is that the World Bank selected Rio in 2010 for its first municipal loan ($1 billion) to support on-going health and educational initiatives. (See: web.worldbank.org/WBSITE/ EXTERNAL/NEWS/0,,contentMDK:22636897~pagePK:34370~piPK:34424~theSite PK:4607,00.html).
3.   The growth of *favela* populations outpaced population growth for the city as a whole by roughly eight times; there was a 3.4 per cent overall growth rate from 4,765,621 to 4,929,723 between 2000 and 2010 in Rio de Janeiro.

4. Throughout the early 1980s, many countries and particularly cities in the global North were experiencing the first wave of HIV infections and municipal and national programmes emerged. For example, the US Centres for Disease Control defined the term Acquired Immune Deficiency Syndrome (AIDS) in 1982, the same year the Gay Men's Health Crisis Center in New York City began the first treatment of infected individuals and the City and County of San Francisco, working with activists and the San Francisco AIDS Foundation, developed a model of community-based care and in-home treatment (Engel, 2006). The first international AIDS conference was held in 1985 in Atlanta and the Global Programme on AIDS was launched by the World Health Organization in 1987.

5. Compulsory licensing is when a government allows someone else to produce a patented product or process without the consent of the patent owner. It is one of the flexibilities on patent protection included in the World Trade Organization's agreement on intellectual property, technically known as the TRIPS (Trade-Related Aspects of Intellectual Property Rights) Agreement.

6. Today Brazil also exports yellow fever and meningitis vaccines and produces over 85 per cent of all vaccines used domestically.

7. Brazilian Constitution. Article 198. 'Health actions and public services integrate a regionalized and hierarchical network and constitute a single system, organized according to the following directives:

    I. decentralization, with a single management in each sphere of government;

    II. full service, priority being given to preventive activities, without prejudice to assistance services;

    III. participation of the community.'

8. The success of Favela-Bairro has inspired similar initiatives for improving the lives of the urban poor in at least six other countries: Argentina (National Neighborhood Upgrading Programme), Ecuador (Housing Sector Support Programme), Bolivia (Housing Sector Reform Programme), and Uruguay (Municipal Development and Integration of Informal Settlements).

9. The Gini index measures the extent to which the distribution of income or consumption expenditure among individuals or households within an economy deviates from a perfectly equal distribution (see http://data.worldbank.org/indicator/SI.POV.GINI/).

10. Recipients must qualify for benefits; this is not an entitlement programme. They must also comply with the conditions to receive payment. Social workers are trained to visit families and survey them for compliance. If a family is non-compliant, they get a first warning. A second letter notifying of temporary suspension of benefits is issued if family compliance falls below 85 per cent and no acceptable justification is given. As a 'debit card' is used to access cash through banks the programme is able to block payments. Benefits are paid as soon as the situation is resolved. If non-compliance continues for a further two months, the specific benefit is suspended, such as those linked to school attendance. After a year of continual noncompliance, the benefit is permanently cancelled. Since the inauguration of *Bolsa Família*, only 4.5 per cent of beneficiaries have had one or more of their benefits permanently cancelled (Soares, 2012, p.11).

Chapter 5

Collaborative Planning in Nairobi's Slums

There was a loud commotion about halfway through our community planning meeting in St. Teresa's Church in the Mathare informal settlement in Nairobi. Mathare is one of close to 200 slums in Nairobi without such basic services as water and sanitation. The massive shantytown is an informal settlement, so for decades it has been ignored by government and service providers. Working tirelessly through its labyrinth of muddy, unpaved streets, jam-packed sheet-metal roofed and dirt floor huts, community groups have organized to plan for a better future. The meeting was the culmination of years of organizing, surveying, mapping and generating specific proposals for improving the lives, living conditions and health of Mathare residents.

Voices of teenagers yelling could be heard outside the meeting and some of the older men in the meeting ran outside. The electricity had just come back on after a rolling blackout had hit the area and delayed the meeting for two hours. As the engine from our portable generator went silent, the commotion outside was impossible to ignore. The 500 or so community members and others turned to see what was happening.

Teenagers were arguing with middle-aged men, pointing fingers and waving hands. A man sitting next to me whispered, 'Mungiki'. The Mungiki are a notorious gang in Kenya, often violent, and they control security and services in the slums where the police and army, not to mention utility companies, just will not go. Two years earlier they had been accused of inciting a riot in Mathare after a disputed presidential election and in this community were blamed for such atrocities as chopping off legs and skinning heads. They intimidate and extort. They also recruit young people in slums like Mathare, where one in five children do not live to see their fifth birthday, close to 40 per cent do not attend school, and two-thirds of girls have reportedly been forced to trade sex for food. Being connected to a gang in Mathare can make all this different: a toilet rather than defecating in the open, a TV rather than a paraffin lamp, food rather than an empty stomach.

Suddenly, the argument outside stopped. The men turned and left. Many of the teenagers stood around and a few wandered inside the meeting. The man sitting next to me seemed very nervous.

The community meeting was being run by a civil society group called *Muungano wa*

Wanavaijiji – the over 60,000 strong federation of the urban poor in Kenya – and Pamoja Trust – their sister NGO. Their skilled facilitator, Kimani, kept the meeting going even though the teenagers at the back of the room seemed to have most others on edge. The community dialogue continued with a discussion of drinking water service, sewers, new roads, electricity service and day care centres. For three more hours residents discussed the details of these proposals – the youth incident a distant memory.

Near the conclusion of the meeting, a representative from the Nairobi City Council stood and addressed the crowd. He stated that the Council was prepared to endorse the community plan and begin the process of issuing land titles and supporting the upgrading of roads, water and sewer infrastructure as proposed. The crowd was cautiously optimistic that something was about to change in their community.

As the meeting adjourned, I was approached by 16 year old, Gabriel, one of the teenagers outside. He told me his gang had been paid by the men, slum landlords in Mathare, to come and break-up our meeting. The youth took the money and when they got here, Gabriel told me, 'we saw what you guys were doing and we want that stuff too'. He said the argument was about the structure owners wanting their money back. 'No refunds in the slums', Gabriel smiled.

He reached into his pocket, pulled out a business card and handed it to me. His mates called for him and he hustled out the back door of the church. He called back, 'Hey Prof. Text me'. Smiling, I turned over his business card. It read: *Gabriel. Mathare. Executive Producer*.

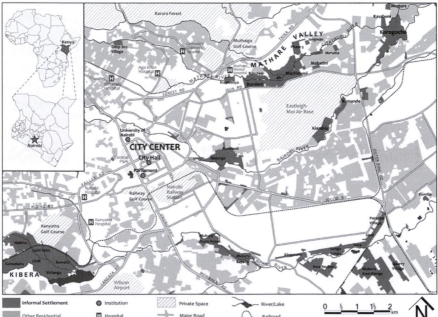

NAIROBI   *Residential Areas & Informal Settlements*

Figure 5.1. Nairobi: residential areas and informal settlements, 2011. (*Source*: GIS data jointly developed by University of California, Berkeley, Muungano Support Trust and University of Nairobi, 2011)

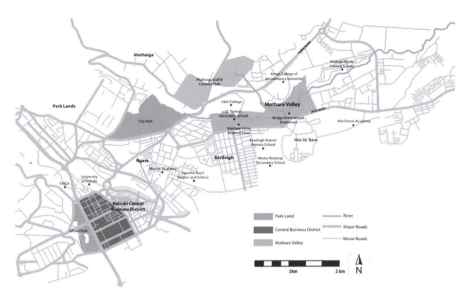

Figure 5.2. Location of Mathare informal settlement in Nairobi. (*Source*: GIS data jointly developed by University of California, Berkeley, Muungano Support Trust and University of Nairobi, 2011)

Figure 5.3. Living conditions in Mathare informal settlement. (*Photo*: Author)

The agreements reached in the community meeting held that day in St Theresa's church emerged after 2 years of organizing and planning by and with Mathare residents. This chapter analyzes the processes of collaborative planning in this Nairobi slum and highlights how in places where the state is largely absent, civil society groups are organizing processes for healthy city planning. In a place as complex as Mathare, a key to success is collaboration among different groups and institutions, and I will reveal some of the strengths and limitations of the collaborative planning process. This can only be understood through an organizational and institutional analysis of *Muungano Wa Wanavijiji*. Muungano and their partners, Muungano Support Trust (MuST) and

Slum Dwellers International (SDI) – a global network of the urban poor. Together these groups are attempting to redefine planning in Nairobi and beyond, using an integrated approach to analysis and solution generation. The journey to understand today's planning must begin with a review of how the present situation was achieved. Nairobi's informal settlements did not occur by chance or accident, and these historical forces bear heavily on contemporary efforts for healthy and equitable city planning.

Nairobi: The Place of Cold Waters

In the late nineteenth century, the British settled an area elevated from the heat of the African savannah and the humidity of the trading port city of Mombasa on the Indian Ocean. For centuries, the Athi, Kikuyus, Kambas and Maasai, and other tribes moved their caravans through this area and often stopped for food, to graze their cattle and to trade.

The location was also strategic for expanding the railway that the British imperialists had built using imported Indian labourers. The British Uganda Railway Committee decided in 1895 to build a railway connecting the heart of East Africa at Lake Victoria – a major source of the White Nile River – to the Indian Ocean coast at Mombasa. The British plan was to extract natural resources from the region and transport them to the coastal port. The resources would fuel the expansion of the British Empire. In 1895 the British declared control over this area stretching from the Indian Ocean across the African continent to the far western edge of the Rift Valley and called the region the East African Protectorate. The managing town was called 'Enkare Nyrobi', 'Cold Water' in the Maasai language (Morgan, 1976).

European housing was built on the highest elevations in town. The colonists borrowed from their experiences in India, where camps built on higher elevations were throught to have fewer pests carrying tropical diseases (Curtain, 1985). Racially segregated planning in Nairobi was soon adopted and linked to medical beliefs of the day. As Curtain (1985, p. 606) notes, the medical advisory committee to the Colonial Office for Tropical Africa declared in 1911:

It has been proved that the separation of Europeans from natives is one of the most efficient means of protection against disease endemic amongst native races. Even partial separation, such as sleeping outside the native quarter at night time, affords a very considerable degree of security.

After a case of the bubonic plague in 1897 and another in 1902, British colonial leaders sought to identify the cause and to prevent future deaths. Sir Charles Eliot, Colonial Administrator and Commissioner of British East Africa, 1900–1904, blamed the Indian settlements, stating:

The Indians had built their houses so close together that they neutralized the natural advantages of air and light and then allowed the most disgusting filth to accumulate on a small area. (Quoted in Hill, 1949, p. 227)

The Indian Bazaar, Nairobi's hub of residential and economic activity for non-

Europeans, ultimately blamed for disease, was burned to the ground and relocated further away from European settlements. According to reports by Medical Officers in Nairobi in 1902 and 1904, the Indian Bazaar was:

damp, dark, unventilated, overcrowded dwellings on filth-soaked and rubbish-bestrewn ground housed hundreds … tin sheds used indiscriminately as dwelling houses, shops, stores, laundries, wash houses, opium dens, bakeries, brothels, butchers' shops, etc, etc … rats abounded and the general conditions of life of the 1,500–2,000 inhabitants were miserable and filthy in the extreme. (Quoted in White *et al.*, 1948, pp. 14–15)

W.J. Simpson of the London School of Hygiene and Tropical Medicine was enlisted to study the problem and devise a solution for the health of the white colonialists. Simpson's 1914 report known as the *Simpson Plan* articulated that land-use control was the central issue for colonial rule. A layout plan was needed that demarcated land for specific uses and where Europeans, Indians and Africans would be allowed to live separately. Maps were drawn (cf. figure 5.4) demarcating boundaries and spatial control. Simpson's report would declare:

The haphazard growth of the town which is being permitted, have brought about such a condition of insanitation that Nairobi, although scarcely 14 years old, and aspiring to be a European town, is in its commercial area one of the most insanitary I have seen. (Quoted in White *et al.*, 1948, p. 16)

In addition to the removal of the Indian Bazaar, Simpson recommended the separation of functions and ethnic groups, justified on public health grounds:

In towns where the nationality of the same, town planning resolves itself into arranging for residential, commercial and manufacturing areas, which are further governed in character by rental and class, and in such a way as to secure convenience, good transit, pleasing amenities and permanent healthiness for all. Something more than this is required in town, such as those

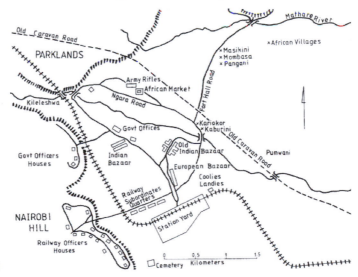

Figure 5.4. Map
of Nairobi, 1910s.
(*Source*: Hake, 1977)

in East Africa, where nationalities are diverse and their customs and habits different from one another. Though the same objects have to be aimed at, it has to be recognized that the standard and mode of life of the Asiatic, except in the highest class, do not consort with those of European ... and that the customs of the primitive African, unfamiliar with and not adapted to the new conditions of town life, will not blend in with either. In the interest of each community and of the healthiness of the locality and country, it is absolutely essential that in every town and trade centre the town planning should provide well-defined and separate quarters for European, Asiatic and African. (Simpson, 1914)

Simpson's racist recommendations were grounded in the dominant colonial medical belief that the African city was like a sick patient in need of curing (Olumwullah, 2002). The planner's solution, much like that of the physician at the time, was immunization and separation; either treat malaria with quinine or isolate the sick from the healthy. The result in 1913 was a segregation plan organized by ethnicity and functions called 'Nairobi: Sketch-map of Segregation Proposals'. The plan was signed and endorsed by A.M. Jeevanjee, one of two Asian members of Nairobi's Municipal Committee, and included six zones: European residential; high-class commercial; Asiatic residential; middle-class commercial and swamp; African and protective zones (Barnow et al., 1983). The land area demarcated for Europeans and 'high-class' activities was more than double that for Asians and more than ten times the area for Africans (figure 5.5). Thus racial residential and economic segregation took hold in Nairobi, in part justified by prominent public health and medical scientists.

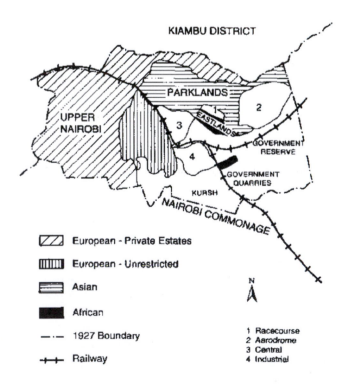

Figure 5.5. Segregated districts, Nairobi, 1910s. (*Source*: Obudho, 1997, p. 300)

Colonial Planning and African Segregation

Kenya became an official British colony in 1920, the same year the Native Pass Law and Vagrancy Ordinance were adopted. These laws restricted residence in Nairobi to those employed by Europeans or Indians (Morgan, 1976). The profits of colonialist farms depended on cheap African labour and the British were intent on keeping Africans away from the growing city. Yet, by 1923, official policy justifying racial segregation on sanitary grounds shifted:

Following up on Professor Simpson's report, a policy of segregation was adopted in principle, and it was proposed by Lord Milner to retain this policy both on sanitary and social grounds. So far as commercial segregation is concerned, it has already been generally agreed that this should be discontinued... It is now the view of the competent medical authorities that, as a sanitation measure, segregation of Europeans and Asiatics is not absolutely essential for the preservation of the health of the community; the rigid enforcement of sanitary, police and building regulations without any racial discrimination, by the Colonial and municipal authorities will suffice. It may well prove that in practice the different races will, by natural affinity, keep together in separate quarters, but to effect such separation by legislative enactment except on the strongest sanitary grounds would not, in the opinion of His Majesty's Government, be justifiable. (*Kenya Law Gazette*, 17 August 1923, quoted in White *et al.*, 1948, p. 15)

Enforcement of this directive was non-existent since it rested in the hands of a newly created town council in Nairobi that included nine elected European councillors, seven Indians (elected but nominated by the British Governor), two government nominated members and one administrative officer intended to represent or 'safeguard native interests' (White *et al.*, 1948, p. 17). It was not until 1946 that Africans had two directly elected representatives on the town council (Achola, 2001).

The health of Africans living in Nairobi remained an issue for Europeans who depended on their cheap labour. Waterborne diseases continued because the British dominated council refused to allocate the financial resources to build a drainage and water delivery system recommended by engineers in the 1910s (Leys, 1973). By 1923, disparities in crude death rates were increasingly apparent and documented by the Annual Reports of the Medical Officer of Health: 8.4/1,000 for Europeans; 16.5/1,000 for Asians, and 33.5/1,000 for Africans (*Ibid.*, p. 289). Rising mortality rates and the rapid expansion of unplanned African villages throughout Nairobi led the colonialists to build the first housing for Africans (Achola, 2001).

A planned community called Pumwani, meaning resting place, was constructed in 1922 and was the first area in Nairobi planned and built by the British specifically for Africans. Roads, latrines and ablution blocks were constructed along with housing plots in a rectangular grid (McVicar, 1968). Pumwani was intended to be the one official place where all Africans living in Nairobi would stay (White, 1990, p. 48). The location was selected to house the African labour force in close proximity to the industrial area while increasing the distance between African and European settlements (McVicar, 1968). Pumwani was physically separated from the rest of Nairobi by a river and the Old Caravan Road, a major commercial route. The Europeans hoped that the plan for the settlement and its sanitary services (along with a 10pm–5am curfew) could quell increasing African demands for political participation and reduce 'depravity', particularly prostitution and sexual relations (White, 1990). Africans were forcibly relocated from other squatter areas to Pumwani. While residents were responsible for building their own homes, they were required to follow the newly created British building and planning rules for the area that defined house size and forbade subletting. In practice, most Africans built as they wished, subletting was common due to the transient nature of work, and social bonds among residents increased (McVicar, 1968).

Public Health in the Colonial Town

By 1929 Nairobi had its own Public Health Committee and a municipal Public Health Department under the direction of the National Ministry of Health. Each section of the committee was headed by a European Officer, but with mostly Indian technical staff. The Department had oversight of the municipalities' health care institutions, communicable and non-communicable diseases, urban sanitation, and housing and hygiene investigation. The Public Health Department's remit would expand to include many urban planning functions, such as the siting and regulation of municipal markets, dispensaries and health centres, day nurseries, funerals, and ambulance services (Achola, 2001). In one dispute between the Pubic Health Department and the town council, the health agency demanded that the council allocate resources to address the ongoing insanitary conditions at the Indian Bazaar and other African living areas. Specifically, the Health Department wanted the council to replace mud and wattle housing with permanent materials. The council refused, claiming the Health Department's request was financially impractical (*Ibid.*, p. 131).

Reports of the Medical Officer for Health throughout the 1940s revealed consistently higher rates of infant mortality for Africans compared to Asians and Europeans (table 5.1). Infant mortality was and remains an important indicator of how social conditions and social inequities impact the most vulnerable, namely newborns under one year old, and chronic disparities between groups suggest on-going social injustices. While not advocating for greater social justice, the Ministry of Health, according to Achola (*Ibid.*, p. 124), 'repeatedly stressed to [their] European compatriots that the health of the town was in large measure determined by the health of the urban African population'. The European run Nairobi Town Council refused to spend money on services for Africans arguing that since they were not taxpayers, Africans had little entitlement to municipal services. The Council also legislated rules limiting Africans from owning property (Obudho, 1997).

Yet, Chaiken (1998) argues that the colonial medical and public health system established a decentralized system of primary care organized around clinics and dispensaries and trained thousands of Africans in primary prevention; a legacy that runs counter to the narrative of colonists always acting to degrade the health of Africans. For example, a report in 1933 by the Chief Medical Officer in Nairobi, R.A. Paterson, emphasized the importance of community-based prevention and service delivery:

Table 5.1. Infant Mortality (per 1,000 live births) in Nairobi, 1939–1945.

Year	Europeans	Asians	Africans	European: African Disparity*
1939	35	174	217	6.2
1940	56	174	248	4.4
1941	20	146	180	9.0
1942	33	127	165	5.0
1943	36	95	207	5.8
1944	49	62	154	3.1
1945	33	56	131	4.0

Note: * Disparity calculation = African rate/European rate.
Source: Achola, 2001, compiled from Medical Officer of Health Annual Report, 1945.

Of even greater importance than the relief of sickness is its prevention, and with the latter object in view both doctors and nurses, and midwives, as well as health visitors and sanitary inspectors, must come into the most intimate contact with the people in their own homes from day to day; and if the behests of these workers are to carry weight … so medical workers must live among the people in all quarters of the area to be served; and they must be sufficient in number, and so posted that there is intimate and easy contact between the whole of the personnel of the medical service and the folk of the countryside… Facilities for treatments must, therefore, be brought almost to their doors, while teaching must be taken actually over their doorsteps. For these purposes the primary health centers have been established. (Quoted in Chaiken 1998, p. 1705)

In the 1950s a post-war colonial policy was adopted to train and hire African women that brought their own 'healthy living knowledge' to positions as health visitors, based on a similar UK lay public health visitor model (Porter, 1999).

According to Moradi (1998), by the time Kenya gained independence, the colonial medical services had eradicated or nearly eliminated cholera, plague, typhus, onchocerciasis, and relapsing fever. In a study of height of Kenyans from different regions and tribal groups from the 1880s to the 1990s, Moradi (1998) found that all groups experienced significant nutritional and height gains. According to his study, Kenya performed on par with other developing countries, such as India, Indonesia, Mexico and Ghana, from 1900 through 1970, but progress came to a halt in the 1980s and 1990s (Ibid., p. 1118). In a separate study of mortality due to malaria in Nairobi, significant racial disparities existed during the colonial era but seemed to have declined radically by independence in the 1960s (Mudhune et al., 2011).

The 1948 Colonial Master Plan

Rapid growth (see figure 5.6) and a desire for modernization led the Mayor of Nairobi to invite a South African team of architects to generate a new master plan for the city. The plan, published in 1948 as, Nairobi Master Plan for a Colonial Capital, wanted the city to 'develop naturally out of the present land usage and particularly the present land values' (White *et al.*, 1948, p. 57). In reality, the plan imposed a Euro-centric City Beautiful and Garden City model onto the growing capital. At the heart of the plan was a civic centre modelled after other capital cities the architects revered, such as Paris and Canberra, and reflected the modernism of popular designers of the day such as Le Corbusier (see figures 3.6 and 3.7). The architects' enthusiasm for simple, geometric design, repetition and uniformity reflected their faith that a modern civic design would modernize the people of Nairobi. Using Paris as a model, the architects proposed a Kenya Centre and Parkway, both with grand parallel boulevards, and lined with buildings that would house government functions and be the tallest in the city (see figure 3.9).

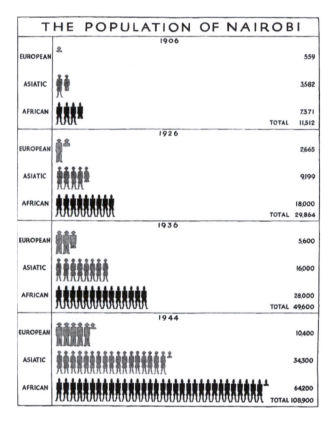

Figure 5.6. Nairobi population growth. (*Source*: White *et al.*, 1948)

The 1948 planners defined their task as purely technocratic:

The Master Plan however, is able to be completely neutral on the subject of racial segregation by being confined to the principles of planning which take their measure on the human and technical needs. It is concerned with the satisfaction of the wants which all men require such as privacy, open space, education, protection from through-traffic, water supplies, etc. The more attention that can be devoted to what is common to man the more likely are we to concentrate on what can to-day be planned in the light of reason while leaving to political and educational action and to the individual to sort out the rest. If the Plan has a bias it is this humanistic one. (*Ibid.*, p. 49)

Yet, by defining planning as pure reason separate from politics, the 1948 plan left colonial racial segregation unchanged and unchallenged. The idea that Africans had been planning their own functional communities within Nairobi for decades, surviving in the face of widespread racial discrimination and physical isolation, went unnoticed by the 1948 planners (Hake, 1977). Planning is couched as a science (however imperfect) and neutral technology. The Europeans' status and imperial authority was left unquestioned.

Informality as Urbanization in Post-Independence Nairobi

The 1948 Master Plan was never fully adopted but a post-war economic boom contributed to rapid development including squatter settlements in Nairobi. The colonial administration grew increasingly suspicious that the informal settlements were centres of opposition political movements, so they were targeted for demolition (Obudho, 1997). A State of Emergency was declared in 1952 as Africans moved to oust the imperial British occupiers. According to Hake (1977), the inadequate and unsanitary state of African urban housing was one of the reasons behind the Mau Mau revolt, a Kikuyu-lead anti-colonist armed resistance against the British between 1952 and 1960. While the British won the physical battle with the Mau Mau, they lost the war. The uprising and resistance were a major force behind Kenya achieving independence in 1962.

During the State of Emergency, the colonists used urban demolitions to exert force and arrest potential agitators. According to Hake (1977) the informal settlement in Nairobi's Mathare Valley, north of Eastleigh along the Mathare River, was a particular target for the British and at least 150 homes were destroyed during the resistance. The emergency and demolitions controlled the urban population in ways the colonists were unable to do through racial segregation; services were directed almost entirely to Europeans while Africans were resettled in new squatter settlements according to their tribe (Obudho, 1997).

Yet, the informal economy in Nairobi continued to grow after independence as the new Kenyan government struggled to manage urban growth and related health challenges. Operation Clean Up was one of the first policies passed by the post-independence Nairobi City Council and enforced the removal of 'undesirable elements' across the city. What this meant was slum clearance (Caminos and Goethert, 1978). Etherton et al. (1971) estimated that by 1970 at least one-third of Nairobi's population was living in informal settlements across the city (figure 5.7). As Hake (1977) notes, the Kenyan government continued to tear down shacks with the aim of improving what they thought was an unhealthy and unsightly blight on the newly independent Kenya, displacing over 50,000 people in just one year (1971). An article in the *Sunday Nation* newspaper in 1971 quoted a Mathare Valley resident:

We thought that after Uhuru ... we would be no longer molested. We have been hoping against hope. It is only the stranger in Nairobi that does not know us. Now and then it is either Mathare or Majengo that makes headlines in papers. We are an enemy of the City Council for ever. But

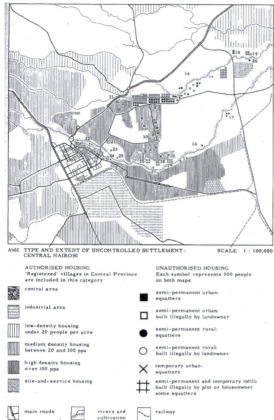

Ab02 TYPE AND EXTENT OF UNCONTROLLED SETTLEMENT: SCALE 1 : 100,000
CENTRAL NAIROBI

AUTHORISED HOUSING
'Registered' villages in Central Province
are included in this category

UNAUTHORISED HOUSING
Each symbol represents 500 people
on both maps

central area

industrial area

low-density housing
under 20 people per acre

medium density housing
between 20 and 100 ppa

high density housing
over 100 ppa

site-and-service housing

main roads   rivers and
cultivation

semi-permanent urban:
squatters

semi-permanent urban:
built illegally by landowner

semi-permanent rural:
squatters

semi-permanent rural:
built illegally by landowner

temporary urban:
squatters

semi-permanent and temporary infill:
built illegally by plot or houseowner
some squatters

railway

Figure 5.7. Informal Settlements (with
population estimates) in Nairobi 1970.
(*Source*: Etherton *et al.*, 1971, p. 5)

where to go? ... If they were replacing them with houses of their taste and allowed us to live in them ... but you know what they do. They are simply chasing us. They do not want us. We are an eye-sore. But where shall we go?[1]

In a collaborative effort to stop demolitions and more displacement of Mathare's population, Etherton and colleagues at the University of Nairobi embarked on a detailed study of the area to document life and living conditions and recommend policies for improving life for thousands of slum dwellers in Mathare and across Nairobi (Etherton *et al.*, 1971).

The Mathare Informal Settlement, 1970

The Mathare settlement grew on the banks of the Mathare and Gitathuru Rivers alongside a rock quarry. While informal settlements or villages as they are often referred to in Nairobi had been present in the Mathare Valley since at least the 1920s, the settlement had a population explosion in 1969, doubling in just over 16 months (Etherton *et al.*, 1971, p. 10). This was due in part to Africans returning to Mathare after the Emergency but many others were forced to relocate in Mathare after being

Table 5.2. Population growth in Nairobi, 1906–1989. (*Source*: Obudho and Aduwo, 1992)

Year	Africans Pop.	%	Europeans Pop.	%	Asians Pop.	%	Total Pop.
1906	6,351	60.4	579	5.5	3,582	34.1	10,512
1928	19,112	64.0	1,492	5.0	9,260	31.1	29,864
1931	26,761	55.8	5,195	10.8	15,988	33.4	47,944
1936	27,700	55.8	5,357	10.8	16,549	33.4	49,606
1948	66,336	55.8	10,830	9.1	41,810	35.1	118,976
1962	157,865	59.2	21,476	8.0	87,454	32.8	266,795
1969	421,079	82.6	19,185	3.8	69,022	13.6	509,286
1979	768,032	92.8	19,050	2.3	40,693	4.9	827,775
1989	1,260,149	95.1	15,822	1.2	48,599	3.7	1,324,570

moved from Eastleigh Section VII to allow for the expansion of Pumwani and after the Nairobi City Council set fire to and burned down the Kaburini settlement (*Ibid.*). To the surprise of many urban squatters in Nairobi, the new Kenyan government followed the colonial practices of demolition and eviction of their communities (Obudho and Aduwo, 1989). Nairobi's population and the proportion that were squatters grew rapidly during the 1960s, with the overall population increasing from about 267,000 in 1963 to over 500,000 by 1969, and Mathare's population reached over 34,000 across nine distinct villages by 1969 (Etherton *et al.*, 1971; Obudho, 1997, p. 301).

The households in Mathare organized into cooperatives to purchase the land they occupied with the hope of protecting themselves from future evictions. This was an innovative and new strategy for urban squatters. The cooperatives allowed members to purchase shares and their original intent was to secure land tenure for all squatters (Etherton *et al.*, 1971). However, all but one of the cooperatives became companies and began building rental housing units to satisfy the rapidly increasing demand.

The housing built by the companies was haphazard but dense. According to Etherton *et al.* (1971, p. 48), 'the objective of all the companies seems to have been to concentrate as many lettable rooms as possible on the site'. This was accomplished by building long structures divided into four to eight, 3 m x 3 m rooms. Very few of the companies provided adequate public services. Four of the companies did not provide any water but six provided and paid for water for residents. The average number of residents per water tap in 1970 Mathare was 870, while the average number of people per pit latrine was 136, but ranged across villages from 22 to 3,555 per latrine (*Ibid.*, p. 49). In short, the companies that built housing in Mathare, 83 per cent of which was occupied by non-company renters, provided very few services.

Health in 1970 Mathare

A health survey of Mathare residents visiting a local clinic and stool samples taken from primary school children provided an overview of the health status of residents. The stool samples found that 81 per cent of children had roundworm and 62 per cent bilharzia or schistosomiasis. These are both parasitic diseases linked to exposure to poor sanitation and, while rarely fatal, can impair children's growth and cognitive development. The Mathare clinic staff reported that the biggest health issue for children was malnutrition and that they most frequently distributed vitamins and milk to visiting patients. Over 55 per cent of children visiting the clinic suffered from a chronic cough and over 43 per cent from a stomach ailment and/or diarrhoea (*Ibid.*, p. 41).

The 1970 report on Mathare provided a set of recommendations for improving the settlement that included water supply, sanitation, road access, refuse collection and electricity service (*Ibid.*, p. 65). Etherton summed up the primacy of health concerns in recommending infrastructure improvements: 'The essential minimal improvements suggested for the Valley would go a long way to help prevent the worms and stomach upsets, for it is not the insides of people's rooms that are dirty as much as the outside where children crawl and run around' (*Ibid.*, p. 41). The report included national policy recommendations for rural development assistance to prevent internal migration to Mathare, support for the informal economic and employment sector, and ending the policy of demolition and resettlement of urban squatter communities. The recommendations went unanswered and the Kenyan government continued to use public hygiene arguments to tear down slums. A campaign called *Turudi Mashambani* ('Let's return to the rural areas') was adopted to discourage migration into cities and included an official policy of slum clearance (Obudho and Aduwo, 1992).

Mathare in the 1990s

While few of the Etherton recommendations were implemented, Kenya's National Development Plan in the mid-1970s put a halt to demolitions (Huchzermeyer, 2011). The World Bank began a 'sites and services' loan programme to Kenya that required housing and utility services to be coupled in development projects (Bassette, 2003). Under this scheme, the Nairobi City Council would retain control of the squatter land and after the Bank financed services and housing were built, new residents (former squatters) were expected to pay rent to the city to 'pay back' the loan. Some slum upgrading resulted in tenement housing being built by the National Housing Corporation in the 1980s, but the limited housing supply failed to meet the growing need (Huchzermeyer, 2011). By the 1990s, slum demolitions were common again, displacing an estimated 30,000 residents in 1991 (Weru, 2004, p. 48).

In Mathare 4A, one village in the larger settlement, the German Development Bank financed a pilot upgrading project in 1992. The project was overseen by the Catholic Church which was granted the land in Mathare 4A by the Kenyan government. The Church commonly filled a vacuum left by an absent state by providing a range of services, from health care to education, and this gave it legitimacy in the eyes of both the government and international donors. To ensure local participation, a project management organization, *Amani Housing Trust*, was created to run the day-to-day implementation and steward the new housing. The initial phase of the project replaced temporary structures with over 1,400 more permanent units with access to water and sanitary infrastructure (Kamau and Ngari, 2002). In a second phase, the absentee landlords who were letting most of the structures in Mathare 4A, were to be expropriated and compensated with between 4,000 and 12,000 Kenyan shillings (KES) per structure. In exchange, the structure owners were required to sign over their properties to the Church as well as any future claims to land in 4A (Rodriguez-Torres, 2010, p. 71).

Father Klaus Braunreute, who was in charge of the Benedictine Church just across Thika Road from Mathare 4A, was the leader of the project. Using its stature as a service provider, its relationship with the German Embassy and support from Zacharia Maina, the Kenya African National Union (KANU) member of parliament who represented Mathare 4A, the Church secured the funds to implement the project. As the group began the project in 1993, a first challenge was getting existing residents to leave their homes so the new construction could begin. Youth gangs were enrolled to remove reluctant families forcibly (Lamba, 2005). Displaced residents were temporarily resettled in another area, but had to pay rent to the Church for their new accommodation. The displaced residents protested, as did the landlords, who did not like being forced to give up their lucrative business (Kamau and Ngari, 2002).

Opposition to the project continued after the first set of new houses were built. Rents were up to 800 KES per month, more than double what residents had been paying before the upgrading. The Church allocated a number of new units to workers and others who were not living in Mathare 4A before the project began. This stoked more opposition and resentment (Huchzermeyer, 2011)

Protest and resistance to the Church-led project increased and some residents accused Father Klaus, a white priest, of using colonial tactics and political favours to his financial advantage (Rodriguez-Torres, 2010, p. 77). Litigation ensued, as residents and former landlords formed an unlikely alliance against the Church, and demanded a return of their land. After six months of hearings, the Makadara Court rejected the requests of the residents and landlords. Protests followed and project employees were attacked. By 1998 150 new houses had been built with access to a toilet, shower and electricity. A new dispensary, two day-care centres and thirty business kiosks had also been constructed. However, police were deployed to the area as different gangs fought over the project and on 27 January 1999 the Nairobi City Council and the Ministry of Public Works ordered the suspension of the project (Rodriguez-Torres, 2010; Weru, 2004).

Impact of the Mathare 4A Project on Informal Settlement Planning

The Mathare 4A project was seen by many as symptomatic of a larger political challenge in Kenya; namely under the presidency of Daniel Toroitich Arap Moi and thereafter, land was increasingly used for political favours and patronage (Wrong, 2009). In a series of corruption scandals, government officials were accused of allocating public land that was already occupied by informal settlements to their supporters (Chege, 1981). The state, in many cases the Nairobi City Council and police, was used to forcibly evict residents from their homes and trading places, despite slum dwellers fighting the evictions with the assistance of the Legal Advice Center or *Kituo cha Sheria* (Weru, 2004; Wrong, 2009). The lack of transparency and the accusations of patronage in the Mathare 4A project reflected a wider frustration among the urban poor and Kenyans more generally with land-related corruption in politics. Slum dwellers were seeking an alternative model where they would be active shapers and direct beneficiaries of planning and improvement schemes that went beyond 'boutique' projects and instead instituted lasting improvements for the millions of slum dwellers who were now living in Nairobi's informal settlements.

Twenty-First-Century Informal Settlement Planning in Nairobi

By 2010, over 65 per cent of Nairobi's estimated 3.5 million people were living in the city's informal settlements. Seeking to ensure slum dwellers were leading, not just responding to, government and international organization projects, Slum Dwellers International (SDI) helped create Muungano Wa Wanavijiji. The slum dweller federation was supported by an NGO, Pamoja Trust, founded in 2000 by human rights lawyer Jane Weru, but is now supported by the NGO Muungano Support Trust (MuST). Pamoja Trust was founded to help the urban poor oppose demolitions and quickly evolved into generating alternative solutions to the related challenges of housing, services, human rights and health (Weru, 2009). According to Weru:

Stopping evictions was critical but it was only a small part of the change that was necessary. The laws and policies were broken. We needed to also be clear about what was causing the evictions and lack of services. Namely, lack of policies, planning and investment in the urban poor, you see. We began enumerating and mapping the settlements to document the extent of the challenge. The federation was organized to build local accountable institutions that built power for social change.

The structure of Muungano helped move the work from protest to short and longer term solutions. Muungano's core function is organizing daily savings groups. Joining a group is voluntary. Members are required to deposit a small amount of money each day into their own account held by the group. Resources are pooled to provide a financial safety net for members, such as when an emergency medical expense occurs. According to Jack Makau of SDI (2011):

The savings group strategy says slum dwellers have some resources that, if pooled together, can leverage other assets and begin to finance their own projects. It rejects the notion that the poor have to wait for someone else's handout. It wasn't that we didn't want government and donor support. Being able to use some of their own money to finance projects helps the poor get a better seat at the table. So the savings groups are a community organizing strategy to build power, with the added benefit of building financial capital for slum dwellers.

The combination of the political and financial capital is one of the innovations of savings groups as defined by Muungano and SDI, compared to more popular micro-credit schemes (Satterthwaite, 2002). Micro-credit has had mixed results in building a lasting community base of accountable institutions, as well as providing financial resources for a range of community service needs beyond micro-enterprise (Roy, 2011).

The Muungano savings groups in each village, often led by women, organize daily savers and meet weekly to discuss progress and build trust. Everyone in a village is invited to participate and the organization usually builds slowly. According to Joseph Kimani, a community organizer with MuST word of mouth and small projects build interest:

When we start, people are rightly skeptical. Why should I give money to this group? Will they steal it? What are they doing? Transparency, accountability and trust are at the heart of the organization for these reasons. Community members are leaders, manage the accounts, and keep one another accountable. We discuss community priorities and what we can do in the short term. Of course, many issues come up for people struggling in the slums, so these discussions about priorities and sharing of stories builds trust and community. (Kimani, 2011)

Within each savings group, there are at least six teams which execute the core functions of Muungano's mission: surveying and mapping; welfare; savings and loans; land and housing; advocacy; and auditing (Karanja, 2010a). The survey and mapping team organizes members also, as David Mathenge of MuST described, 'making the invisible visible'. With the support of MuST, this team trains members to conduct house-to-house enumerations, collecting detailed information on each household and compiling these data for community 'ground truthing' (Karanja, 2010b). These data are crucial for documenting which people are living in the informal settlements and the living conditions they face. According to Mathenge (2011):

The enumerations go to every household and we return to validate the data. Then we post the findings in the community. This is real peer review. We not only need to know how many people live where, but to also know who would benefit as projects and planning occurs. We put this demographic information into maps of every meter of the village. We do what the census and planners in NCC have avoided or just do not have the will to do.

The other teams within each Muungano savings group are equally important to the organizing and social change mission. The welfare team discusses how the group should spend resources to support members that need assistance, such as payment for emergency hospitalization, a funeral or food assistance. The savings and loan team keeps track of savings issues and reviews requests for individual loans and repayment while the auditing team reviews finances. The auditing team works with Muungano's fiscal agent, Akiba Mashinani Trust (AMT) which supports the village-level groups and networks of savings groups with professional financial services (amtkenya.org).

The land and housing team focuses on tenant and structure owner issues and disputes, while building a negotiated agreement among the entire community for securing tenure and land rights. The idea is that each village has its own land-use and allocation histories involving a range of stakeholders, from tribal chiefs to religious institutions to political parties. Land rights and control issues are intimately wrapped into these politics and Muungano recognizes that no one model of securing land tenure and housing security will apply in every informal settlement or village within a settlement (Mathenge, 2010). All the teams coordinate to develop advocacy strategies but focus on building coordinated campaigns among the entire network. The Muungano network structure is shown in figure 5.8.

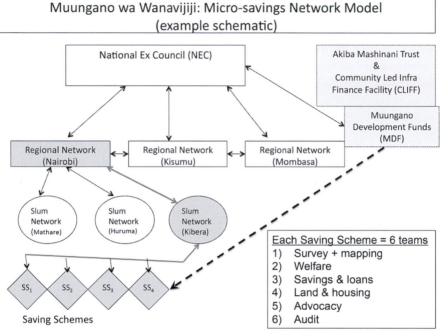

Figure 5.8. Muungano network structure. (*Source*: www.mustkenya.org).

Network Epistemologies for Slum Health: Slum Dwellers International

The Muungano advocacy work builds on the Shack/Slum Dwellers International (SDI) model of network power. According to Jack Makau, a Director at SDI working to coordinate networks across all of Africa, the approach for Muungano and its sister supportive organization MuST, reflects the core social change model of SDI:

The SDI model is fluid but built on the idea that international development, as defined by donors and other professionals, tends to fragment what must be brought together. For SDI, organizing is the base. Organizing allows for the human technology – counting, mapping, planning, house modelling – that delivers short-term improvements. Planning is about negotiating a different future. Partnerships are woven into all this, since we recognize communities can't do this alone.

Government needs to be partner since they are the ones with the resources and responsibility to bring our innovations to scale. Our networks of slum dwellers have exchanges, or content-focused visits. This is often where innovations come. It's incremental. It builds power. It leads to real change. (Makau, 2011)

The exchanges Makau mentions are a crucial component of the SDI model and something the organization calls horizontal exchanges. These exchanges include trips where small groups of slum dwellers travel to other slums, often in another country, to learn from other slum dwellers about what is possible in their own place. In this way, the local struggle in one community becomes 'translocal' and relational, as knowledge and innovations from multiple sites around the world are shared and emerge into a network of strategies and on-going knowledge creation.

For example, in Mumbai, a powerful network of SDI affiliates also learn among themselves since they have different strategies for improving the lives and conditions of slum dwellers. The National Slum Dwellers Federation, a rights-based group, *Mahila Milan* ('Women Together'), a micro-savings group focused on housing and infrastructure, and the Society for Promotion of Area Resources Centres (SPARC), a more broad-based NGO, have come together. They share a resource centre in Byculla, central Mumbai, where the constant flow of people and phone calls ensures that the groups share information about breaking crises, policy initiatives, and what is happening with other SDI networks around the world (Appadurai, 2002). With the long-standing experiences and range of local expertise, the Mumbai Alliance acts as one hub for information sharing across the global network of SDI.

Learning the City by (Re)Making It

Residents in Mathare were once again facing eviction in 2008. This time it was a United Nations Environment Programme (UNEP) and Kenyan National Environment Ministry project aimed at cleaning-up the Nairobi River. One of the first places to be 'cleaned' was along the Mathare and Gitathuru Rivers that were tributaries to the Nairobi River. The Kenyan government called for a standard 30 metre riparian buffer to be cleared on each side of all rivers, an environmental standard left over from the British. Tens of thousands of Mathare residents would be displaced with no place to go. Muungano and Pamoja Trust were already organizing residents when the river clean-up project was announced and they mobilized to stop the slum clearance.

Mathare was just emerging from some of its worst violence since the State of Emergency. Post election conflicts flared across Kenya in 2007–2008 after a disputed presidential election; Kikuyus and Luos fought and killed hundreds. In Nairobi, Mathare was ground zero for the ethnic violence. As the *New York Times* reported in 2007:

The bloodshed began with a bootlegging dispute, but it has been fueled by ethnic rivalry. The epicenter is Mathare, a cluster of slums with approximately 500,000 people, crammed between downtown Nairobi and an affluent neighborhood where many ambassadors live. Mathare is a landscape of rust – thousands of shacks squeezed together with rusted metal roofs and rusted metal sides, and the occasional rusted metal bridge between. Even the mud here, where not a blade of grass grows, is rust red. The area is notorious as a pocket of anarchy in a relatively orderly city, a place where street gangs levy taxes and teenage boys with machetes and dreadlocks shake down people at checkpoints. Most days, the police are nowhere to be found. Residents say it has been like this for years.

Mathare residents were also blamed for stealing water and the Nairobi Water and Sewerage Company (NWSC) responded by closing the water main that supplied Mathare with drinking water. Within a day children were sick and diarrheal disease spiked. Dehydration and hospitalizations followed. Mathare residents took to the streets to demand the water be turned back on. They closed a major highway, Thika Road, adjacent to the settlement causing traffic in the city to come to a standstill. According to Jane Weru, then Executive Director of Pamjoa Trust, 'more violence and a major crisis was looming. We had to intervene and called a meeting with the City and water company. We marched to City Council and demanded the meeting'.

Out of Crisis: A Healthy Planning Process

The meeting at the City Council was tense as the streets were still occupied. According to Jack Makau, then Communication Director of the Trust and now regional director of SDI:

Fires were literally still burning. The memory of the post-election and more recent violence was fresh in everyone's mind. Mathare was capable of blowning-up. We demanded that the water be turned back on immediately and for a halt the riparian evictions. They [Nairobi City Council] had almost no other option but to engage and meet our demands. I guess it helped that we also had Mathare residents waiting outside. (Makau, 2010)

The meeting was a success. Pamoja Trust and Muungano got the NWSC to turn the water back on. In exchange for a halt to the evictions, the groups agreed to work with residents to draft an upgrading plan for Mathare that would be presented to the Council for formal approval.

The groups left the Council meeting intent on building on their successful planning and upgrading project in a neighbouring informal settlement called Huruma. In Huruma, Muungano organized residents to save enough money for new housing down payments and to negotiate with structure owners on the allocation of new plots. The Council owned the land and agreed to construct sanitary infrastructure if the residents could agree on a new housing layout. Pamoja Trust organized a planning process that included enumerating households to determine the current housing need and a design process to come up with the new layout. An economic development plan, where residents would start a business making cement blocks to be used for constructing their own homes was also devised. The building materials would also be sold to raise additional capital. The Huruma, Kambi Moto project was a successful upgrade project that Muungano aimed to replicate in Mathre (Weru, 2004).

Planning for a New Mathare

The planning process began in Mathare in 2008 and focused on four of the villages that were on government land, named Kosovo,[2] 4B, Mashimoni and Mabatini. The Muungano savings group in these communities spent most of 2008 and into 2009 organizing and training residents for the enumerations. By May 2009, over 12,000 households had been surveyed and the community mapped electronically and entered into a geographic information system (GIS). A partnership between the University of Nairobi, Department of Urban and Regional Planning and Pamoja Trust, Muungano and SDI was expanded to include the University of California Berkeley, Department of City and Regional Planning. The universities were enrolled to help analyze the data and draft integrated upgrading proposals that included housing, infrastructure, community facilities, open space, and environmental requirements.

Planning meetings were held weekly among residents. The NGO-university team reported findings from the enumerations and drafted proposals that reflected community-negotiated standards. A decision was made to focus on Kosovo initially and then the other three villages. Four key objectives emerged from the community planning meetings for the improvement plan. The first was that the new project should have no or very limited displacement. This meant that everyone that currently lived in Mathare, 95 per cent of whom were renters, would be offered somewhere to live in the newly designed community. Second, infrastructure was to be designed for in-home water and sewer connections. Third, a land tenure process should be drafted and, finally, an alternative to the 30 m riparian reserve should be explored. After over a year of meetings and draft proposals, three community workshops in July and August 2009 were scheduled to move towards community approval of a final plan.

Figures 5.9. Kosovo-Mathare plan: community dreaming and visioning before and after. (*Source*: Author)

Over a hundred residents attended the first workshop meeting and almost immediately the tension between structure owners and residents surfaced. Structure owners wanted to know how many units and structures they were going to be given and tenants wanted to know who was going to get ground floor apartments and who would be living in a multi-storey structure? The land issues were proving to be a challenge and according to community organizer Joseph Kimani:

Even before the meeting ended, the structure owners wanted to meet separately with us [the planning team]. They were concerned with their investment and we knew from past experiences that this would be the case. But we had strong agreement that everyone, the structure owners and tenants, wanted improved infrastructure and some agreement that a road that was encroached on should be opened back up. (Kimani, 2011)

The planning team and Muungano members discussed the dynamics of the meeting and decided to focus the next meeting on infrastructure and not attempt to sort out the housing and land tenure issue until the community moved towards agreement on infrastructure.

At a second community workshop, organizers focused on the infrastructure improvement proposals; roads, drainage, sanitation and water service were presented and discussed. Water, sewerage, drainage and roads were integrated into a comprehensive plan. The water service proposal included a design for in-home water taps and a series of new public kiosks managed by community members. The village was tapping water 'illegally' from pipes running adjacent to the village, had intermittent and sometimes contaminated water, and regularly faced long walks, high costs and extortion from water vendors. The prospect of new water service with in-home taps – the first slum in Nairobi to propose such a model – galvanized the community planning process. Members of the Athi Water Trust Fund, a capital improvement entity associated with the Nairobi Water and Sewerage Company, proclaimed that if the community could agree to a management and payment scheme, they would initiate and finance the construction with a combination of company and local labour.

The third community meeting was the one held at St. Theresa's church in Mathare – where the youth gang was supposed to interrupt the session (see above). A series of before and after improvements were sketched (figure 5.9) and shared widely among residents. A final plan was developed out of that meeting and, as mentioned earlier, the City Council endorsed this draft plan.

The Kosovo plans and workshop turned into the Kosovo Water Project. According to Kosovo resident and Muungano Secretary, Jason Waweru, the plan opened up a dialogue that was challenging but eventually they reached consensus. The influence of gangs wanting to control water service was ever present, but the new model had community residents in control of water management. According to Waweru:

The 'delegated management model' meant that the community in Kosovo would control all the issues surrounding distribution of the water, including communal collection of fees. Everyone was scared. If we approved the delegated management model would it just allow more militias and gangs to step in. (Waweru, 2011)

The interim solution was first for Muungano and the Water Company to build a pilot kiosk in one area of Kosovo and to implement the community construction and management model. A distribution kiosk was built and each household was required to give a small deposit as a down payment for an in-home water meter. Community residents hired by the Water Company dug trenches and helped lay pipe. The pilot project was a success, as Muungano took the lead in organizing the community management plan and collecting down payments for the water meters. Those who could not afford a meter could collect water at the new community-operated public kiosk. By June 2011, six additional kiosks had been constructed and the informal water network was removed.

Water and Health in Mathare

According to Jason Waweru (2011), the new water kiosk in the community acts as a centre of planning activity:

People come asking how they can get a meter and water in their homes. The youth gang members even want to learn what is happening. The discussion almost always moves to some other need, such as food, electricity or safety or schools. We direct them to services or an upcoming meeting on the subject. This is how we negotiated with the power company for more regular electricity after they were arresting people with informal wires to the power poles. Having this place here is more than managing water. It is a place for answering questions, learning about issues and solving problems together.

As Waweru describes it, the water kiosk is a tangible sign that the community (and MuST in particular) can successfully negotiate with service providers and stop arrests – referring people to services but also learning about issues and mobilizing residents for solutions. He told how the presence of the water kiosk and its staff helped keep the peace after gangs and others were ready to react with violence after the police came into Kosovo in the middle of the night and arrested people with informal electricity connections. The regular day-to-day presence of Muungano members to answer questions and address issues is, according to Waweru, equally important: 'its not just a structure, but a place with people who live here and have the interests of the community at heart'.

An evaluation of the pilot phase of the water project in Kosovo was conducted by Mati and Macharia (2011). Using quantitative survey data and focus group discussions with residents, the evaluation found that the reliance on informal vendors had decreased by 50 per cent. The primary source of water for Kosovo residents had changed significantly from vendors and unmetered taps to metered water in homes and new water kiosks. The percentage of residents with in-home metered water service increased from 7.5 per cent before the pilot project to 35.6 per cent after; over 34 per cent relied on water vendors before the project while 17 per cent used vendors after and over 20 per cent used the new kiosk as their primary water source. Before the project, residents paid 2.5 KES per 20 litre jerry of water. After the project residents using water vendors reported paying less than 2 KES per jerry can. The in-home water service has reduced the distance to the nearest water source and the time spent gathering water for 92 per cent of residents. While only 36 per cent of respondents reported that their health has improved after the water project, 70 per cent reported that their life had improved since the pilot project was completed (Mati and Macharia, 2011, p. 58).

The Mathare Valley Zonal Plan

While the Kosovo water project was moving forward, other villages wanted to benefit from the Muungano-led planning process and infrastructure upgrading. Muungano and MuST, with support from SDI and the university teams, recognized that a village-by-village approach would be too slow and miss the economies of scale, particularly for infrastructure, that would come from investments for the entire community. According to Irene Karanja, the leader of MuST:

We collectively decided that a plan for the entire of Mathare – the zonal plan – was the only way forward to achieve the 'scale' results we focus on. SDI helped share the work in Mumbai by SPARC in Dharavi. We visited there and learned from slum dwellers that this could be done in a complex and contested environment such as Mathare. We established a new Mathare Valley planning process. (Karanja, 2011)

Village-scale planning teams were organized by MuST, and a Mathare Zonal Planning Team was established with at least two representatives from the village teams. A coalition of community-based organizations was organized and a Mathare Planning

Figure 5.10. Community workshops for Mathare Zonal Plan, 2011. (*Source*: Author)

Network was proposed. Additional data were gathered on each village and comparisons were made between Mathare, Mukuru and Kibera, the three largest informal settlements in Nairobi (table 5.3). Maps and results were shared with residents as the planning process moved forward. There were some surprise findings in these data that helped frame the planning process. For example, water costs per month and monthly rents were higher in Mathare than the other informal settlements. Infant mortality was

Table 5.3. Living Conditions in Nairobi's Largest Informal Settlements, 2011.

		Informal Settlements	
Indicators	Mathare	Mukuru	Kibera
Estimated Population	188,183	287,186	377,774
Water accessibility	315 people per water point	208 people per water point	132 people per water point
Water cost per month	437 KES	247 KES	225 KES
Average rent per month	1,245 KES	790 KES	1,150 KES
Average cost for health care per month	792 KES	830 KES	750 KES
Average school fees per month	1,602 KES	1,010 KES	1,333 KES
Cost of latrine access per month	184 KES	226 KES	210 KES
Electricity accessibility	77% supplied by electricity (both formal and informal)	54% supplied by electricity (both formal and informal)	58% supplied by electricity (both formal and informal)
Average electricity cost per month	403 KES	375 KES	348 KES
Infant mortality per 1,000 live births	92.5	46.6	73.1

Source: MuST 2011.

also greatest in Mathare. In some cases, hundreds of people were sharing one toilet, often a pit latrine, while the Sphere International Humanitarian standard is no more than twenty people per toilet (figure 5.11). These new data helped further mobilize the broader community around the urgency of and the need for healthy planning.

Planning as On-Going Monitoring

The first Draft Mathare Valley Zonal Plan included two strategies for ongoing monitoring, recognizing that the complexity of the place could not be addressed in one plan at one point in time. First, a new coalition building process was proposed that identified many of the key stakeholders that needed to either participate in the process or approve some aspect of it. A long-range work plan was developed for this coalition building process, which focused on short, medium and long-term implementation projects.

0   100   200   400   600   800

Meters

• Sanitation Blocks

— Sewer Pipes

Figure 5.11. Distribution of functioning toilets in Mathare, 2012. (*Source*: Author and Muungano Support Trust, University of Nairobi and SDI)

Table 5.4. Mathare Zonal Plan, equity indicators.

Equity Category	Indicators	Measures for Mathare
Living Conditions	Housing	• Percentage of residents in savings program for housing • Ratio of structure owners to tenants • Self-reports of food insecurity
	Water, sanitation and food	• Percentage of households with in-home water and toilet service • Number of new electricity connections installed by utility company • Number of infrastructure projects launched to secure housing on steep slopes and in flood areas
	Environment	• Number of non-charcoal burning cook-stoves sold at subsidized cost
	Safety	• Self reports of safety and violence from women
	Transportation	• Public spending on transport
Economics and Services	Primary health care	• Percentage of free clinics offering maternal and childhood care using in-home community health workers
	Mental/substance care	• Percentage of international health research budgets spent on mental health services/interventions
	Education	• Percentage of families receiving free day care
	Employment	• Percentage of local residents hired to work on government and internationally funded contracts in past year
	Wealth access	• Ratio of slum dweller new bank accounts to all new accounts by local banks in past year
Political Power and Outcomes	Community participation	• Percentage of residents participating in community-based organization
	Government responsiveness	• Number of meetings held in community by Nairobi City Council, Water and Power Company, addressing on-going infrastructure, housing and health issues
	Recognition of minority rights (women)	• Number of women given land rights/housing tenure by City Council
	Health status	• Self-rated health
	Art/Cultural expression	• Percentage of youth and adults participating in cultural programs

Second, a set of monitoring indicators was drafted in the plan to track progress on a number of issues identified by slum dwellers as priority issues. The indicators were grouped into three equity categories: living conditions, economics and services, and political power/outcomes. Under each category specific indicators and measures were included. The aim was to have a plan for tracking change and a way for residents to track the suite of measures that together contribute to greater equity in Mathare (table 5.4).

Conclusions

The Mathare Zonal Plan is still in its early adoption phase, but the process, analyses and recommendations offered healthy city planners insights for what is possible in one of the most inequitable urban environments on the planet. First, in the absence of the state, a mobilized civil society of residents is crucial. Slum dwellers are essentially the planners in Nairobi. Second, networks of organizations share resources and power. The Muungano savings network and the SDI network both supported institutional building and learning that enabled planning to move forward. Third, counting and mapping are important for making an inequitable situation more visible. The data gathering and mapping by MuST and the planning team helped focus attention on the overlapping issues in Mathare and deliver the first household-level water service.

Despite these accomplishments, there is much missing from this case for healthy planning. First, the lack of policy development at the municipal and national scale suggests that more needs to be done to ensure that local plans can go 'to scale' and impact the hundreds of thousands of residents of informal settlements. Second, the planning processes could have more directly engaged clinical service providers and primary health care needs of slum dwellers. Acute care needs can prevent residents from taking advantage of planning processes and built environment improvements. Finally, the Mathare planning process has not figured out a strategy to manage the land rights and tenure issues, nor has it yet addressed the housing tenure situation. While the planning is on a large scale, land control issues in Nairobi more generally are not addressed, and the colonial legacies of segregation and the urban poor's limited access to land, and the wealth and rights this provide, remain an ongoing challenge.

Notes

1. The slum dwellers talking, dam Manyatta reports from Mathare Valley. *Sunday Nation*, 18 April 1971.
2. One community was given the name 'Kosovo' by locals in the 1990s due to its legacy of ethnic violence, similar to the violence in the southeastern European region.

Chapter 6

Planning for Environmental Health Justice in Richmond, California

Seeking Health and Justice in Richmond

'We work with the 1 per cent', asserted DeVone Boggan (2010), describing his work as Director of the Office of Neighborhood Safety (ONS) in Richmond California. The ONS is a community violence prevention and health promotion initiative that aims to address violent crime in the city. In 2009, Richmond had the second highest murder rate of all cities in the United States.

Boggan continued:

The 1% of trigger pullers in this community. Young people who are known to or highly likely to commit a homicide. This doesn't make us popular, but every educational, welfare, public health and other service program we have can't, or doesn't know how to, engage these folks. We go right to them with our street outreach workers. Give them incentives and opportunities that no one else has. We give them an opportunity to be something besides a statistic.

The ONS is an innovative programme run out of the Richmond city government that uses a range of interventions to promote peace and community wellbeing. Located across the Bay from San Francisco, Richmond is a poor, industrial city with one of the largest populations of African-Americans, Latinos and Asians in the Bay Area. Richmond residents face what local activists call the triple threat: poverty, pollution and pistols. In addition to violence, over 22 per cent of the city was unemployed in 2010 and Chevron operates its largest oil refinery in the US across the street from neighbourhood playgrounds.

Yet, the ONS and others in local government, along with environmental and social justice activists, are part of a community-wide coalition that is working to promote greater health equity in the city. Richmond is the first city in California to draft a Health Element, or a policy blueprint, as part of its General Plan Update. Environmental justice activists challenged a planned Chevron expansion and won, using the victory to shift the balance of power in city government. The City, county and school district are leading the Richmond Health Equity Partnership that is developing a 'health in all policies' strategy for the city. And, homicides are down. In less than two years of the

ONS programme (2009–2011) the number of gun-related homicides in Richmond went from forty-five to twenty-six.

This chapter argues that the inter-personal street outreach work of the ONS combined with a vision for healthy policy that emerged during a land-use planning process and is currently being implemented through the Richmond Health Equity Partnership constitute many of the elements of healthy city planning (HCP). As a small city across the Bay from San Francisco, Richmond has historically been the location of the region's most noxious industry and working-class populations. Today, it is emerging from years of deindustrialization, dependency on multinational petrochemical industries and ethnic violence. Reductions in violence and collaboration among previously antagonistic community-based organizations and local government agencies have begun to change the image and opportunities in Richmond. In 2012, the University of California, Berkeley and the Lawrence Berkeley National Laboratories selected Richmond for their second campus, positioning the city to house one of the largest development projects in the State of California.

This chapter explores these and other strategies in Richmond to understand how together they contribute to healthy city planning. Contemporary efforts to promote greater equity in Richmond emerged from decades of struggle and activism by African-Americans, and a brief history of Richmond begins the chapter. From early struggles to gain union membership to forming one of the first environmental justice organizations in the US, racial justice activism has defined equity planning throughout Richmond's history.

Today, sophisticated social movements are helping to shift the roles of government in urban health promotion. Yet, in analyzing the pursuit of health equity in Richmond, I suggest that civil society groups that develop an 'inside-outside' strategy are most effective. This means that community-based organizations need to be strategic as they determine when to work with government, on the inside, and when to remain outside agitators and activists.

Richmond's Industrial History, Land Use and Equity

The City of Richmond's waterfront directly across the Bay from San Francisco made it an ideal location for maritime industry in the nineteenth century. By the 1890s, city leaders were intent on making Richmond the industrial giant of the Pacific Coast, the 'Pittsburgh of the West', and began by giving away land for commercial development. The land was granted to Richmond leaders by the US government, which had in turn taken it from Mexicans who had been granted the land decades earlier. Former agricultural areas in Richmond were subdivided into commercial plots (Whitnah, 1944).

The Santa Fe Railroad made Richmond the terminus of its trans-continental railroad in 1900 and the next year, 1901, Standard Oil built its largest refinery in the US at the time on Richmond's peninsula (Moore, 2000). Over the next decade, a host of industries that would define America's early industrial period located in Richmond, including the Pullman Coach Company, American Radiator, Ford Motor Company, Standard Sanitary Company and Stauffer Chemical Company. Industry lured workers and the population grew from about 3,000 in 1900 to nearly 30,000 by the 1930s.

The African-American population grew to be the largest ethnic group in the City by the 1930s. African-Americans from Louisiana and other Southern States who worked as Pullman porters commonly moved their families to Richmond to avoid the racism of the American South (*Ibid.*). A growing African-American workforce was willing to accept lower wages than most other workers, in part because jobs were scarce in the Jim Crow segregated South (see chapter 3, note 4). The railroad unions rejected African-American members but the Pullman Porter and Santa Fe Railroad companies specifically hired black workers to offset and undercut labour organizing among whites (Moore 2000).

During World War II, the Kaiser Richmond Shipyards became one of the largest military shipbuilding operations in the United States (Hill, 1977). Workers flocked to shipyard jobs and temporary housing was built for the new workers. Richmond's population increased to over 90,000 by 1943. The increase in the African-American population was most dramatic and by 1947, an estimated 14,000 African-Americans lived in Richmond (Moore, 2000, p. 8). Much of the new population was housed in temporary structures. Dormitories, demountable houses, and apartment buildings were quickly built and more than 60,000 people were living in public housing by 1950.

The shipyard work for African-Americans was limited to manual labour. Yet, the shortage of workers during the war led the Kaiser Shipbuilding Corporation to launch an aggressive recruitment campaign (Hill, 1977). In 1942, the company dispatched teams to Southern states to recruit African-American workers. The mechanical cotton picker was displacing thousands of share croppers and white-on-black violence in the South enticed many to seek new opportunities in Richmond 'golden state' California (Moore, 2000, p. 50).

As Moore (*Ibid.*, p. 3) notes:

Figure 6.1. African-American boilermakers shipyard strike. (*Source:* University of California Berkeley, Bancroft Library; http://content.cdlib. org/ark:/13030/hb5z09p0p8/)

Black newcomers to Richmond wanted the opportunity to 'mix and mingle and get along' in California. The history of black Richmondites suggests that unlike the larger eastern and midwestern urban black communities that were defined almost from the outset by rigid boundaries, small black communities in California, and perhaps in other western states, were formed and functioned within broader spatial and cultural parameters.

However, racial tensions existed in Richmond. Whites refused to allow African-Americans to join their labour unions. It would take a landmark ruling by the California Supreme Court in 1945 – *James v. Marinship* – before unions across America gave African-American shipbuilders equal rights to union membership (Hill, 1977). The ruling invigorated a black labour and civil rights movement in Richmond and across the United States (Taylor, 1998).

Figure 6.2. Dorothea Lange, Richmond – *Maritime Commission Housing for Shipyard Workers, c.* 1944. (*Source*: © the Dorothea Lange Collection, the Oakland Museum of California, City of Oakland. Gift of Paul S. Taylor)

Figure 6.3. Richmond activist protests racial discrimination at Lucky's Supermarket in Richmond, 1950. (*Source*: Courtesy of Richmond Historical Museum)

North Richmond: Unincorporated and Excluded

As the City of Richmond grew during the war years, so too did its land area. The city expanded it boundaries and included new industries and residents to expand its tax base and service area. Yet, the one area that remained outside the boundaries of the growing city was North Richmond. North Richmond remained an unincorporated jurisdiction of Contra Costa County, meaning that the elected representatives, city utilities and other services provided by the municipality did not reach it (Bastin, 2003).

Moore (2000) described the living conditions and racial segregation in 1940s North Richmond:

By 1940, therefore, most of Richmond's African-American population was concentrated in and around North Richmond, one third of which lay inside city limits, with the rest located in the unincorporated area. It was in close proximity to a garbage dump, it had few street lights, and its unpaved streets became muddy quagmires in the rain. North Richmond lacked adequate fire and police protection, depending on a single sheriff's car to patrol the entire county section…

According to Henry Clark (2011), a life-long resident of North Richmond and leading activist in the area (see below), this was not by accident but rather predicated on racism:

By the war years North Richmond was already almost entirely African-American. We had barber shops and black-owned businesses. We were like an extension of a black southern town. It was also the only area in Richmond were blacks were allowed to buy property because of racial covenants. So, when we could, our community moved out of the poorly constructed 'temporary' public housing and bought our own homes here in North Richmond.

African-Americans were shut out from surrounding areas and were *de facto* forced to live in North Richmond with its poor services and lack of political representation.

At the end of World War II, the shipyards closed and unemployment defined Richmond. By 1949, 36 per cent of the labour force in North Richmond was unemployed (Moore, 2000, p. 97). The city's employment strategy was to raze the older housing and create more industrial land. In 1950 Richmond city officials and Contra Costa County administrators proposed tearing down all wartime housing projects in the southern sector of Richmond to make way for private commercial and residential developments (Broussard, 1993). This would have displaced 80 per cent of the African-American population in Richmond, since most were still living in the war-era 'temporary' public housing. A 1950 redevelopment plan also called for most of the dwellings in pre-dominantly African-American North Richmond to be razed due to their unhygienic and dilapidated condition (*Ibid.*).

Planners did respond to the housing crisis in 1950 with the government-built Parkchester Village, which was planned as an economically and racially mixed community. The African-Americans who could afford to move into the newly planned development did, and communities such as North Richmond lost their middle-class base and fell deeper into poverty (*Ibid.*). Parkchester quickly became a middle-class, educated and politically astute African-American community which, according to Broussard (1993), only increased the resentment of neighbouring white elites and other ethnic groups, such as Latinos, who did not benefit from new public housing investments.

In 1956, residents organized in North Richmond to fight some of the planned evictions. The North Richmond Neighborhood Council was formed, the first such council in the San Francisco Bay Area to be led by African-Americans (Moore, 2000). However, the residents lost and hundreds of African-American families were displaced from North Richmond and vacant lots replaced homes that were labelled as blighted.

Ten years later, in 1966, a riot that began at Richmond High School between Mexican-Americans, African-Americans and white students spilled over into the community. Activists and social workers from a community group called Neighborhood House helped restore peace. However, the event left a lasting scar on the city and hundreds of white families began fleeing Richmond for newly constructed suburbs (Broussard, 1993). A decade later Richmond's first shopping mall opened, in the Hilltop area along the major Interstate 80 roadway. Both the white flight and mall construction contributed to a rapid decline in commercial activity in Richmond's downtown area.

Early Environmental Health and Justice Activism

In 1979, the Citizens Action League (CAL) of the Association of Community Organizations for Reform Now (ACORN) formed a toxics subcommittee to address

Figure 6.4. Meeting of the Citizen Action League Toxics Subcommittee in Richmond in the 1980s. Chairman and co-founder Ernest Witt, Sr is seated centre of the table. (*Source*: Courtesy of Larson, 2005)

citizen concerns about toxins in the community and their health. One concern was the night-time dumping of waste that was a regular practice in Richmond's poor areas and the air pollution from the neighbouring petrochemical refinery. A new national environmental health activist group, the National Toxics Campaign, made Richmond and a local toxic waste site the focus of one of its first campaigns. According to Henry Clark (2011), Executive Director of the environmental justice organization, West County Toxics Coalition (WCTC):

West County Toxics Coalition was created as an affiliate of the National Toxics Campaign. I became director in 1986. We were at the forefront of the national environmental justice movement as we confronted the pollution from Chevron and other chemical refineries in those days. We were the only group, one of the few in the whole country, led by and focused on toxic pollution and health of people of color in cities.

WCTC organized the African-American community and others in Richmond concerned about the health effects of pollution. The Chevron refinery was a target of much of the early WCTC campaigns and they were soon joined by another environmental group, Citizens (now Communities) for a Better Environment (CBE). Together WCTC and CBE challenged Chevron to disclose the pollutants associated with its practice of flaring, where flammable gases from the oil refining process are released and burned-off. Activists accused Chevron of using the flaring process to release many tons of toxic air pollutants illegally into the neighbouring community.

By 1993, the General Chemical Company, which operated on the same property of the Chevron refinery, submitted an Environmental Impact Report (EIR) for expanding their operation. The Richmond City Council certified the report finding no significant adverse impacts from the company's proposed expansion. As environmental justice activists were challenging the EIR certification, on 23 July a massive chemical leak and explosion occurred. A toxic cloud of sulphuric acid escaped from the plant into the neighbouring community of colour (CCHealth, 2000). Over 24,000 people from Richmond went to the emergency department complaining of coughing, shortness of breath, runny eyes, nausea and other symptoms (Kay, 1996). Thousands of residents were ordered to stay indoors until the toxic cloud dissipated (figure 6.5).

Community residents, labour unions and others joined WCTC and CBE to put pressure on Chevron and General Chemical to respond to the health concerns of residents. Months of negotiations ensued between lawyers representing the activists, General Chemical and the City of Richmond. Activists were concerned that General Chemical would be allowed just to pay a fine and continue with their operation. The community groups targeted the State permitting authority, the California Air Resources Board (ARB). By May 1994, General Chemical and Chevron agreed to sign a Memorandum of Understanding (MOU) with the activists and city, legally binding the company to develop new air monitoring and reporting, an emergency warning system, and to pay for the construction of a new health clinic in North Richmond – the North Richmond Health Center (Kay, 1996). The clinic was built, but toxic emissions from the Chevron facility increased from 200 tons per year in 1994 to over 6,000 tons in 2002 and chemical spills and accidents continued at the same pace as before the agreement (CBE, 2005).

According to Greg Karras (2010), a senior scientist with CBE, the negotiated agreement at the time was ground-breaking but did not deliver on what the community needed:

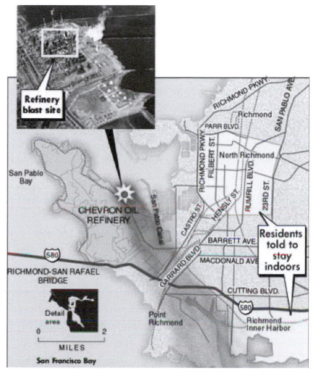

Figure 6.5. Toxic cloud from Richmond Refinery explosion, 1999. (*Source*: Kay, 1996).

Figure 6.6. Playground in North Richmond with Chevron refinery in the background. (*Source*: Photo © Robert Durell, used with permission)

Very few communities, let alone people of color, had negotiated with a multi-national corporation and won concessions at that time. We had the city against us too. That was an important precedent, as was the requirement for them to disclose what chemicals they were using, when they were transporting them and their safety plan. New monitoring stations were proposed and other things that in the end let them off-the-hook. The refinery expanded and pollution in the community got worse. We won the battle but lost the war.

By 2003, the Bay Area Air Quality Management District (BAAQMD) issued a report stating that refinery flares occurred almost daily and contributed 22 tons a day in additional unregulated pollution. The report noted that the Chevron refinery was not consistently measuring its flare emissions (*San Francisco Chronicle*, 2003). Within months of the report, the BAAQMD issued regulations limiting flaring emissions from refineries and requiring periodic reporting.[1] The *San Francisco Chronicle* (*Ibid.*) reported that 'the health risk must be lessened' and the 'refineries must intensify pollution prevention efforts and reduce the poisons that rain down on the homes of their neighbors'. In another study following the 2003 air quality report, Pastor *et al.* (2007) found that communities of colour in the Bay Area, including Richmond, were disproportionately exposed to US Environmental Protection Agency regulated Toxic Release Inventory (TRI) Sites and toxic air pollution, compared to their white neighbours. According to Roger Kim (2010), Director of the Asian-Pacific Environmental Network (APEN) that organizes the large Laotian community in Richmond:

What was confirmed was that people of color in Richmond were and continue to be disproportionately exposed to environmental toxins and corporations and government are negligent. The cumulative effects on our bodies from decades of exposures, from air pollution to illegal waste dumped on our yards to violence in the streets, can't be regulated away by one agency. We needed major change. Many people of color didn't trust the government or Chevron to protect their health.

General Planning for Health Equity

In the context of these environmental health and justice struggles, the City of Richmond launched a planning process to update their General Plan. Under California law, cities and counties must update their general plans periodically and include a series of chapters or elements. A general plan is supposed to be the policy constitution and development blueprint for local government, but can just as easily sit on a shelf and be ignored. The required elements include housing, land use/urban design, circulation/mobility, public facilities/infrastructure, open space, public safety and noise. Many jurisdictions in California choose to add additional elements, and typically address economic development, arts and culture, and education. Richmond's last General Plan was adopted in 1994 and much had changed since that time.

In 1970, Richmond's population stood at roughly 79,000 but by 1980 had declined to 74,600 (City of Richmond, 1994). By 1990 the population had grown to 87,400 and by 1992 the population reached 92,500 (*Ibid.*). Much of the population growth had occurred on the edges of Richmond, particularly the Hilltop, Marina and Point Richmond districts where large investments in high-cost housing had occurred. During the late 1990s and early 2000s Richmond's economy stagnated while the surrounding San Francisco Bay Area's economy grew. Poverty in Richmond remained above 20 per cent and economic hardship was disproportionately burdening the African-American, Latino and Asian-American populations.

By the early 2000s, health disparities between Richmond's African-American and white populations were stark. According to Contra Costa County Health Services, the local public health department, 22 per cent African-American children were hospitalized for asthma compared with less than 9 per cent of white children (CHAPE, 2007). A study by Milet *et al.* (2007) found that asthma rates varied according to how long a family lived in Richmond; for those in Richmond for more than 10 years, family self-reported asthma rates were four times greater than for those that had lived in Richmond less than 2 years. *Contra Costa Times* reporters Suzanne Bohan and Sandy Kleffman found that the ZIP code in central Richmond (94603) had a life expectancy of 71.2 years (the California state average is 78.4 years) while a few miles away in another ZIP code over the Richmond Hills life expectancy was close to 87 years (Bohan and Kleffman, 2010). Contra Costa Health Services also reported that between 2005 and 2007, African-Americans in the county had a life expectancy of 73 years while Asians and Latinos lived to 86 years. Richmond's African-Americans were dying between 13 and 16 years earlier than their neighbours.

Richmond Equitable Development Initiative (REDI)

In part as a response to the environmental, health and economic inequities in Richmond, a coalition of community-based organizations came together to form the Richmond Equitable Development Initiative (REDI) in 2003. Organized by a regional equity-focused non-profit group called Urban Habitat, REDI's membership included the environmental justice organizations that worked to hold Chevron accountable as well as housing advocates, health clinic and service providers and faith-based violence reduction groups.[2] According to former Executive Director of Urban Habitat, Juliet Ellis (2010), REDI used research, policy advocacy, leadership training and community organizing strategies to ensure that the growth and development decisions in Richmond benefited the city's low-income populations and communities of colour. The coalition focused its early efforts on affordable housing and employment opportunities. However, according to Ellis (*Ibid.*), environmental health issues were always part of the challenge. She recalled:

Our members were struggling with housing costs and employment, but health, access to care and pollution issues were always related to jobs. Chronic illness of a resident or family member kept kids out of school and family members away from work. Health care needs and high costs put our families in greater financial hardship. REDI developed a strategy that integrated health promotion into our affordable housing and economic development campaigns.

REDI organized a series of workshops for community residents on affordable housing and green economic development issues. As the General Plan Update proceeded, they held training for residents on the issues the General Plan would cover and how they could participate and advocate for their needs. Emerging from the REDI workshops with community members was a platform for equitable development that included, among other issues:

◆   the clean-up and redevelopment of vacant properties,
◆   energy efficiency, solar energy and sustainable building materials used to rehabilitate housing;
◆   local workforce development and hiring of local people to perform building improvements;
◆   establishing a community land trust;
◆   short and long term tenant protections to prevent evictions (REDI, 2007).

REDI Equitable Development Framework and Principles

The following framework and principles have been developed by the Richmond Equitable Development Initiative (REDI), a diverse coalition of organizations committed to growth that benefits rather than burdens existing residents and that involves low-income residents in the decisions that impact their lives and neighborhoods. Piecing together the intersections among critical elements of the city, including **land use, housing, economic development, transportation** and **health**, will build a path to a vibrant, holistic, and just community. As a foundation, the following framework and principles are REDI's vision of an equitable Richmond.

Richmond Equitable Development Initiative

Figure 6.7. REDI framework and Principles. (*Source*: REDI, 2007)

Incorporating Health Equity in the General Plan

As the community engagement process for the General Plan proceeded REDI members and other community groups participated in planning visioning sessions. A consulting planning firm, Moore, Iacofano, and Goltsman (MIG), was contracted by the City of Richmond to organize the General Plan Update process, drafted early documents and facilitated public meetings. At a series of community planning meetings over the course of the first few months of the process, MIG senior planner Vikrant Sood (2007) recalled:

The key issues for community residents were jobs, environmental justice and health. Yet, we didn't have any specific plan for addressing pollution, a strategy for getting residents back to work or how land use planning could improve public health. Community pressure and critique of our approach forced us to reach out to others in the region that had expertise in these areas. Specifically for health, we engaged with the San Francisco Department of Public Health, and their Environmental Health Director Dr. Rajiv Bhatia, to learn about how to integrate public health into our land use planning. That is essentially how the idea of a specific Health Element emerged.

A partnership between MIG and Dr. Rajiv Bhatia was established and together they approached the California Endowment (TCE), a state-wide health foundation, about possibly supporting an innovation that had never been attempted in the State of California before, namely drafting a Health Element as part of the General Plan Update. TCE was already funding many of the community-based organizations in Richmond, including REDI, and some similar land-use and health work using Health Impact Assessment in San Francisco. According to Dr. Bhatia (2010):

The Endowment was interested in supporting new ways to promote health equity beyond more health care, which we know is insufficient. They were already supporting a health impact assessment process analyzing a proposed rezoning plan in San Francisco, so the prospect of health in a General Plan wasn't too far off from that.

The consulting firm, MIG received financial support from TCE to organize a drafting process as a separate element of the General Plan. A Technical Advisory Group of professionals and civil society groups was established to advise the process and draft the document.[3] The REDI coalition was also funded by TCE to participate in the Health Element process and to organize Richmond residents to engage in and shape the content of the plan.

The first task of the Technical Advisory Group (TAG) was to describe the connections between land-use planning, city management and public health. The TAG also set to work on identifying the existing conditions in Richmond that were likely to be influencing population health. Existing data were gathered, mapped and incorporated into a baseline conditions report. The TAG discussed these findings and generated a set of goals for the Health Element, described in the opening section of a baseline conditions report (MIG, 2007, p. 5):

The Health Element will address health disparities and promote healthy living, and use the General Plan as a vehicle for promoting sound public health and land use policy. The Element will outline a framework and methodology for evaluating and understanding existing community health and wellness conditions, develop goals, policies and implementing actions to address key community issues and opportunities, and create a tool for tracking progress over time. The Element will involve key stakeholders and the Richmond community in the process, and focus on key community needs and opportunities.

Recognizing and addressing health disparities was the first goal of the Element. This was, according to Sheryl Lane of Urban Habitat and a leader of REDI, an important orientation of the work. Lane (2007) noted:

What was different about the Health Element from the beginning was that is was organized around equity, not just the built environment or health care as most planners were advocating. The community coalition and public health experts made this clear during meetings of the TAG. Equity was a core goal.

Other explicit goals for the Health Element were to develop policies, not just land-use or spatial plans and urban designs, to address community health issues. Finally, a third aspect of the Health Element was to incorporate, from the outset, tracking and monitoring of progress over time. All these aspects required, according to the TAG report, community participation and accountability in all aspects of decision-making.

The TAG solicited input from a range of experts to begin drafting the Health Element. An initial analytic step accompanying the Existing Conditions Report in 2007 was to explain and hypothesize about the relationships between place and health inequities in Richmond. According to Lane (2007):

It wasn't enough to repeat what hundreds of public health and community people already knew; that we were more sick and dying early in Richmond. We wanted more specific information and as an equity coalition it was critical we also identified the causes and reasons behind these health inequities.

Maps and data were shared with the group making the connections between place and health inequities in the region, specifically neighbouring Alameda County (ACPHD, 2008) and later Contra Costa County (Bohan and Kleffman, 2010) (figure 6.8). The maps revealed the geography of health inequities in the Bay Area and showed that places with high poverty and low property values mapped almost perfectly with high rates of chronic disease and low life expectancy. They also helped the group and decision-makers connect the day-to-day decisions in local government with public health in new ways. According to Bill Lindsey, City Manager of Richmond, the

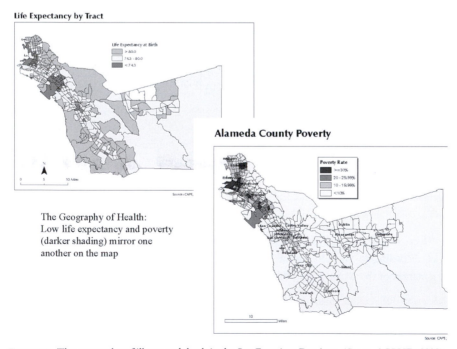

Figure 6.8.   The geography of illness and death in the San Francisco Bay Area. (*Source*: ACPHD, 2008)

presentations helped a 'light bulb' go off for him that every city agency and decision was partially responsible for health and equity. According to Lindsey (2011):

I remember watching the maps and slides and hearing the discussions of health equity and it just clicked for me, an economist, that I was in the business of health promotion. Everything we did, or didn't do, in the City could have an influence on health for certain populations. Of course, there were other things we couldn't control, but it became clear that if we aligned and leveraged all that we did do in local government towards health, we could make a significant difference in people's lives, make this city more livable and save residents and government lots of money. That was a defining 'Ah ha' moment for me.

The presentations also included a series of maps correlating mortality rates in a specific census tract with certain features of the place, such as the type of housing stock it had, what the neighbourhood looked like, and employment, economic, home ownership and ethnic status (figure 6.9). What became clear was that the places with the highest life expectancy had the best socio-demographic outcomes and *vice versa*. For Sheryl Lane (2007):

The maps were about the overlapping and cumulative burdens we face in communities of color in this region. You can't separate race from place from health. The Health Element couldn't just focus on one disease or economic issue. It was clear to us that we needed an integrated strategy for equity that took racism and its place-based health impacts seriously.

The TAG used these data and maps to inform their recommendations in the first draft of the Health Element, which was issued in 2008.

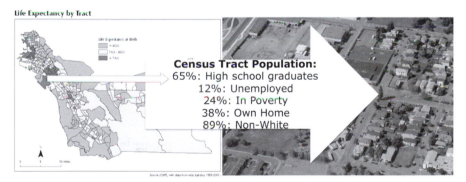

Figure 6.9. Health and place in the San Francisco Bay Area. (*Source*: ACPHD, 2008)

The Health and Wellness Element

The 2008 Health and Wellness Element (HWE) draft aimed to be comprehensive and integrative, using ten aspects of healthy planning articulated by the TAG as an organizing framework. The major topics ranged from access to healthy food and medical services to economic opportunities and environmental quality (figure 6.10). Under each broad healthy planning topic, specific goals influenced desired outcomes and the policies and implementing actions that were necessary to achieve the desired goals.

By early 2009, a second draft of the Element was released. In this draft, the goals had been changed and restated as:

The Community Health and Wellness Element sets a critical path for improving conditions that will foster the physical health and emotional well-being of Richmond residents. The Element defines healthy living determinants, reviews current conditions in Richmond relative to healthy determinants and prescribes specific policies and implementing actions tailored to critical health needs in the community.

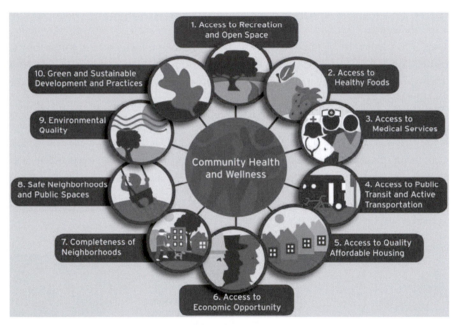

Figure 6.10.   Richmond Health & Wellness Element, Community planning objectives. (Source: City of Richmond, www.ci.richmond.ca.us/index.aspx?NID=2412)

Members of the REDI coalition viewed this as an attempt by the city to shift the focus away from equity to more general wellness. According to Michael Katz (2011) of the REDI coalition, the group went through and compared both the 2008 and 2009 versions of the Health Element to discover the two versions were radically different. REDI requested a meeting with the Planning Director in Richmond to understand what had happened. Of particular concern to REDI was that the content of the document had been altered to minimize the issue of equity. References in the document to 'dramatic inequalities' and 'residents are at high risk' were removed. Other changes included removing recommendations calling for evening safe-ride public transit, the development of green and clean industries, a commitment to partnerships with local renewable energy businesses, and support for continuation of the Office of Neighborhood Safety.

For CBE and REDI, another significant change was the removal of air quality monitoring and language such as "cumulative environmental burdens." According to Nile Malloy of CBE, this raised suspicions that the Richmond Council of Industries and particularly Chevron were starting to take notice of the Health Element. Malloy recalled:

> We had seen this before, where industry pushes back against community planning and our right to know. We had agreed that the Health Element would establish a citywide monitoring and reporting program to assess the cumulative impacts of air pollution and toxins on human and environmental health, and monitor exposure of sensitive uses such as homes, parks, schools and childcare facilities to pollutants. All this was edited-out of the new version of the Health and Wellness Element. (Malloy, 2010)

Another significant deletion from the first draft of the Health Element was phrasing committing the City to be a leader in using health-based criteria to review and approve development projects and to work to maximize the health benefits and minimize or eliminate health impacts of development. For REDI, many of the changes significantly weakened the document and left them uncertain about the efficacy of a Health Element for promoting equity in Richmond.

Yet, for Richmond Planning Director Richard Mitchell the text changes were minor and were intended to streamline the document so that it would be consistent with the other Elements in the General Plan. Mitchell (2007) noted:

> The Health Element emerged as a document that referenced almost every other aspect of the General Plan. That made sense, since the way we had come to define health, it cut across all sectors of planning. We needed to make a document that was turning into volumes more manageable. Mostly redundancies were removed.

Under pressure from REDI, CBE, the California Endowment, and many of the professionals who volunteered their time as TAG members, the City committed to work with REDI to revise the 2009 draft and re-insert many of the items that had been removed. The work delayed a final draft of the Health Element for another 6 months, encouraged many community-based groups to withdraw from the healthy planning process, and weakened the trust and partnerships that the Health Element drafting process had built between the city and community activists.

Confronting Multinational Corporate Power … and Winning

Environmental Justice activists continued to monitor Chevron and another proposed facility expansion opened the door for more legal challenges. In 2005, Chevron had submitted a plan to expand its refinery operations to process heavy crude oil with high sulphur content. Chevron's environmental review found no significant environmental impacts from the proposed expansion and in June 2008, both the Richmond Planning Commission and City Council (by a 5 to 4 vote), approved the project and issued the necessary permits for the project to proceed.

In September 2008, CBE, WCTC, and the Asian Pacific Environmental Network filed a petition for *writ of mandate* against the City and Chevron, arguing that the environmental review of the project was flawed because Chevron failed to disclose, analyze and mitigate all the potential environmental impacts of the refinery's new processes. Specifically, CBE argued that the Chevron project did not disclose the amount or type of heavy crude oil they would be processing. CBE argued that an environmental assessment could not be approved if the pollutants were not fully disclosed. CBE also argued that Chevron failed to analyze and provide adequate mitigation for greenhouse gas emissions from their planned expansion and they did not analyze cumulative impacts, both requirements under California's Environmental Quality Act (CEQA, 2010).

A trial court agreed with the community coalition in 2009, and ordered Chevron to stop construction of the project (Barker, 2009). Chevron had already hired more than 1,000 workers at the construction site and had committed to pay $61 million to City Council defined community benefit projects. According to Nile Malloy of CBE, the payment was a symbol of how corrupt Richmond officials had become since the pay-off was negotiated behind closed doors. Malloy (2010) noted:

After the community benefit agreement we negotiated with Chevron in the 1990s, we had no faith that they would abide by any of their commitments this time. Of course, they refused to engage with us or our environmental justice partners. They essentially bought-off council and planning commission members for their vote certifying the environmental review. We decided as a coalition to pursue the legal route and stop the project until they disclosed and analysed impacts.

Roger Kim (2010) noted that the initial ruling by the judge seemed to catch Chevron off-guard and galvanized the community:

Our lawsuit said 'you, Chevron must disclose what you'll be doing before saying there won't be any impacts'. That was a message everyone could relate to in the community. The environmental groups that seemed more concerned with climate change than the health of local poor people also got behind us. The $61 Million payout was negotiated behind closed doors and we used all this to hold elected officials accountable. We mounted a massive get-out-the-vote campaign and put forward our own candidates for council and planning commission. The lawsuit provided us with media attention and that, combined with the Obama campaign excitement, allowed us to compete against Chevron's campaign donations.

As the controversy of the Chevron case moved into the courts, community groups won at the ballot box. In November 2008, three of the council's seven members who had voted to approve the Chevron project were voted out of office. Despite donating over $1 million to their preferred candidates, Chevron lost and the APEN supported candidates won, including a cardiologist named Jeffery Ritterman who campaigned on environmental, health and social justice issues. In addition, voters passed ballot Measure T, also called 'A Fair Share for Richmond', which called for a re-assessment of business license fees for large manufacturers based on the value of their raw materials and property. The ballot measure was drafted by community groups in direct response to Chevron's $61 million payout to the City.

By April 2010 the California Court of Appeals exhausted Chevron's final appeal of the CBE lawsuit. The judge ruled that Chevron must submit a new environmental review that disclosed the type and amount of heavy crude it will use and how the refinery will reduce its greenhouse gas emissions. In 2012, Chevron also lost its appeal of Measure T and will have to start paying new annual fees to the City of Richmond.

Community Health Indicators

Capitalizing on the electoral and legislative victories, community groups in Richmond partnered with others in the San Francisco Bay Area to gather new data on environmental health issues. CBE launched a household exposure study and survey to identify the contaminants that people of colour in Richmond were breathing in their homes. They worked with researchers from University of California, Berkeley to develop a hypothesis about how cumulative environmental and social burdens at both the individual and community level adversely impacted health (figure 6.11). The model called 'The Big Picture: Understanding Health in Richmond' suggested that the cumulative interplay of community-level stressors, such as air pollution, fear for one's safety and lack of healthy food access, combined with individual-level stressors, such as access to health care, poverty and education, to impact health inequities in Richmond (Cohen et al., 2012). The household survey was designed and administered by community residents. It revealed that elevated levels of metals and air toxics

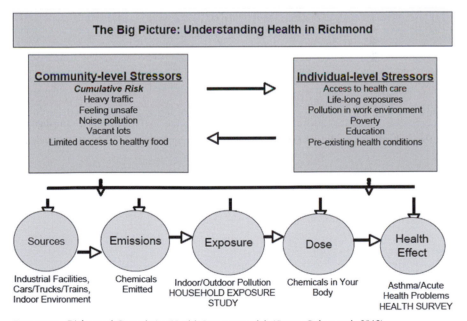

Figure 6.11. Richmond Cumulative Health Impacts model. (*Source*: Cohen *et al*., 2012).

attributable to refinery operations, not other stationary or mobile source polluters, were disproportionately impacting families living adjacent to the Chevron refinery.

A second project also employed community members to measure hazardous exposures and health outcomes experienced in Richmond. The Pacific Institute, West County Toxics Coalition and other organizations launched a year long effort to define what they thought were the indictors of a healthy and socially just Richmond. They gathered oral histories along with publically available data into a report entitled, *Measuring What Matters: Neighborhood Research for Economic and Environmental Health and Justice* (Pacific Institute *et al.*, 2009) (figure 6.12).

The report reflected a broad set of community assets and challenges, from lead paint in homes to waterfront access, to freight transportation, to liquor stores and prisoners returning to the community. A new regional health equity coalition, the West County Indicators Project, was created to track progress on the group's indicators. According to lead author Eli Moore (2010) the aim and result were to take a holistic approach to health and justice in the community:

Residents defined the issues and the measures. We didn't try to segment issues into traditional boxes; housing, environment, transportation, etc. In people's daily lives, access to the waterfront, pollution from a flare at Chevron, employment and services for returning, formerly incarcerated folks, and tax revenues to support parks, playground, streetlights and other necessities were all related.

Figure 6.12. Measuring What Matters report. (*Source*: Pacific Institute *et al.*, 2009)

The report and its findings were widely influential. Contra Costa Health Services used the information and methods in the report for its epidemiological surveillance system. Members of the West County Indicators Project used their findings to influence the drafting of a city wide monitoring programme to track the implementation of the Health and Wellness Element.

From Planning to Action for Health Equity

Leaders from the drafting group, including REDI, agreed that a pilot implementation phase could help move the Health and Wellness Element from plan to action. While it seemed awkward to being implementing a policy and planning document that had yet to be approved by the City, the partners agreed and were encouraged by the community-based initiatives described above to move forward. According to Lina Velasco (2011), a senior planner with the City of Richmond, the City Manager and community groups did not want the City to lose the momentum and institutional memory from the drafting process. She reflected:

Many of us, myself included, were asked to be leaders of the implementation but we hadn't participated in the drafting of the Health Element. We quickly learned that city planners and management staff hardly knew what the health department did in Richmond and the health department knew very little about planning, community development and city management. We spent the first six or more months learning from one another, touring their offices, explaining our constraints and discretionary actions. We also ran trainings for one another about the field and for us the idea of the social determinants of health was powerful and important.

Emerging from the implementation programme, known as Phase II of the Health and Wellness Element, or the Implementation Phase, was a work plan consisting of three components: neighbourhood schools as pilot sites; policy initiatives; and data tracking and monitoring. A steering committee of city and county government staff and representatives from community-based organizations – with facilitation by the non-profit organization called PolicyLink – selected two neighbourhood elementary schools, Peres and Chavez, to act as anchors for delivering services, crafting policies and engaging residents in healthy city planning. According to Gabino Arredondo (2011), a planner hired to lead the community health efforts at the schools, these two schools were in communities with some of the greatest challenges facing Richmond:

The Iron Triangle neighbourhood has some of the worst violence, environmental pollution and poverty in the city. So we selected that community and the primary schools to bring families and young people more into the centre of the planning process. Our approach was not to impose our agenda, but organize parents and teachers, learn about their most pressing needs and engage with the Health and Wellness Element implementation in that way.

Arredondo began organizing parents and attending their existing meetings, such as parent-teacher association (PTA) meetings and English as a Second Language (ESL) coffee hours. Most of the families were Latino, many new immigrants, and employment, housing, food, health care, crime and safety were constant concerns. City planners, the health department and parents drafted neighbourhood action plans specific to community-defined priorities. Yet, the families were sceptical that the City was actually interested in their concerns, and tested their willingness to help on multiple occasions. According to Arredondo:

The parents said a path was very dangerous because it wasn't paved and had not lights. We did a 'walk audit' with them and they showed us the issues. Within a week I was able to get the engineering and public works departments to the site to make changes. We delivered on compost and recycling, held fairs with music and food and got a mobile health care clinic to visit the school and serve parents and kids. We began to redefine their relationship with government.

The small actions built upon one another until parents and community residents living around the schools were calling the city planners asking them for advice on services and when they were next coming back to their neighbourhood. According to Velasco, that is when the planning team recognized how fragmented service delivery could be for Richmond's least well-off neighbourhoods:

Since we had built relationships with the community, planners were the face of government to them, but we didn't know about all the services they were asking us about. They would call us for food stamp information or free health care for their kids or passport information or housing subsidies. It was clear to us that we needed to expand our partnership and also change policies that created barriers for these residents.

The policy group in Phase II focused on drafting ordinances and city policies that emerged from the Health and Wellness Element (HWE) planning stage. Four policies were initially targeted, including senior housing guidelines, an urban agriculture assessment, a healthy street vendors ordinance, and a healthy development checklist. While community groups did not participate in the selection of these policies, the urban agriculture assessment garnered significant community interest. A series of workshops and public forums were held to discuss the urban agriculture challenges and opportunities in Richmond and how the issue might address some of the health inequities residents in the city were experiencing. By the end of the two-year implementation phase, only rough drafts of these policy issues were completed. As one community organization participant noted:

The policy issues were the most vague and disorganized aspect of this process. I thought they could have worked more closely with residents and public health to prioritize issues. This was also a lost opportunity to engage from the outset with the Office of Neighborhood Safety (ONS). In the end, I'm not sure what policies were developed.

What did emerge from the Policy team was that the City and County needed to commit to and draft a policy to integrate health equity into all functions of the city, from budgeting to garbage collection. With the encouragement of the State of California's Department of Public Health and University of California, Berkeley professors, the City began exploring the idea of adopting a Health in All Policies (HiAP) strategy. At the conclusion of the two-year implementation phase, the City Manager committed the city to drafting and adopting a HiAP strategy.

A data work group was the third pillar of the HWE implementation phase. This group explored the Measuring What Matters report and more traditional planning and public health data with the aim of drafting a manageable set of indicators to track progress towards health equity as the HWE is adopted and implemented. A detailed final report spelled out data sources and recommendations for indicators, but no immediate actions were taken.

The most successful aspect of the Implementation Phase was the neighbourhood pilot projects at the two elementary schools and the fact that city staff and the county health department were now regularly working together on place-based equity issues. The partners began writing new grant proposals to government and private foundations to continue their work and for the third time, the California Endowment, agreed to fund a third stage of the project called the Richmond Health Equity Partnership (RHEP). The objectives of the RHEP are to refocus the work of the city, county and school district around health equity, train staff in how to do this, have local governments implement an HiAP strategy and for the school district to adopt a full service community schools governance model (richmondhealth.org).

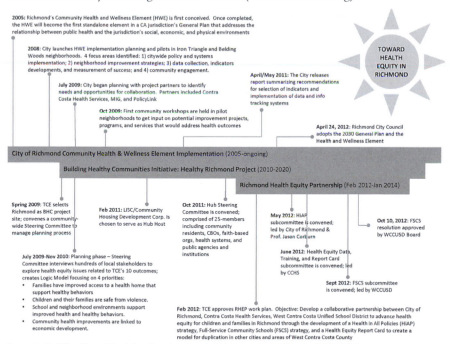

Figure 6.13. Timeline of healthy city planning in Richmond, California, 2005–2012.

The Richmond Health Equity Partnership

The Richmond Health Equity Partnership aims to coordinate existing health promotion activities better, focus them around a health equity strategy, and link them to the city's budgeting process. The first objective of the RHEP is to draft and implement a HiAP strategic plan and implementing ordinance for the City of Richmond.

The RHEP defines health equity as the goal of achieving the highest level of health for all people by addressing avoidable inequalities and equalizing the conditions for health for all groups, especially for those who have experienced socioeconomic disadvantage and historical injustices, such as racism. Trainings among RHEP participants and City staff focused on how to reframe conventional policy and public health questions using a structural racial racism lens (Box 6.1).

Box 6.1: From Conventional to Health Equity Questioning: Some Examples

Conventional: How do we connect isolated individuals to a social network?
Health Equity: What institutional policies and practices maintain rather than counteract people's isolation from social supports?

Conventional: How can we create more green space, bike paths, and farmers' markets in vulnerable neighbourhoods?
Health Equity: What policies and practices by government and commerce discourage access to transportation, recreational resources, and nutritious food in neighbourhoods where health is poorest?

Conventional: How can we encourage people to make healthier choices, like not smoking and eating more healthily?
Health Equity: What social conditions and economic policies predispose people to the stress that encourages smoking?

Conventional: How can individuals protect themselves against health disparities?
Health equity: What kinds of community organizing and alliance building are necessary to protect communities?

The RHEP also adopted a model of change that aims to integrate internal institutional change with new policies and to increase and support community-based organizing and capacity (figure 6.14). The institutional and policy changes, along with new services, programmes and data gathering are all central components of how the RHEP envisions achieving greater health equity. While only launched in 2012, the RHEP is aiming to extend previous efforts at two primary schools in Richmond as well as city, county and community-based partnerships to better coordinate activities that can move toward more healthy and equitable city planning.

Conclusions

This chapter has highlighted some of the strategies for environmental health justice in Richmond. Activists groups have used a range of strategies from research and organizing to lawsuits and participating with local government, to integrate equity into

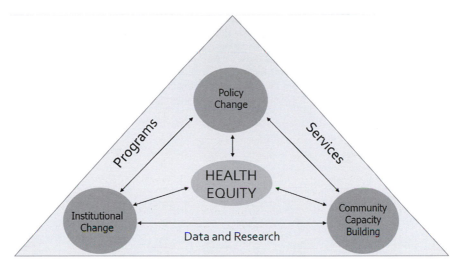

Figure 6.14. Richmond Health Equity Partnership, model of change.

planning processes. The work of activists helped ensure local government focused explicitly on equity and social justice issues and pushed these institutions to look inward for change as well as outward. The case also highlights that HCP demands implementation activities, not just report drafting, to move toward 'learning by doing'. The HWE implementation phase forced local government planners and health officials to learn how they could function together in new ways that could promote equity and what barriers existing within each 'institutional culture' for even greater steps toward health equity.

The RHEP suggests that the City has made a new commitment to an integrated, multi-issue approach, where learning and monitoring is valued. However, it may be too early to tell if it will result in significant change. What is clear is that environmental justice activism was and remains instrumental in shifting Richmond city planning to focus on health equity.

Notes

1. Regulation 12, Rule 11, Flare Monitoring at Petroleum Refineries, on 4 June 2003; Regulation 12, Rule 12, Flares at Petroleum Refineries, was adopted on 20 July 2005.
2. The members of REDI include: Alliance of Californians for Community Empowerment (ACCE); Contra Costa Faith Works; Contra Costa Interfaith Supporting Community Organization (CCISCO); East Bay Alliance for a Sustainable Economy (EBASE); Greater Richmond Interfaith Program (GRIP); Urban Habitat; Asian-Pacific Environmental Network (APEN); Laotian Organizing Project (LOP); Communities for a Better Environment (CBE). See: http://urbanhabitat.org/richmond.
3. The TAG also included representatives from the Contra Costa Health Services Department (CCHS); the Environmental Health Investigation Branch (EHIB) of the California Department of Health Services; and the Department of Public Health, City and County of San Francisco. Members included: Richard Jackson MD, MPH, Adjunct Professor, School of Public Health, University of California, Berkeley; Richard Kreutzer MD, Branch Chief, Environmental Health

Investigations Branch, California Department of Health Services; Wendel Brunner, MD, Public Health Director, Contra Costa Public Health; Poki Stewart Namkung MD, MPH, Public Health Officer, Santa Cruz County Health Services Agency and President of the National Association of County and City Health Officials (NACCHO); Dennis M. Barry, Director, Contra Costa County Community Development; Richard Mitchell, Planning Director, City of Richmond; Victor Rubin, PolicyLink; Sharon Fuller, Ma'at Academy; Sheryl Lane, Urban Habitat; Barbara Becnel, North Richmond Neighborhood House; Delphine Smith, Communities for a Better Environment.

Chapter 7

Towards a Planet of Healthy and Equitable Cities

From the *favelas* of Rio to the slums of Nairobi to the streets of California, activists are working to make city planning more healthy and equitable. By knowing their history and where they came from, activists and governments are aiming to promote greater equity from neighbourhoods to the nation. Yet, as all the cases here suggest, the work is incomplete and ongoing. This contemporary reality reflects the history of modern urban health; the state, professionals and activists struggle to understand what makes places and populations more healthy while acting with incomplete information. Healthy city planning is a politics and process of engaging with all aspects of city governance, but where the expertise and experiences of civil society organisations is at the centre. HCP never was, nor currently is, primarily about physical plan making.

As the planet urbanizes and the urban population outpaces the rural, learning how to plan for health and equity under conditions of uncertainty is crucial for our survival. The frameworks and cases offered here are intended to extend a conversation about what it means to actively seek more healthy and equitable places for everyone. Yet, my approach and the cases highlight, that reversing a century or more of urban planning and policy inequities that have contributed to health inequities will not be easy.

I opened this book with a call for approaching cities as complex systems. What the cases highlight is that embracing all the complexity of cities is challenging but possible by connecting neighbourhood-based social movements to national policy initiatives. The butterfly effect concept of systems thinking demands that healthy city planners move away from professional expert-defined concepts and embrace practices of community-based experts who know their communities and navigate daily challenges to survive and thrive.[1] In other words, neighbourhood actors and institutions must be the health and equity stimulating butterflies in the complex system of a city and its metropolitan region. Yet, as the cases make clear, the institutions of planning and public health must work at the national, regional and municipal scales to create the enabling conditions for the butterfly to take flight and stimulate change for the better. Thus, the starting point for creating systems change for healthy city planning, as this book has argued, is knowing how the histories of the disciplines, in general and in specific places, has worked to enable or stymie social justice and to identify contemporary practices – in bureaucracies, scientific and legal institutions – that act to either promote or derail efforts for greater health equity.

Hybrid Science for the Healthy City

The laboratory and field site views of the city are important metaphors for understanding the impact that science – as an organizing principle – has had on the histories of both city planning and public health. While most histories of city planning and public health have treated science and technology as either independent of the development of city governance and institutions or as neutral with respect to their impact on urban politics, this book has argued that a critical history of science and technology can reveal the institutional encoding of urban health theories, cultural norms and the structure of city management. Contemporary efforts to promote healthy city planning must learn how scientific norms and practice shaped the physical, social and institutional characteristics of the city and how practices today either reify or confront scientific norms that perpetuate racial, ethnic and class-based inequities that manifest themselves so acutely in city neighbourhoods around the world.

As importantly, the history offered here suggests that 'science' was never one overarching ideology and there was contestation, critique and compliance with the field site and laboratory views of the city throughout the nineteenth and twentieth centuries. While one view tended to dominate research and practice, healthy city planners have much to learn about how the hybrid applications of both field and lab views of the city came to be, were implemented, impacted urban dwellers and were either institutionalized or marginalized. I suggested that the community health centre movement was one such hybrid practice that combined the field and laboratory views of the city and, depending on their organization, could have significant positive impacts on the health and wellbeing of the urban poor. As I described in the case on Rio de Janeiro, community health centres staffed with lay outreach workers, networked across *favelas* in the city and, supported by a national health system, enabled the centres to serve the needs of the urban poor. In this case, the enabling conditions for the success of community health centres as facilitators of neighbourhood health come from both the Federal government in Brazil and neighbourhood organizing and accountability groups like CEDAPS. This was one example of a hybridization of the field and laboratory views of the city that was made possible by actions in the neighbourhood and at the national policy scale.

Adaptive Urban Health Justice

Returning to my framework for Adaptive Urban Health Justice outlined in Chapter 1, I examine aspects of the cases that help highlight the core constructs.

1.   Democratic Participation: In each case, democratic participation was a central organizing feature. However, each case offered slightly different models for participation, suggesting to planners that there is no one-size-fits-all model for democractic healthy city planning. In Rio, CEDAPs built networks of existing organizations in *favelas* and use their Shared Construction of Solutions in Health model for group dialogues. In Nairobi, *Muungano wa Wanavijiji*, the Kenyan network of the urban poor, used community savings processes to organize residents. Participation in Richmond was a combination of activists' direct action, such as when challenging Chevron and gathering community indicators, and collaborating with government to draft the Health Element. The cases suggest that knowing the cultural context of planning is important for organizing accountable democratic participation.

2.   *Integrated Decision-Making*: All the cases aimed to promote health equity through integrated decision-making. In Rio, the state is sponsoring integrated policies such as *Favela-Bairro*, *Bolsa Família* and the Family Health Units of the national health system. Each of these policies includes an integrated set of projects and objectives, rather than just focusing on one, such as poverty. Importantly, integrated decisions in Brazilian policy are enabled by community action for health promotion, such as CEDAPS's strategies around building the Rio Healthy City Network. In Nairobi, the Mathare planning processes were not limited to one issue, but sought to integrate infrastructure, housing, environment, livelihoods and other community issues. The Kosovo water project integrated a physical plan with *Muungano* facilitiating a model of community-based management of this life-supporting basic service. The Health Element in Richmond integrated a suite of social determinants of health and the Richmond Health Equity Partnership aims to integrate a range of issues and institutions in their work.

Integrated decision-making was not just about substantive issues but also included integrating action at multiple scales of government, from the local to national. In Brazil, Municipal Health Councils act as intermediaries between the national health system, the municipality, and neighbourhood-scale prevention and care. In Richmond, the pilot implementation phase of the Health Element included a set of strategies organized around two neighbourhood schools and city-scale policy development. The city of Richmond, county and school district are integrating decision-making through the Health Equity Partnership.

3.   *Multidimensional Monitoring*: In adaptive urban health justice, monitoring should track specific decisions and progress towards health equity goals. While less transparent to community members, *Bolsa Família* has evaluation and monitoring built into the policy that tracks not just the number of participants but also what factors act to enable or stymie compliance with the conditions of the cash transfer programme. In the *Measuring What Matters* report from the Richmond case, activists defined equity goals and selected indicators from a multi-dimensional perspective. In Nairobi, the Mathare Zonal Plan included a coalition-building process for monitoring and indicators for tracking implementation and broader social changes likely to promote equity. However, all the cases suggest that multidimensional monitoring is a major challenge and this was one of the weaker aspects of the ongoing work in each city.

4.   Social Learning: The cases suggest that social learning for urban adaptive health justice should occur within a particular context and among organizations not just individuals. The networked organizational structures described in each case facilitated learning. The organizations within the CEDAPS network learned from and with each other. Slum Dwellers International (SDI) played a key role in facilitating learning among the *Muungano* network and in organizing exchanges of slum dwellers in their global network. The Mathare slum dwellers and their collaborative planning partnership with universities enabled learning by gathering and analyzing details about their community through enumeration and mapping. The Richmond Equitable Development Initiative (REDI) was a network of organizations that learned different ways to advocate for equity though the healthy planning processes in Richmond. The City of Richmond learned how to implement the Health Element at neighbourhood schools through small-scale, incremental projects. All the cases emphasize that learning Healthy City Planning (HCP) is best done through incremental, tangible practices linked together, not one-off boutique projects.

Yet, learning is not just about epistemology, but simultaneously is a political process for social change, as John Dewey, Paulo Freire and others so cogently argued.[2] This can come when an entire community or city learns together, such as in the participatory budgeting process in Brazil. Learning as social change is also discovering new possibilities among community residents seeking change or when formerly fragmented government agencies 'learn' new ways of working together and with the urban poor. Healthy city planning can contribute to transformative learning when it helps 'make visible' to those not experiencing inequality but who are in position to alleviate suffering how people and groups in disadvantaged communities experience inequality.

5.   Adjustment and Innovation: All the cases suggest that adjustment and innovation are about people and ideas rather than things. The work of CEDAPS not only adjusts health promotion strategies that come from state-run clinics, but through their lay community health promoters created a process for imagining what a more equitable city could be. In Nairobi, *Muungano* and partners adjusted their planning strategies in Mathare as circumstances changed, shifting from a primary focus on housing to infrastructure. Yet, they also adjusted their water infrastructure strategy, rejecting the notion that the urban poor should only be served by communal facilities, and designed, implemented and managed the first in-home water service project for an informal settlement in Nairobi. The Richmond Health Element was made possible, in part, by the city adjusting from its original 'off-the-shelf' template for the General Plan. This shift helped trigger future innovations oriented not just toward linking planning and health, but integrating health in all policies and practices of city management.

Planning with Soul

In 1938, the American philosopher, education and social reformer John Dewey (1938, p. 49) called for an approach to learning that was much more than just acquiring new knowledge and skills. Dewey wanted us to focus on the meanings of our experiences, what was worthwhile in life, the values we stood for, and on taking action in the world, not just studying it. This, for Dewey, meant not losing our 'soul'. The twenty-first century healthy and equitable city will demand planning with soul.

Jazz is an often-cited expression of soul, and the musical metaphor offers some insights for healthy city planning practice (Corburn, 2005). Jazz is about improvisation and adapting to, while also helping to build, a new group sound. The effective jazz musician knows the history of the genre: the African-American struggle for recognition, the innovators who defined the sound, and its core repertoires. Yet, playfulness, experimentation and spontaneity are essential, but so too are the accepted rules of procedure in jazz, such as when to solo, how to yield to another musician, to break with tone but to also 'bring back the rhythm'. Jazz is not anything goes. Jazz emphasizes succession and accumulation – of techniques, experiences and interactions with other musicians. Ultimately, jazz is about change, reinvention and transgressing accepted boundaries with indeterminate outcomes.

I opened this book with the metaphor of the city as a machine and called for planners to stop treating the city's parts at the expense of the complexity of the whole. I suggested that small actions in the complex system of cities can have a big impact – the butterfly effect. Yet, this requires enabling conditions, which are actively made and remade by people and the institutions of science and politics. I close with jazz, hoping to encourage a more soulful, healthy and just practice of city planning.

Notes

1. The term 'butterfly effect' was coined by Edward Lorenz in the 1970s. See http://en.wikipedia.org/wiki/Butterfly_effect.
2. See *en.wikipedia.org/wiki/John_Dewey* and http://*en.wikipedia.org/wiki/Paulo_Freire*

References

Abrams, C. (1955) *Forbidden Neighbors: A Study of Prejudice in Housing*. New York: Harper and Brothers, *1955*

Abramson, M. and the Young Lords Party (1971) *Palante: Young Lords Party*. New York: McGraw-Hill.

Abreu, M. (2008) *Evoluçao Urbana do Rio de Janeiro*, 4th ed. Rio de Janeiro: Pereira Passos.

Acheson, D., Barker, D., Chambers, J., Graham, H., Marmot, M. and Whitehead, M. (1998) *The Report of the Independent Inquiry into Health Inequalities*. London: Stationery Office. Available at: http://www.archive.official-documents.co.uk/document/doh/ih/contents.htm.

Achola, M.A. (2001) Colonial policy and urban health: the case of colonial Nairobi. *Azania: Archaeological Research in Africa*, **36/37**(1), pp. 119–137.

Ackerknecht, E. (1953) *Rudolph Virchow: Doctor, Statesman, Anthropologist*. Madison, WI: University of Wisconsin Press.

Adashi, E.Y., Geiger, J., and Fine, M.D. (2010) Health care reform and primary care – the growing importance of the community health center. *New England Journal of Medicine*, **362**, pp. 2047–2050.

APHRC (African Population and Health Research Centre) (2002) *Population and Health Dynamics in Nairobi Informal Settlements*. Nairobi: APHRC.

Agache, A. (1930) *Cidade do Rio de Janeiro: extensão, remodelacão, embellezamento. Organisacão projectadas pela administracão*. Rio de Janeiro: Pris, Foyer brésilien.

ACPHD (Alameda County Public Health Department) (2008) *Unnatural Causes: Health and Social Inequality in Alameda County*. Alameda, CA: ACPHD. Available at: www.acphd.org/media/53628/unnatcs2008.pdf.

Alkire, S. and Foster, J. (2011) Counting and multidimensional poverty measurement. *Journal of Public Economics*, **95**, pp. 476–487.

Anderson, W. (2006) *Colonial Pathologies: American Tropical Medicine, Race, and Hygiene in the Philippines*. Durham, NC: Duke University Press.

APHA (American Public Health Association) (1938) *Basic Principles of Healthful Housing. Committee on the Hygiene of Housing*. Chicago, IL: Public Administration Service.

APHA (1948) *Planning the Neighborhood: Standards for Healthful Housing. Committee on the Hygiene of Housing*. Chicago, IL: Public Administration Service.

Appadurai, A. (2002) Deep democracy: urban governmentality and the horizon of politics. *Public Culture*, **14**, pp. 21–47.

Argyris, C. and Schon, D. (1974) *Theory in Practice: Increasing Professional Effectiveness*. San Francisco, CA: Jossey-Bass.

Argyris, C., and Schön, D. (1996) *Organizational Learning II: Theory, Method and Practice*. Reading, MA: Addison Wesley.

Arredondo, G. (2011) Personal communication.

Avila De Matos, E.A. (2008) 'Alliance For Progress': Civilizing Speech and Press in Professional Education Paraná – Brazil. Proceso Civilizing International Symposium: Civilización Culture and Instituiciones. Buenos Aires, pp. 359–367.

Babcock, R.F. (1966) *The Zoning Game: Municipal Practices and Policies*. Madison, WI: University of Wisconsin Press.

Baer, W. (2001) *The Brazilian Economy: Growth and Development*. Westport, CT: Praeger.

Bamberger, L. (1966) Health care and poverty: what are the dimensions of the problem from the community's point of view? *Bulletin of the New York Academy of Medicine*, **42**, pp. 1140–1149.

Banerjee, T. and Baer, W.C. (1984) *Beyond the Neighborhood Unit: Residential Environments and Public Policy*. New York: Plenum.

Barnow, N.F., Wittus Hansen, N., Johnsen, M., Poulsen, A., Rønnow, V. and Sølvsten, K. (1983) *Urban Development in Kenya: The Growth of Nairobi 1900–1970*. Copenhagen: Kunstakademiets Arkitektskole.

Barker, D. (2009) Judge: Chevron must halt Richmond expansion. *San Francisco Chronicle*, 3 July, p. B-1. Available at: http://sfgate.com/cgi-bin/article.cgi?f=/c/a/2009/07/03/BALT18IENG.DTL.

Bassette, E.M. (2003) *Informal Settlement Upgrading in Sub-Saharan Africa: Retrospective and Lessons Learned*. Washington DC: World Bank. Available at: http://web.pdx.edu/~bassette/docs/wblitreview-Jan03_web.pdf.

Bastin, D. (2003) *Richmond: Images of America*. Mount Pleasant, SC: Arcadia Publishing.

Bastos, I.P.M. (2010) Personal communication.

Batty, M. (2008) The size, scale, and shape of cities. *Science*, **319**, pp. 769–771.

Bauer, C. (1945) Good neighborhoods. *Annals of the American Academy of Political and Social Science*, **242**, pp. 104–115.

Bear, N. (2009) Personal communication.

Becker, D., CEDAPS Director (2011) Personal communication.

Becker, D., Edmundo, K., Nunes, N.R., Bonatto, D. and Souza, R. (2004) Empowerment e avaliação participativa em um programa de desenvolvimento local e promoção da saúde. *Cien Saude Colet*, **9**(3), pp. 655–667.

Becker, D., Edmundo K.B., Guimarães, W., Vasconcelos, M.S., Bonatto, D., Nunes, N.R. and Baptista, A.P. (2007) Network of healthy communities of Rio de Janeiro, Brazil. *Promotion & Education*, **14**(2), pp. 101–102.

Bellin, L. (1966) Obligatory alliance – the urban renewal authority and the city. *American Journal of Public Health Nations Health*, **56**(5), pp. 776–784.

Betancur, J.J. (2007) Approaches to the regularization of informal settlements: the case of PRIMED in Medellín, Colombia. *Global Urban Development*, **3**(1), pp. 1–15.

Betts, R.F. (1971) The establishment of the Medina in Dakar, Senegal, 1914. *Africa: Journal of the International African Institute*, **41**, pp.143–152.

Bhatia, R., Director, Environmental Health, San Francisco Department of Public Health (2005, 2006, 2007, 2010) Personal communications.

BMH (Brazilian Ministry of Health) (2001) *AIDS: The Brazilian Experience. National STD/AIDS Programme*. Brasilia: Ministry of Health. Available at: www.bma.org.uk/ ap.nsf/Content/Healthenvironmentalimpact~Recommendations.

Boccolini, C, Rio de Janeiro Human Breast Milk Programme (2011) Personal communication.

Boggan, D. (2010, 2011) Personal communications.

Bohan S. and Kleffman, S. (2010) Shortened lives: where you live matters for health. *Contra Costa Times*, 26 January.

Bourdieu, P. (1990) *The Logic of Practice*. Cambridge: Polity Press.

Boyer, C. (1983) *Dreaming the Rational City: The Myth of American City Planning*. Cambridge, MA: MIT Press.

Broussard, A.S. (1993) *Black San Francisco: The Struggle for Racial Equality in the West, 1900–1954*. Lawrence, KS: University Press of Kansas.

Burawoy, M. (1998) The extended case method. *Sociological Theory*, **16**(1), pp. 4–33.

Burgos, M.B. (1999) Dos Parques Proletários ao Favela-Bairro: as políticas públicas nas favelas do Rio de Janeiro, in Zaluar, A. and Alvito, M. (eds.) *Um século de favela*. Rio de Janeiro: Fundação Getúlio Vargas.

Bush, V. (1945) *Science: The Endless Frontier. United States Office of Scientific Research and Development*. Washington DC: US Government Printing Office.

Caiaffa, W., Almeida, M.C., Oliveira, C. *et al.* (2005) The urban environment from the health perspective: the case of Belo Horizonte, Minais Gerais, Brazil. *Cad Saúde Publica*, **21**(3), pp. 958–967.

Cain, L. (1972) Raising and watering a city: Ellis Sylvester Chesbrough and Chicago's first sanitation system. *Technology and Culture*, **13**, pp. 353–372.

Caminos, H. and Goethert, R. (1978) *Urbanization Primer: Project Assessment, Site Analysis, Design Criteria for Site and Services or Similar Dwelling Environments in Developing Areas*. Cambridge, MA: MIT Press.

Cardoso, A.L. (2007) Avanços e desafios na experiência brasileira de urbanização de favelas. *Cadernos Metrópole*, **17**, pp. 219–240.

Carson, R. (1962) *Silent Spring*. New York: Houghton Mifflin.

Cavallieri, F. (2010) Personal communication.

CBE (Communities for a Better Environment) (2005) *Flaring Hot Spots: Assessment of Episodic Local Air Pollution Associated with Oil Refinery Flaring Using Sulfur as a Tracer*. Huntington Park, CA: CBE.

CCHealth (Contra Costa Health Services) (2000) Major Accidents at Chemical/Refinery Plants. Available at: http://cchealth.org/groups/hazmat/accident_history.php.

CEDAPS (2012) *Platform of Urban Centers*. Available at: http://www.cedaps.org.br/ Platform_of_Urban_Centers.

Central Housing Advisory Committee (1944) *Design of Dwellings (Dudley Report) including Report of a Study Group of the Ministry of Town & Country Planning on Site Planning and Layout in relation to Housing*. London: HMSO.

CEQA (California Environmental Quality Act) (2010) Available at: ceres.ca.gov/ceqa.

Chadwick, E. (1842) *Report on the Sanitary Condition of the Labouring Population of Great Britain*. Edinburgh: Edinburgh University Press.

Chaiken, M.S. (1998) Primary health care initiatives in colonial Kenya. *World Development*, **26**(9), pp. 1701–1717.

CHAPE (Community Health Assessment Planning and Evaluation) (2007) *Health Disparities in Contra Costa County, CA*. Contra Costa County, CA: Public Health Division, Contra Costa Health Services. Available at: http://cchealth.org/groups/rhdi/pdf/health_disparities_in_cc.pdf.

Chege, M. (1981) A tale of two slums: electoral politics in Mathare and Dagoretti. *Review of African Political Economy*, **20**, pp. 74–88.

City of Richmond (1994) *General Plan*. Richmond, CA: Planning Department.

Clark, H. (2011) Personal communication.

Clark, W.C. and Dickson, N.M. (2003) Sustainability science: the emerging research program. *Proceedings of the National Academy of Science*, **100**(14), pp. 8059–8061.

Coehlo, V., Pozzoni, B. and Montoya, M. (2005) Participation and public policies in Brazil, in Gastilis, J. and Levine, P. (eds.) *The Deliberative Democracy Handbook: Strategies for Effective Civic Engagement in the Twenty-First Century*. San Francisco, CA: Jossey-Bass.

Cohen, A., Lopez, A., Malloy, N. and Morello-Frosch, R. (2012) Our environment, our health: a community-based participatory environmental health survey in Richmond, California. *Health Education and Behavior*, **39**(2), pp. 198–209.

Coleman W. (1982) *Death is a Social Disease. Public Health and Political Economy in Early Industrial France*. Madison, WI: The University of Wisconsin Press.

CSDH (Commission on Social Determinants of Health) (2008) *Closing the Gap in a Generation: Health Equity through Action on the Social Determinants of Health. Final Report of the Commission on Social Determinants of Health*. Geneva: World Health Organization.

Corburn, J. (2005) *Street Science: Community Knowledge and Environmental Health Justice*. Cambridge, MA: MIT Press.

Corburn, J. (2009) *Toward the Healthy City: People, Place & the Politics of Urban Planning*. Cambridge, MA: MIT Press.

Cronon, W. (1992) *Nature's Metropolis: Chicago and the Great West*. New York: Norton.

Cronon, W. (1995) The trouble with wilderness; or, getting back to the wrong nature, in Cronon, W, (ed.) *Uncommon Ground: Rethinking the Human Place in Nature*. New York: Norton, pp. 69–90.

Cueto, M. (1994) (ed.) *Missionaries of Science: The Rockefeller Foundation and Latin America*. Bloomington, IN: Indiana University Press.

Curtain, P.D. (1985) Medical knowledge and urban planning in tropical Africa. *The American Historical Review*, **90**(3), pp. 594–613.

Da Cunha, E. (1944) *Rebellion in the Backlands* (translated by Samuel Putnam). Chicago, IL: University of Chicago Press.

Davila, J. and Daste, D. (2012) Medellín's Aerial Cable-Cars: Social Inclusion and Reduced Emissions. Development Planning Unit, University College London.

Deegan, M.J. (2002) *Race, Hull-House, and the University of Chicago: A New Conscience against Ancient Evils*. Westport CT: Praeger.

Dewey, J. (1938) *Experience and Education*. New York: Collier Macmillan.

DHHS (Department of Health and Human Services) (1980) *Inequalities in Health: Report of a Research Working Group* (The Black Report). London: HMSO.

Donnangelo, M.C.F. (1975) *Medicina e sociedade: o médico e seu mercado de trabalho*. São Paulo: Pioneira.

Diamond, J. (1997) *Guns, Germs and Steel: The Fates of Human Societies*. New York: Norton.

Du Bois, W.E.B. (1906) *The Health and Physique of the American Negro: A Sociological Study Made Under the Direction of Atlanta University by the Eleventh Atlanta Conference*. Atlanta, GA: Atlanta University Press.

Duffy, J. (1990) *The Sanitarians: A History of American Public Health*. Chicago, IL: University of Illinois Press.

Duhl, L.J. and Hancock, T. (1988) *A Guide to Assessing Healthy Cities*. WHO Series Healthy Cities Paper No.3. Copenhagen: FADL.

Dye, C. (2008) Health and urban living. *Science*, **319**, pp. 766–769.

Edmundo, K., CEDAPS Director (2011) Personal communication.

Edmundo, K., Guimarães, W., Vasconcelos Mdo, S., Baptista, A.P. and Becker, D. (2005) Network of communities in the fight against AIDS: local actions to address health inequities and promote health in Rio de Janeiro, Brazil. *Promotion and Education*, Supplement 3, pp. 15–19.

Ellis, J. (2010) Personal communication.

Emirbayer, M. (1997) Manifesto for a relational sociology. *American Journal of Sociology*, **103**, pp. 281–317.

Engel, J. (2006) *The Epidemic: A Global History of AIDS*. Washington DC: Smithsonian Institution.

Engels, F. (1968) *The Condition of the Working Class in England* (translated and edited by W.O. Henderson and W.H. Chaloner). Stanford, CA: Stanford University Press.

Epstein, S. (1996) *Impure Science: AIDS, Activism, and the Politics of Knowledge*. Berkeley, CA: California University Press.

Escobar, A. (2001) Culture sits in places: reflections on globalism and subaltern strategies of localization. *Political Geography*, **20**, pp. 139–174.

Etherton, D., Jorgensen, N., Steele, R. and Mulili, M. (1971) Mathare Valley: A Case of Uncontrolled Settlement in Nairobi. Housing Research and Development Unit, University of Nairobi.

Fairfield, J.D. (1994) The scientific management of urban space: professional city planning and the legacy of progressive reform. *Journal of Urban History*, **20**, pp. 179–204.

Fanon, F. (1968) *The Wretched of the Earth*. New York: Grove Press.

Fernandes, E. (2007) Constructing the 'Right To the City' in Brazil. *Social Legal Studies*, **16**(2), pp. 201–219.

Fernandes, E. and Valencia, M.M. (eds.) (2004) *Urban Brazil*. Rio de Janeiro: Editora Mauad.

Ferrez, M., Ferrez, G. and Santos, P.F. (1982) *O álbum da Avenida Central: um documento da construção da Avenida Rio Branco, Rio de Janeiro, 1903–1906*. São Paulo: Editora Ex Libris.

Fischler, R. (1998) For a genealogy of planning. *Planning Perspectives*, **13**(4), pp. 389–410.

Ford, G.B. (1915) *The City Scientific. Proceedings of the Fifth National Conference in City Planning*. Boston: National Conference on City Planning, pp. 31–39.

Fraser, N. (2009) *Scales of Justice: Reimaging Political Space in a Globalizing World*. New York: Columbia University Press.

Freedman, D. (2010) Lies, damned lies and medical science. *Atlantic Monthly*, November. Available at: http://www.theatlantic.com/magazine/print/2010/11/lies-damned-lies-and-medical-science/8269/.

Freire, P. (1972) *Pedagogy of the Oppressed*. Harmondsworth: Penguin.

Fukuyama, F. and Colby, S. (2011) Half a miracle: Medellín's rebirth is nothing short of astonishing. But have the drug lords really been vanquished? *Foreign Policy*, May/June.

Fullilove, M.T. (2004) *Root Shock: How Tearing up City Neighborhoods Hurts America and What We Can Do about It*. New York: Ballantine.

Fung, A. (2006) *Empowered Participation: Reinventing Urban Democracy*. Princeton, NJ: Princeton University Press.

Funtowicz, S. and Ravetz, J. (1993) Science for the post-normal age. *Futures*, **25**(7), pp. 739–755.

Gagen, E.A. (2000) Playing the part: performing gender in America's playgrounds, in Holloway, S.L. and Valentine, G. (eds.) *Children's Geographies: Playing, Living, Learning*. London: Routledge, pp. 213–229.

Galton, F. (1904) Eugenics: its definition, scope, and aims. *The American Journal of Sociology*, **10**(1), pp. 1–25.

Galvao, J. (2005) Brazil and access to HIVAIDS drugs: a question of human rights and public health. *American Journal of Public Health*, **95**, pp. 1110–1116.

Gandy, M. (1999) The Paris sewers and the rationalization of urban space. *Transactions of the Institute of British Geographers*, **24**, pp. 23–44.

Gasnier, A. (2010) Brazil passes racial equality law but fails to endorse affirmative action. *Guardian*, 29 June. Available at: http://www.guardian.co.uk/world/2010/jun/29/brazil-race.

Geiger, J. (2005) The unsteady march. *Perspectives in Biology and Medicine*, **48**(1), pp. 1–9.

Geronimus, A. (1992) The weathering hypothesis and the health of African-American women and infants: evidence and speculations. *Ethnicity and Disease*, **2**(3), pp. 207–221.

Gibbons, M., Limoges, C., Nowotny, H., Schwartzman, S., Scott, P. and Trow, M. (1994) *The New Production of Knowledge: The Dynamics of Science and Research in Contemporary Societies*. London: Sage.

Gieryn, T.F. (1999) *Cultural Boundaries of Science*. Chicago, IL: University of Chicago Press.

Gillette Jr., H. (1983) The evolution of neighborhood planning: from the Progressive Era to the 1949 Housing Act. *Journal of Urban History*, **9**(4), pp. 421–444.

Gohlke, J.M. and Portier, C.J. (2007) The forest for the trees: a systems approach to human health research. *Environmental Health Perspective*, **115**(9), pp. 1261–1263.

Goodman, R. (1971) *After the Planners*. New York: Simon and Schuster.

Gottlieb, R. (1993) *Forcing the Spring. The Transformation of the American Environmental Movement*. Washington DC: Island Press.

Gouveia, G.C., Souza, W.V., Luna, C.F., Souza-Júnior, P.R. and Szwarcwald, C.L. (2005) Health care users' satisfaction in Brazil, 2003. *Cad Saude Publica*, Supplement 21, pp. 109–118.

Gulyani, S. and Bassett, E.M. (2007) Retrieving the baby from the bathwater: slum upgrading in Sub-Saharan Africa. *Environment and Planning C*, **25**(4), pp. 486–515.

Gulyani, S. and Basset, E. (2008) Revisiting … Retrieving the baby from the bathwater: slum upgrading in Sub-Saharan Africa. *Environment and Planning C*, **26**, pp. 858–860.

Hake, A. (1977) *African Metropolis: Nairobi's Self-Help City*. New York: St. Martin's Press.

Hamilton, A. (1943) *Exploring the Dangerous Trades: The Autobiography of Alice Hamilton*. Boston, MA: Northeastern University Press.

Hancock, T. and Duhl, L. (1986) *Promoting Health in the Urban Context*. World Health Organization, Healthy Cities Paper 1. Copenhagen: FADL Publishers.

Hancock, T. and Duhl, L. (1988) *WHO Healthy Cities Project: A Guide to Assessing Healthy Cities*. Copenhagen: FADL Publishers.

Harpham T. (2009) Urban health in developing countries: what do we know and where do we go? *Health and Place*, **15**, pp. 107–116.

Harris, M. and Haines, A. (2010) Brazil's family health programme. *British Medical Journal*, **341**, pp. 1171–1172.

Healey, P. (1998) Building institutional capacity through collaborative approaches to urban planning. *Environment and Planning A*, **30**(5), pp. 1531–1556.

Healey, P. (2003) Collaborative planning in perspective. *Planning Theory*, **2**(2), pp. 101–123.

Health of Towns Association (1844) *Address to the Inhabitants of Manchester and Salford: Why are Towns Unhealthy?* Manchester: Cave and Sever.

Hill, H. (1977) *Black Labor and the American Legal System I: Race, Work, and the Law*. Washington DC: BNA Books.

Hill, M.F. (1949) *Permanent Way*, Vol. 1. *The Story of the Kenya and Uganda Railway*. Nairobi: East African Literature Bureau.

Hirsh, A.R. (1983) *Making the Second Ghetto: Race and Housing in Chicago, 1940–1960*. Cambridge: Cambridge University Press.

Hoffman, F.L. (2004 [1896]) *The Race Traits and Tendencies of the American Negro*. Clark, NJ: Lawbook Exchange.

Howard, E. (1965 [1902]) *Garden Cities of Tomorrow*. Cambridge, MA: MIT Press.

Huang, C., Vaneckova, P., Wang, X., FitzGerald, G., Guo, Y. and Tong, S. (2011) Constraints and barriers to public health adaptation to climate change. *American Journal of Preventative Medicine*, **40**(2), pp. 183–190.

Huchzermeyer, M. (2011) *Tenement Cities: From 19th Century Berlin to 21st Century Nairobi*. Trenton, NJ: Africa World Press.

Hull-House, Residents of (2007 [1895]) *Hull House Maps and Papers: A Presentation of Nationalities and Wages in a Congested District of Chicago, Together with Comments and Essays on Problems Growing out of the Social Conditions*. Champaign, IL: University of Illinois Press.

Hylton, F. (2007) Medellín's makeover. *New Left Review*, **44**, pp. 71–89.

IBGE (Instituto Brasileiro de Geografia e Estatística) (1980, 1991, 2000, 2010, 2011) *Census Reports*. Available at: http://www.ibge.gov.br/home/.

ICSU (International Council Science Union) (2011) *Science Plan on Health and Wellbeing in the Changing Urban Environment: A Systems Approach*. Available at: http://www.icsu.org/asia-pacific/news-centre/news/announcement-science-plan-on-hwcue.

IDB (Inter American Development Bank) (2010) *Rio de Janeiro Low-Income Neighborhood*. Urban Development Program, Stage Iii (Br-L1175). New York: IDB.

Innes, J.I. and Booher, D.E. (2010) *Planning with Complexity: An Introduction to Collaborative Rationality for Public Policy*. London: Routledge.

IOM (Institute of Medicine) (1988) *The Future of Public Health*. Washington DC: National Academy Press.

Isaacs, R. (1948) The neighborhood unit is an instrument of segregation. *Journal of Housing*, **5**, pp. 215–219.

Jacobs J. (1961) *The Death and Life of Great American Cities*. New York: Random House.

Jasanoff, S. (2004) The idiom of co-production, in Jasanoff, S. (ed.) *States of Knowledge: The Co-production of Science and Social Order*. London: Routledge, pp. 1–45.

Jasanoff, S. (2005) *Designs on Nature: Science and Democracy in Europe and the United States*. Princeton, NJ: Princeton University Press.

Johnson, S. (2006) *The Ghost Map*. Harmonsworth: Allen Lane.

Kamau, H.W. and Ngari, J. (2002) Integrated Urban Housing Development Assessment of the Mathare 4A Development. Programme Against The Sustainable Livelihoods Approach. Working Paper 4. Available at: https://practicalaction.org/docs/shelter/iuhd_wp4_mathare_4a_assessment.pdf.

Karanja, I. (2010*a*) An enumeration and mapping of informal settlements in Kisumu, Kenya, implemented by their inhabitants. *Environment & Urbanization*, **22**(1), pp. 217–239.

Karanja, I. (2010*b*) Personal communication.

Kark, S.L. and Kark, E. (1983) An alternative strategy in community health care: community-oriented primary health care. *Israeli Journal of Medical Science,* **19**(8), pp. 707–713.

Karras, G. (2010) Personal communication.

Kates, R., Clark, W., Corell, R., Hall, J., Jaeger, C., Lowe, I., McCarthy, J., Schellnhuber, H-J., Bolin, B., Dickson, N., Faucheux, S., Gallopin, G., Grubler, A., Huntley, B., Jager, J., Jodha, N., Kasperson, R., Mabogunje, A., Matson, P. and Mooney, H. (2001) Sustainability science. *Science*, **292**, pp. 641–642.

Katz, M. (2011) Personal communication.

Kauffmann, J. (2009) Advancing sustainability science: report on the International Conference on Sustainability Science (ICSS) 2009. *Sustainability Science*, **4**, pp. 233–242.

Kay, J. (1996) Richmond plant safety pact OK'd. *San Francisco Examiner*, 7 February, pp. A-5.

Kelly, M. (1897) *A Review of Hoffman's Race Traits and Tendencies of the American Negro*. Washington DC: The American Negro Academy.

Kevles, D.J. (1985) *In the Name of Eugenics: Genetics and the Uses of Human Heredity*. New York: Knopf.

Kim, R. (2010) Personal communication.

Kimani, J. (2011) Personal communication.

Klinenberg, E. (2002) *Heat Wave: A Social Autopsy of Disaster in Chicago*. Chicago, IL: University of Chicago Press.

Koppitz, U. (2005) Constructing urban infrastructure for multiple resource management: sewerage systems in the industrialization of the Rhineland, Germany, in Schott, D., Luckin, B. and Massard-Guilbaud, G. (eds.) *Resources of the City: Contributions to an Environmental History of Modern Europe*. Farnham: Ashgate.

Kraut, A. (1988) Silent travelers: germs, genes, and American efficiency, 1890–1924. *Social Science History*, **12**, pp. 377–393.

Kreidler, A.G. (1919) A community self organized for preventive health work. *Modern Medicine*, **1**, pp. 26–31.

Krieger, N. (1994) Epidemiology and the web of causation: has anyone seen the spider? *Social Science and Medicine*, **39**, pp. 887–903.

Krieger, N. (2011) *Epidemiology and the People's Health*. New York: Oxford University Press.

Krumbiegel, E.R. (1951) Hygiene housing. *American Journal of Public Health and the Nations Health*, **41**(5), pp. 497–504.

Lamba, A. (2005) Land Tenure Management Systems in informal Settlements: A Case of Nairobi. Thesis, Delft University of Technology.

Lane, S., Urban Habitat (2007) Personal communication.

Latour, B. (1987) *Science in Action: How to Follow Scientists and Engineers through Society*. Cambridge, MA: Harvard University Press.

Lear, L. (1997) *Rachel Carson: Witness for Nature*. New York: Henry Holt.

Leavitt, J.W. (1992) Typhoid Mary strikes back: bacteriological theory and practice in early twentieth-century public health. *Isis*, **83**, pp. 608–629.

Lee, K.N. (1993) *Compass and Gyroscope: Integrating Science and Politics for the Environment*. Washington DC: Island Press.

Lefkowitz, B. (2007) *Community Health Centers: A Movement and the People Who Made It Happen*. New Brunswick, NJ: Rutgers University Press.

Lemann, N. (1991) *The Promised Land: The Great Black Migration and How It Changed America*. New York: Knopf.

Lerner, J. (2010) The Participatory Budgeting Project, www.Menegat, Rualdo. 'Participatory democracy and sustainable development: integrated urban environmental management in Porto Alegre, Brazil'. *International Institute for Environment and Urbanization*, **14**(2), pp. 181–206.

Levi, G.C. and Vitória, M.A. (2002*)* Fighting against AIDS: the Brazilian experience. *AIDS*, **16**, pp. 2373–2383.

Lewis, N.P. (1916) *The Planning of the Modern City: A Review of the Principles Governing City Planning*. New York: Wiley.

Leys, N. (1973) *Kenya*. London: Frank Cass.

Lindsey, B. (2011) Personal communication.

Logan, T. (1976) The Americanization of German zoning. *Journal of the American Institute of Planning*, **42**(4), pp. 377–385.

McEwen, B.S. (2000) Allostasis and allostatic load: implications for neuropsycho-pharmacology. *Neuropsychopharmacology*, **22**(2), pp. 108–124.

McVicar, K.G. (1968) Twilight of an African Slum: Pumwani and the evolution of African Settlement in Nairobi. PhD thesis, University of California, Los Angeles.

Majone, G. (1989) *Evidence, Argument and Persuasion in the Policy Process*. New Haven, CT: Yale University Press.

Major Greenwood (1935) *Epidemics and Crowd-Diseases: An Introduction to the Study of epidemiology*. London: Macmillan.

Makau, J. (2010, 2011) Personal communications.

Malloy, N. (2011) Personal communication.

Markowitz, G. and Rosner, D. (2002) *Deceit and Denial: The Deadly Politics of Industrial Pollution*. Berkeley, CA: California University Press.

Marsh, B. (1909) *An Introduction to City Planning: Democracy's Challenge to the American City*. New York: Committee on Congestion of Population in New York.

Massey, D.S. and Denton, N.A. (1993) *American Apartheid: Segregation and the Making of the Underclass*. Cambridge, MA: Harvard University Press.

Mathenge, D. (2010, 2011) Personal communications.

Mathews, T.J. and MacDorman, M.F. (2012) Infant mortality statistics from the 2008 period linked birth/infant death data set. *National Vital Statistics Reports*, **60**(5). Available at: http://www.cdc.gov/nchs/products/nvsr.htm#vol60.

Mati, E. and Macharia, D. (2011) *Influence of Water Supply on Quality of Life for Urban Slum Dwellers: The Case of Kosovo-Mathare Pilot Water Project in Nairobi, Kenya*. Saarbrucken: Lambert Academic Publishing.

Meade, T.A. (1989) Living worse and costing more: resistance and riot in Rio de Janeiro, 1890–1917. *Journal of Latin American Studies*, **22**(2), pp. 241–266.

Meade, T.A. (1997) *Civilizing Rio: Reform and Resistance in a Brazilian City, 1889–1930*. University Park, PA: Pennsylvania State University Press.

Melendez, M. (2003) *We Took the Streets: Fighting for Latino Rights with the Young Lords*. New York: St. Martin's Press.

Melosi, M. (1980) *Pollution and Reform in American Cities, 1870–1930*. Austin, TX: University of Texas Press.

Melosi, M. (2000) *The Sanitary City: Urban Infrastructure in America from Colonial Times to the Present*. Baltimore, MD: Johns Hopkins University Press.

Milet, M., Tran, S., Eatherton, M., Flattery, J. and Kreutzer, R. (2007) *The Burden of Asthma in California: A Surveillance Report*. Richmond, CA: California Department of Health Services, Environmental Health Investigations Branch. Available at: http://www.ehib.org/paper.jsp?paper_key=Asthma_Burden.

Millward, R. and Bell, F. (2001) Infant mortality in Victorian Britain: the mother as medium. *Economic History Review*, **54**(4), pp. 699–733.

Mitchell, R., Director of City Planning, City of Richmond (2007) Personal communication.

Monsanto (1962) The desolate year. *Monsanto Magazine*, October, pp. 4–9.

Moore, E. (2010) Personal communication.

Moore, S.A.W. (2000) *To Place Our Deeds: The African American Community in Richmond, CA 1910–1963*. Berkeley, CA: California University Press.

Moradi, A. (1998) Confronting colonial legacies – lessons from human development in Ghana and Kenya, 1880–2000. *Journal of International Development*, **20**, pp. 1107–1121.

Morgan, W.T.W. (1976) *Nairobi: City and Region*. Nairobi: Oxford University Press.

Mudhune, S.A., Okiro, E.A., Noor, A.M., Zurovac, D., Juma, E., Ochola, S.A. and Snow, R.W. (2011) The clinical burden of malaria in Nairobi: a historical review and contemporary audit. *Malaria Journal*, **10**(138).

Murray, C.J. and Lopez, A.D. (1997) Mortality by cause for eight regions of the world: Global Burden of Disease Study. *The Lancet*, **349**, pp. 1269–1276.

Nachman, R.G. (1977) Positivism and revolution in Brazil's first republic: the 1904 revolt. *The Americas*, **34**(1), pp. 20–39.

Needell, J.D. (1987) The Revolta Contra Vacina of 1904: the revolt against 'modernization' in Belle-Époque Rio de Janeiro. *The Hispanic American Historical Review*, **67**(2) pp. 233–269.

Nelson, N.A. (1919) Neighborhood organizing vs. tuberculosis. *Modern Medicine*, **1**, pp. 515–521.

Norris, T. and Pittman, M. (2000) The healthy communities movement and the coalition for healthier cities and communities. *Public Health Reports*, **115**, pp. 118–123.

Norton, B.G. (2005) *Sustainability: A Philosophy of Adaptive Ecosystem Management*. Chicago, IL: University of Chicago Press.

Nott, J.C., Gliddon, G.R., Morton, S.G., Agassiz, L., Usher, W. and Patterson, H.S. (1854) *Types of Mankind: Or, Ethnological Researches: Based Upon the Ancient Monuments, Paintings, Sculptures, and Crania of Races, and Upon Their Natural, Geographical, Philological and Biblical History, Illustrated by Selections from the Inedited Papers of Samuel George Morton and by Additional Contributions from L. Agassiz, W. Usher, and H.S. Patterson*. Philadelphia, PA: J.B. Lippincott, Grambo.

NRC (National Research Council) (1999) *Our Common Journey: A Transition Toward Sustainability*. Washington DC: National Academies Press.

NRC (2004) *Adaptive Management in Water Resources Project Planning. Panel on Adaptive Management for Resource Stewardship*. Washington DC: National Academies Press.

Nunn, A.S., Fonseca, E.M., Bastos, F.I. and Gruskin, S. (2009) AIDS treatment in Brazil: impacts and challenges. *Health Affairs*, **28**, pp. 1103–1113.

Obudho, R.A. (1997) Nairobi: national capital and regional hub, in Rakodi, C. (ed.) *The Urban Challenge in Africa*. Tokyo: UN University Press, pp. 292–334.

Obudho, R.A. and Aduwo, G.O. (1989) Slums and squatter settlements in urban centres of Kenya: towards a planning strategy. *Netherlands Journal of Housing and Environmental Research*, **4**(1), pp. 17–29.

Obudho, R.A. and Aduwo, G.O. (1992) The nature of the urbanization process and urbanism in the city of Nairobi, Kenya. *African Urban Quarterly*, **7**(1/2), pp. 50–62.

Oliveira-Cruz, V., Kowalski, J. and McPake, B. (2004) Viewpoint: the Brazilian HIV/AIDS 'success story' – can others do it? *Tropical Medicine and International Health*, **9**(2), pp. 292–297.

Olmsted, F.L. Jr. (1910) City Planning: an introductory address at the second national conference on city planning and the problems of congestion, Rochester, NY, May 2. American Civic Association, Department of City Making, series 2, no. 4.

Olmsted, J.C. (1894) Organization and management of a city engineer's office. *Journal of the Association of Engineering Societies*, **13**, pp. 594–595.

Olumwullah, O.A. (2002) *Dis-ease in the Colonial State: Medicine, Society, and Social Change Among the AbaNyole of Western Kenya*. Westport, CT: Greenwood.

Pacific Institute *et al.* (2009) *Measuring What Matters: Neighbourhood Research for Economic Health and Justice in Richmond, North Richmond, and San Pablo*. Oakland, CA: Pacific Institute. Available at: http://www.pacinst.org/reports/measuring_what_matters/index.htm.

Paim, J., Travassos, C., Almeida, C., Ligia Bahia, L. and Macinko, J. (2011) The Brazilian health system: history, advances, and challenges. *The Lancet*, **377**, pp. 1778–1797.

Palmer, S. (2010) *Launching Global Health: The Caribbean Odyssey of the Rockefeller Foundation*. Ann Arbor, MI: University of Michigan Press.

PAHO (Pan-American Health Association) (2011) Resolution Cd51.R4. Strategy and Plan Of Action On Urban Health. Available at: http://new.paho.org/hq/index.php?option=com_content&view=article&id=6035%3Alaunching-pahos-10-year-strategy-and-plan-of-action-on-urban-health-in-the-americas-at-the-10th-international-conference-on-urban-health&catid=4066%3Asde-international-conference-on-urban-health&lang=en.

Parisse, L. (1969) *Favelas do Rio de Janeiro – evolução – sentido*. Rio de Janeiro: Centro Nacional de Pesquisas Habitacionais (caderno do CENPHA, 5).

Parker, R. (2003) Building the foundations for the response to HIV/AIDS in Brazil: the development of HIV/AIDS policy, 1982–1996. *Divulgacão em Saúde para Debate*, **27**, pp. 143–183.

Parker, R. (2009) Civil society, political mobilization, and the impact of HIV scale-up on health systems in Brazil. *JAIDS: Journal of Acquired Immune Deficiency Syndrome*, **52**, pp. 49–51.

Pastor, M.J., Saad, J., and Morello-Frosh, R. (2007) Still Toxic after All These Years: Air Quality and Environmental Justice in the San Francisco Bay Area. Center for Justice, Tolerance and Community, University of California, Santa Cruz. Available at: http://cjtc.ucsc.edu.

Payne-Sturges, D.C., Burke, T.A., Breysse, P., Diener-West, M. and Buckley, T.J. (2004) Personal exposure meets risk assessment: a comparison of measured and modeled exposures and risks in an urban community. *Environmental Health Perspectives*, **112**, pp. 589–598.

Perlman, J. (2010) *Favela: Four Decades of Living on the Edge in Rio de Janeiro*. New York: Oxford University Press.

Perry, C.A. (1929) City planning for neighborhood life. *Social Forces*, **8**(1), pp. 98–100.

Peterson, J. (1979) The impact of sanitary reform upon American urban planning, 1840–1890. *Journal of Social History*, **13**, pp. 83–103.

Peterson, J. (2003) *The Birth of City Planning in the United States, 1840–1917*. Baltimore, MD: Johns Hopkins University Press.

Pluntz, R. (1990) *A History of Modern Housing in New York City: Dwelling Type and Social Change in the American Metropolis*. New York: Columbia University Press.

Pomeroy, J.J. (1929) Health center development in Los Angeles County. *Journal of the American Medical Association*, **93**, pp. 1546–1550.

Porter, D. (1999) *Health, Civilization and the State: A History of Public Health from Ancient to Modern Times*. London: Routledge.

Riis, J. (1890) *How the Other Half Lives: Studies among the Tenements of New York*. New York: Penguin.

Robertson, J. (1840) *Report of the Committee on the Health of Towns*, No. XI. London.

Rocha, I., CEDAPS Director of Monitoring and Evaluation of Projects (2011) Personal communication.

Rodriguez-Torres, D. (2010) Public authorities and urban upgrading policies in Eastlands: the example of Mathare 4A slum upgrading project, in Charton-Bigot, H. and Rodriguez-Torres, D. (eds.) *Nairobi Today. The Paradox of a Fragmented City*. Dar es Salaam: Mkuki Na Nyota Publishers, pp. 61–94.

Rosen, G. (1971) The first neighborhood health center movement – its rise and fall. *American Journal of Public Health*, **61**, pp. 1620–1637.

Rosen, G. (1993) *A History of Public Health*. Baltimore, MD: Johns Hopkins University Press.

Ross, K. (1995) *Fast Cars, Clean Bodies. Fast Cars, Clean Bodies: Decolonization and the Reordering of French Culture*. Cambridge, MA: MIT Press.

Roy, A. (2011) *Poverty Capital: Microfinance and the Making of Development*. London: Routledge.

Rydin, A. *et al.* (2012) Shaping cities for health: complexity and the planning of urban environments in the 21st century. *The Lancet*, **379**, pp. 2079–2108.

San Francisco Chronicle (2003) Air of concern. 16 February, p. D4. Available at: http://www.sfgate.com/cgi-bin/article.cgi?f=/c/a/2003/02/16/ED208619.DTL.

Santos, C.N.F. dos (1981) *Movimentos Urbanos no Rio de Janeiro*. Rio de Janeiro: Zahar Editores.

Santos, W.G. dos (1979) *Cidadania e Justiça*. Rio de Janeiro: Editoria Campus.

Sardell A. (1988) *The U.S. Experiment in Social Medicine: The Community Health Center Program, 1965–1986*. Pittsburgh, PA: University of Pittsburgh Press.

Satterthwaite, D. (2002) Local funds, and their potential to allow donor agencies to support community development and poverty reduction in urban areas: Workshop report. *Environment and Urbanization*, **14**(1), pp. 179–188.

Schultz, S. and McShane, C. (1978) To engineer the metropolis: sewers, sanitation and city planning in late nineteenth century. *American Journal of American History*, **65**(2), pp. 389–411.

Scott, J.C. (1998) *Seeing Like a State: How Certain Schemes to Improve the Human Condition Have Failed*. New Haven, CT: Yale University Press.

Scott, M. (1971) *American City Planning Since 1890*. Berkeley, CA: California University Press.

Sennett, R. (1995) *Flesh and Stone: The Body and the City in Western Civilization*. London: Faber & Faber.

Silkin, L. (1948) Address by the Rt. Hon. Lewis Silkin, M.P. *Journal of the Town Planning Institute*, **34**, pp. 151–152.

Silva, M.L.P. da (2005) *Favelas Cariocas, 1930–1964*. Rio de Janeiro: Contraponto.

Simone, A. (2004) People as infrastructure: intersecting fragments in Johannesburg. *Public Culture*, **16**(3), pp. 407–429.

Simpson, W.J. (1914) *Sanitary Matters in the East Africa Protectorate, Uganda and Zanzibar*. Report by Professor W.J. Simpson, CMG, MD, FRCP. London: Colonial Office.

Slum/ShackDwellers International (nd) *Making Cities Inclusive*. Available at: http://www.sdinet.org/method-inclusive-cities/.

Smith, S. (1995) *Sick and Tired of Being Sick and Tired: Black Women's Health Activism in America, 1890–1950*. Philadelphia, PA: University of Pennsylvania Press.

Snow, J. (1854) The cholera near Golden Square, and at Deptford. *Medical Times Gazette*, **9**, pp. 321–322.

Snow, J. (1855) *On the Mode of Communication of Cholera*, 2nd ed. London: John Churchill.

Soares, F.V., Ribas, R.P. and Osório, R.G. (2010) Evaluating the impact of Brazil's Bolsa Família: conditional cash transfers in perspective. *Latin American Research Review*, **45**(2), pp. 173–190.

Soares, F. and Soares, Y.S.D. (2005) *The Socio-Economic Impact of Favela-Barrio. What do the Data Say*. OVE Working Paper 0805. New York: Inter-American Development Bank, Office of Evaluation and Oversight. Available at: http://idbdocs.iadb.org/WSDocs/getdocument.aspx?docnum=600835&Cache=True.

Soares, S. (2012) Bolsa Família, Its Design, Its Impacts and Possibilities for The Future. Working Paper 89. International Policy Centre for Inclusive Growth. United Nations Development Programme, Brasilia.

Sood, V., Project Director, MIG Planning (2007) Personal communication.

Sparer, G. and Johnson, J. (1971) Evaluation of OEO neighborhood health centers. *American Journal of Public Health*, **61**(5), pp. 931–942.

Steenland, K. and Armstrong, B. (2006) An overview of methods for calculating the burden of disease due to specific risk factors. *Epidemiology*, **17**, pp. 512–519.

Stepan, N. (1976) *The Beginnings of Brazilian Science: Oswaldo Cruz, Medical Research and Policy, 1890–1920*. New York: Neale Watson Academy Publications.

Susser, M. (1993) A South African odyssey in community health: a memoir of the impact of the teachings of Sidney Kark. *American Journal of Public Health*, **83**(7), pp. 1039–1042.

Susser, M. and Stein, Z. (2009) *Eras in Epidemiology: The Evolution of Ideas*. Oxford: Oxford University Press.

Tarr, J.A. (1996) *The Search for the Ultimate Sink: Urban Pollution in Historical Perspective*. Akron, OH: University of Akron Press.

Taubes, G. (2008) *Good Calories, Bad Calories*. New York: Anchor Books/Random House.

Taylor, Q. (1998) *In Search of the Racial Frontier: African Americans in the American West 1528–1990*. New York: Norton.

Townsend, P. and Davidson, N. (eds.) (1982) *Inequalities in Health: The Black Report*. Harmondsworth: Penguin.

Tsouros, A. (1995) The WHO Healthy Cities Project: state of the art and future plans. *Health Promotion International*, **10**(2), pp. 133–141.

Tsoukas, H. (2005) *Complex Knowledge: Studies in Organizational Epistemology*. Oxford: Oxford University Press.

UN-HABITAT-WHO (2009) *Hidden Cities: Unmasking and Overcoming Health Inequities in Urban Settings*. Geneva: World Health Organization and United Nations Human Settlement Programme.

UN-HABITAT (2011) Urban Indicators. Available at: http://www.unhabitat.org/content.asp?typeid=19&catid=646&cid=8383.

Valdez, L., CEDAPS Plataforma organizer (2011) Personal communication.

Valladares, L. and Ribeiro, R. (1994) The return of the favela: recent changes in intrametropolitan Rio. *Urbana*, Nos. 14/15, pp. 59–73.

Velasco, L. (2011) Personal communication.

Vigneron, E. (2011) *Les inégalités de santé dans les territoires français, état des lieux et voies de progrès*. Paris: Editions Elsevier Masson.

Villermé, L.R. (1830) De la mortalité dans divers quartiers de la ville de Paris. *Annales d'hygiène publique et de médecine légale*, **3**, pp. 294–341.

Vinten-Johansen, P., Brody, H., Paneth, N., Rachmane, S. and Rip, M. (2003) *Cholera, Chloroform, and the Science of Medicine: A Life of John Snow*. New York: Oxford University Press.

Vlahov, D., Agarwal, S.R., Buckley, R.M., Caiaffa, W.T., Corvalan, C.F., Ezeh, A.C., Finkelstein, R., Friel, S., Harpham, T., Hossain, M., de Faria Leao, B., Mboup, G., Montgomery, M.R., Netherland, J.C., Ompad, D.C., Prasad, A., Quinn, A.T., Rothman, A., Satterthwaite, D.E., Stansfield, S. and Watson V.J. (2011) Roundtable on Urban Living Environment Research (RULER). *Journal of Urban Health*, **88**(5), pp. 793–857.

Waitzkin, H., Iriart, C., Estrada, A. and Lamadrid, S. (2001) Social medicine then and now: lessons from Latin America. *American Journal of Public Health*, **91**(10), pp. 1592–1601.

Wareru, J. (2010, 2011) Personal communications.

Weiss, M.A. (1980) The origins and legacy of urban renewal, in Clavel, P., Forester, J.

and Goldsmith, W.W. (eds.) *Urban and Regional Planning in an Age of Austerity*. New York: Pergamon Press, pp. 53–80.

Weru, J. (2004) Community federations and city upgrading: the work of Pamoja Trust and Muungano in Kenya. *Environment and Urbanization*, **16**(1), pp. 47–62.

Weru, J. (2010) Personal communication.

White, L. (1990) *The Comforts of Home: Prostitution in Colonial Nairobi*. Chicago, IL: University of Chicago Press.

White, L.W.T., Silberman, L. and Anderson, P.R. (1948) *Nairobi: Master Plan for a Colonial Capital*. London: HMSO.

Whitnah, J.C. (1944) *A History of Richmond, California: The City that Grew from a Rancho*. Richmond: Chamber of Commerce.

WHO (2010a) *Urban Health Equity Assessment and Response Tool (HEART)*. Available at: www.who.or.jp/urbanheart.html.

WHO (2010b) Brazil's march towards universal coverage. *Bulletin of the World Health Organization*, **88**(9), pp. 641–716.

Wilkinson, C. (2012) Social-ecological resilience: insights and issues for planning theory. *Planning Theory*, **11**(2), pp. 148–169.

Williams, D. (1999) Race, socioeconomic status, and health: the added effects of racism and discrimination. *Annals of the New York Academy of Sciences*, **896**, pp. 173–88.

Williams, M.T. (1991) *Washing 'The Great Unwashed': Public Baths in Urban America, 1840–1920*. Columbus, OH: Ohio State University Press.

Willis, C. (1992) How the 1916 zoning law shaped Manhattan's central business districts, in New York City Department of City Planning and the City Planning Commission (eds.) *Planning and Zoning New York City: Yesterday, Today and Tomorrow*. DCP 92-03, pp. 1–19.

Wing, S. (2005) Environmental justice, science, and public health. *Environmental Health Perspectives*, **110**(5), pp. 437–444.

Winslow, C.E.A. (1926) Public health at the crossroads. *American Journal of Public Health*, **16**, pp. 1075–1085.

Wohl, A.S. (1984) *Endangered Lives: Public Health Reform in Victorian Britain*. London: Methuen.

Wood, E.E. (1931) *Recent Trends in American Housing*. New York: Macmillan.

Woods, R.A. (ed.) (1898) *The City Wilderness: A Study of the South End*. Boston, MA: Houghton Mifflin.

World Bank (2010) *Bolsa Família: Implementation Completion and Results Report*. IBRD-72340. Report No. ICR00001486. Available at: http://documents.worldbank.org/curated/en/2010/06/12568141/brazil-bolsa-familia-project.

Wrong, M. (2009) *It's Our Turn to Eat: The Story of a Kenyan Whistleblower*. New York: Harper.

Wurthwein, R., Gbangou, A., Sauerborn, R. and Schmidt, C.M. (2001) Measuring the local burden of disease. A study of years of life lost in sub-Saharan Africa. *International Journal of Epidemiology*, **30**, pp. 501–508.

Zalvar, A. and Alvito, M. (1999) *Um século de favela*. Rio de Janeiro: Editora FGV.

Index